British and Commonwealth Armies 1939–45

Supplement 2

Helion Order of Battle
Volume 4

Mark Bevis

HELION & COMPANY

Helion & Company
26 Willow Road
Solihull
West Midlands
B91 1UE
England
Tel. 0121 705 3393
Fax 0121 711 4075
Email: publishing@helion.co.uk
Website: http://www.helion.co.uk

Published by Helion and Company, 2005

Designed and typeset by Bookcraft Ltd, Stroud, Gloucestershire
Cover designed by Bookcraft Ltd, Stroud, Gloucestershire
Printed by The Cromwell Press, Trowbridge, Wiltshire

© Helion and Company 2005

ISBN 1 874622 38 8

British Library Cataloguing-in-Publication Data.

A catalogue record for this book is available from the British Library.

For details of other military history titles published by Helion & Company contact the above address, or visit our website:
http://www.helion.co.uk.

We always welcome receiving book proposals from prospective authors.

Front cover photograph – Sherman Fireflies of the 1st Polish Armoured Division move through an
unidentified village during the winter of 1944/45. Photograph courtesy of the Imperial War
Museum, London (B13400).

CONTENTS

PART 3   AFRICAN THEATRES 1941–1945

PART 4   "SPECIAL FORCES" ALL THEATRES 1940–1943

INTRODUCTION

This is the fourth volume in a series dedicated to tables of organisation and equipment (TOE) of armies of the world in the 20th Century. This volume follows on from Volumes 1, 2 and 3 by covering British, Canadian, Australian, New Zealand and Indian forces, from 1939 to 1945, that were not included in the first three volumes. In this volume, several garrison formations are considered for some 'might have been' situations. For example, 'what if' there had been a German invasion of England in late 1940 (Operation Sealion). There 'might have been' an invasion of Australia at the end of 1941. 'What if' the Egyptian Army had fought Rommel, alongside remnants of the Commonwealth army in the Nile Delta.

I was first introduced to the concept of accurate TOEs when wargaming at Polytechnic in the 1980s. It soon became apparent that existing TOE charts produced for wargamers, were incomplete and riddled with errors, or were produced for certain rules. These current lists resulted from frustrations, at that time, with existing publications. Then, much TOE data was only accessible through academic literature and archives. It was therefore out of reach of most wargamers and military enthusiasts. Whilst this has changed since 1990, much of what has been recently produced on WW2 has been from contemporary handbooks (not the most reliable of sources), or German WW2 archives. In addition, much data is presented in a top-down format, depicting the number of brigades, regiments and companies within a division. When TOE information for companies and platoons, has been presented it has often been within text, and not consistent between authors and publishers.

The approach for this series has been manifestly different. The TOE charts depicted here, were originally designed for wargamers who are most interested in the unit organisations at the sharp end. Therefore information is presented giving details of combat battalions and combat support unit organisations at higher levels. Organisations within a battalion are presented in a standard user-friendly format. This allows for instant comparisons between opposing forces at a particular time, and quick access to particular levels of units. No peculiar symbols or box diagrams to learn! Brigade, Divisional and Corps support units are all detailed. This presents a clear view of combat support units available to Divisional commanders at a given time. It must be stressed that the emphasis is on combat units. Researchers looking for details on pay corps or veterinary units, for example, will find such lists wanting. However, other wargamers, modellers and researchers will find the current lists ideal. There are no pages of text to read through to find the details they need.

In addition, a unique first is a separate chapter on so-called 'Special Forces'. In many cases, this is be the first published attempt to draw together in one place the TOEs of all Special Forces. This is particularly so for British and Commonwealth WW2 formations.

The format of these charts allows for easy updates, corrections and new information to be incorporated into future volumes, if required. Already, there is sufficient information collected for a further thirty volumes, covering all theatres of war in the 20th Century.

Combat battalions are listed under Main Combat Elements. Brigade and Divisional support units occur under their own headings within Support Units. Accompanying notes cover the allocation of radios, infantry anti-tank weapons, weapons in service dates (IOC – initial operational capability), variations, and other miscellaneous notes. In many publications the levels of issue of radios and training levels are sometimes overlooked. However, these factors can drastically alter the combat ability of a unit, regardless of how well equipped it is in weapons. Here, such considerations are given priority.

For ease, all the various non-combat elements of Headquarters' units are grouped together as rifle squads per HQ. Combined, these usually represent signallers, intelligence staff, service personnel, batmen, cooks, artillery survey units etc. In an emergency, such personnel can be used as extra riflemen. Similarly, vehicles are assumed to have a crew in addition to any troops noted, eg lorry drivers are not included in manpower totals. Supply trucks, wagons, tankers, bread vans etc are also not noted, as they are not direct combat elements, but should be assumed to be there on a general level. See Appendix Two for details of using the charts.

Each volume will be separated into Theatres of Operations for the relevant title, and will follow a standard content for each theatre: Armoured Divisions, Armoured Brigades, Independent Armoured and Armoured Recce units, Mechanised Divisions and Brigades, Motorised Divisions and Brigades, Infantry Divisions, Infantry Brigades, Airborne Brigades/Divisions, Horsed Cavalry formations, Corps support units, Army support units, Special Forces

Further information will be welcomed for updated editions, and should be sent to the author care of the publishers.

NOTE ON ABBREVIATIONS AND NOMENCLATURE

ABBREVIATIONS

AA	anti-aircraft		H/T	halftrack
AALMG	LMG mounted on tripod for AA purposes		HVAP	see APCR
A/C	armoured car		IP	Indian Pattern
ACV	armoured command vehicle		LAD	Light Aid Detachment
AFV	armoured fighting vehicle		LCA	Landing Craft Assault
AP	armour piercing shell, or solid shot, no explosive burst		LCM	Landing Craft, Mechanised
			LMG	light machine gun (Bren, etc)
APC	armour piercing, capped (solid shot with piercing cap)		LP	Local Pattern
			LSI	Landing Ship Infantry
APCBC	armour piercing with cap and ballistic cap		MMG	medium machine gun on tripod of rifle calibre, e.g. Vickers
APCNR	armour piercing composite non-rigid			
APCR	armour piercing, composite rigid (HVAP in American parlance) – tungsten core		MNBDO	Royal Marine Naval Base Defence Organisation
			NZ	New Zealand
APDS	armour piercing discarding sabot		OP	Observation Post, also known as FOO
ARV	armoured recovery vehicle		PHQ	Platoon headquarters
A/T	anti-tank		Pl HQ	Platoon headquarters
AVLB	armoured bridge layer		RCL	Recoilless Rifle (also RR)
BAR	Browning Automatic Rifle		RHQ	regimental headquarters
BHQ	Battlegroup headquarters		RTR	Royal Tank Regiment
Boys	Boys anti-tank rifle		S/C	scout car
Btn HQ	Battalion headquarters		sec	section
Btn	Battalion		SHQ	squadron headquarters
CBW	Chemical, Biological Warfare (usually recce/detection units)		S/L	searchlight
			SMG	sub-machine gun
CHQ	company headquarters		smk	smoke
COPP	Combined Operations Assault Pilotage Parties		SP	self-propelled
CS	close-support		SPG	self-propelled gun
demo	demolition		sqd	squad or section of about 10 men
DHQ	Division headquarters		sqdn	squadron
ECM	Electronic Counter Measures		Trp HQ	troop headquarters truck w/LMG
EW	Electronic Warfare			this was the most common Commonwealth tank in 1940–41, and was usually a 15cwt truck with closed cab and open-backed cargo body, with a pintle-mounted Bren gun just behind the cab. Crew would be a driver and passenger in the front cab with rifles, and one or two men in the back manning the Bren gun and carrying rifles. The prime purpose of the vehicle would be to teach driving skills and group manoeuvring, this being important when it is considered that most people at that time could not drive.
FC	fire control (see 'Notes for wargamers' section)			
flamegun	flamethrower			
FOO	see OP			
HE	high explosive			
HEAT	high explosive anti-tank (hollow charge anti-tank round)			
HKSA	Hong Kong Singapore Artillery			
HMC	howitzer motor carriage			
HMG	heavy machine gun on tripod, 12.7mm or similar class of calibre			
HQ	headquarters		WP	White Phosphorous

ARTILLERY FIRE CONTROL

Artillery batteries are described as having one of three types of fire control, these being Obsolete, Assigned, and Flexible. All are Flexible type unless stated otherwise. For descriptions please see the appendix 'Notes for Wargamers'.

MORALE AND TRAINING VALUES

These are very important in judging the ability of the force in question, and take the form of a descriptive grading. Training includes fieldcraft ability (i.e. the ability or lack thereof to use cover when advancing and hiding), accuracy of firing, and the knowledge of modern combined arms tactics. The latter is significant when trying to form mixed battlegroups tasked to achieve certain objectives. The following criteria are used:

Excellent Training Specialists with over 6 months training in their specialism – e.g. Commandos, Paratroops. Very good levels of initiative, whereby units will continue to operate even with major officer/NCO losses, or where local commanders can improvise new plans on the spot, and carry them out. Good fire discipline with high levels of marksmanship, and extra training in melee combat. Very good fieldcraft skills, with an ability to use cover and concealment for advancing. Have the ingenuity and perseverance to use captured weapons immediately.

Good Training Usually combat veterans with at least 3 months effective training or 6 months combat experience, or with effective combined arms training. Capable of responding to order changes effectively and improvisation under combat stress even with some leader losses. Good fieldcraft skills or experience, able to use terrain instinctively to aid defence and attack. Above-average firing accuracy or good melee skills, and able to use captured weapons with some effect.

Average Training The bulk of British and Commonwealth troops, typically about 8–10 weeks training in basic combat skills. Very much reliant on officers and NCOs in order to function effectively. Capable of following an initial battle plan, and also of combined arms actions, but with limited ability to respond quickly to circumstance, especially when under combat stress and suffering casualties. Average shooting skills and limited fieldcraft skills; would be able to carry out ambushes and create interlocking earthworks for defence given a few hours.

Poor Training Conscripts with rushed training, 6 weeks or less (told how to march and shoot and little else), with inexperienced officers and NCOs. Very often troops being used for something other than they were trained for, e.g. using pioneers, trained to dig, as infantry. Totally incapable of using terrain to aid an advance, and usually indifferent or poor shooting skills. Poor camouflage skills. No enthusiasm for melee combat. Very reliant on officers and NCOs to keep semblance of order, will be poor at changing orders once in combat, and will have little or no training in combined arms combat.

Bad Training Not common in British and Commonwealth armies, basically civilians shown how to use a rifle and told to get on with it! Alternatively, native volunteers with more enthusiasm/bravado than skill, such as Arab tribesmen. Although particular individuals may have military ability, the unit will have no fire discipline, no knowledge of use of cover, and no training in battle planning. Attempting to change orders once under fire or expecting the use of initiative would be disastrous.

Morale is a much more subjective statement, but here it is seen primarily as the ability of a unit to withstand casualties before suffering a morale reverse (i.e. halts if advancing under fire, breaks off and withdraws if defending), and is based loosely on the following:

Excellent Morale Elite troops with high motivation and disregard for casualties, will typically sustain 70% casualties before collapsing. Very capable of continuing to function even with heavy officer/NCO losses. However, will suffer a major drop in enthusiasm if not used in action. Usually highly or well-trained.

Good Morale Veteran troops or troops with well known "warrior" status, can typically take 50% casualties before failing, especially in defence. Capable of continuing to function despite some officer/NCO losses. Typical of many non-English British and Commonwealth units, which were noted for their above-average valour. Indeed, one observer in the Far East commented that an infantry brigade with a Gurkha battalion and an Australian battalion either side of a British battalion, would be capable of dealing with anything.

Average Morale The vast bulk of conscript regular infantry of the period, with sufficient training and motivation to carry out orders at first, but will often halt at 10–15% casualties, and may break at 30% losses, especially if suffering significant officer/NCO losses.

Poor Morale Troops that have had less than 4 weeks training, or have not had any time to co-ordinate with other units, or where motivation is lacking, or the troops are unwilling to advance. Will often halt whilst under fire, even with very light losses. Can still be acceptable in defence, but will break on 15–30% losses.

Bad Morale Not common in British and Commonwealth armies, usually untrained militia, unenthusiastic troops and civilians. Will often break and run even if only receiving ineffective fire. Completely unmotivated troops, such as some of the Australians at Singapore, might be classed thus.

Note that a unit can be described as poor in training but good in morale. Very often troops with indifferent or poor skills would still have high motivation, especially in defence. In certain cultures (especially outside Europe) losses have less effect on unit morale even in poorly trained units or armies – many Soviet and Japanese units would take enormous losses and still try to carry out their orders.

AMMUNITION

Whilst it has been emphasised that troop quality, doctrine and radio allocation are just as important as equipment quality, there is another equipment factor that is often overlooked, i.e. ammunition type issued to anti-tank weapons. Much criticism has been directed towards the 2pdr anti-tank gun and tank gun, especially for the early-war period, yet when its stated penetration figures are examined it can be seen that for its calibre of 40mm, it had an excellent penetration performance, especially when issued with later types of ammunition. It should also be noted that the British 2pdr and 6pdr did have high explosive rounds available to them, although these were rarely issued due to doctrine, and production delays. Here then is a general guide to the various types of anti-tank ammunition issued at different dates:

2pdr 40mm – AP (1938); APC (May 1942); APCBC (September 1942); HE (November 1942).

2pdr Littlejohn – from early 1943, any 2pdr-equipped vehicle could have the Littlejohn adaptor fitted, firing APCNR (armour piercing composite non-rigid) squeezebore rounds.

6pdr 57mm – AP (1941); APC (1941); APCBC (September 1942); HE (January 1943); APCR (October 1943); APDS (May 1944).

17pdr 76.2mm – AP, APC, APCBC (January 1943); HE (June 1944); APDS (August 1944).

25pdr field gun – HE, smoke, mustard gas (1938); AP (early 1942).

37mm M6 tank gun – AP, HE (1938); APC (May 1941); APCBC (September 1942); canister (only Far East, 1944+, when in British/Commonwealth service).

75mm QF tank gun – APC, HE (1942); APCBC (February 1943).

75mm M2, M3 tank guns – APC, HE (1942); APCBC (late 1942).

76mm M1, 3" M7 tank guns – APC, APCBC, HE (1942); HVAP (October 1944).

During the first three months following its introduction, the newer ammunition would be rare and would be used alongside the older standard round, perhaps at the rate of 3–6 rounds per tank or gun. Thus, for example, it can be assumed that British tanks in June 1942 would primarily have 2pdr AP, with a few APC rounds; by August they would mainly have APC, with a few rounds of APCBC available from September 1942. Late 1944 Fireflies would only have 2–3 rounds of APDS, the rest being APCBC and some HE, although by 1945 the allocation was probably greater. Initially there were a lot of problems with the APDS round, as it suffered from grave dispersal problems over 600 metres. These problems were more or less sorted out by 1945, when the Comet came into service.

Note that the 25pdr field gun, often used as an anti-tank gun in the desert, did not have an AP shot until 1942; up until then it had to use plain HE with impact fuses, which, being of 25lb (11kg) weight, would have been quite effective against tanks if a direct hit was scored. The Close Support tanks with 3.7" and 3" howitzers never had an anti-tank round, relying on HE and smoke rounds only.

PART 1
BRITISH HOME FORCES 1939–1943

1.1 BRITISH 1ST ARMOURED DIVISION, BRITAIN, MARCH 1939–MARCH 1940

The Division's main combat elements were:

> 1st Heavy Armoured Brigade (2nd RTR, 3rd RTR, 5th RTR Heavy Armoured Regiments)
> 2nd Light Armoured Brigade (Queen's Bays, 9th Lancers, 10th Hussars Light Armoured Regiments)
> 2 Divisional Motor Infantry Battalions (1st Btn Rifle Brigade, 2nd Btn King's Royal Rifle Corps)

Troops are rated at average training and average morale.

SUPPORT UNITS

Divisional Support

Included:

1st Royal Horse Artillery Regiment (April–October 1939) then the 2nd Royal Horse Artillery Regiment:
(1939–January 1940) each:
> RHQ (4 rifle secs, 3 lorries, radio van, 4 AALMG, 1 Boys)
> 2 Batteries, each: Battery HQ (2 rifle secs, 4 trucks, 2 AALMG)
>> 2 Troops, each: 4 × 25pdr Mk.1, 4 trucks, radio truck, 4 AALMG

1st Field Engineer Squadron: Sqdn HQ (2 rifle secs, 1 lorry, 1 motorcycle)
> Troops, each: 4 (12 man) rifle/engineer secs, 3 LMG, 2 lorries

1st Field Park Troop, Royal Engineers: stores, workshop sections

60th Anti-Tank Regiment (December 1939–February 1940 only):
> 3 A/T Batteries, each: Battery HQ (1 rifle sec, 1 truck)
>> 3 Troops, each: 4 × 2pdr, 4 trucks

101st Mixed Anti-Tank/Anti-Aircraft Regiment (February 1940+):
> 2 A/T Batteries, each: Battery HQ (1 rifle sec, 1 truck)
>> 3 Troops, each: 4 × 2pdr, 4 trucks, 2 LMG
> 2 AA Batteries, each: Battery HQ (1 rifle squad, 1 truck)
>> 3 Troops, each: 4 × 40mmL60 Bofors, 4 trucks

Brigade Support

1st Heavy Armoured Brigade HQ (6 × Vickers VIB, 4 × A-13 Mk.1 Cruisers)
2nd Light Armoured Brigade HQ (6 × Vickers VIB, 4 × A-9 Cruisers)

MAIN COMBAT ELEMENTS

Light Armoured Regiment

RHQ (4 × Vickers VIC, 3 recovery trucks)
2 Squadrons, each: Sqdn HQ (1 × Vickers VIC, 2 × Vickers VIB)
> 5 Troops, each: 3 × Vickers VIA/B
1 Squadron: Sqdn HQ (1 × Vickers VIC, 2 × Vickers VIB)
> 1 Troop: 3 × A-9 Cruiser
> 4 Troops, each: 3 × Vickers VIB

Heavy Armoured Regiment

RHQ (2 × A-13 Mk.1, 2 × A-9 CS tanks, 3 recovery trucks)
3 Squadrons, each: Sqdn HQ (1 × Vickers VIC, 2 × A-10 Cruisers)
> 1 1/2-Squadron: HQ (1 × Vickers VIB)
>> 2 Troops, each: 3 × Vickers VIB
> 1 1/2-Squadron: HQ (1 × A-10 or A-13 Mk1 Cruiser)
>> 2 Troops, each: 2 × A-10 or A-13 Mk.1

Actual 3rd Royal Tank Regiment, September–November 1939

RHQ (2 × A-9, 1 recovery truck)
A Squadron: Sqdn HQ (1 × A-9 with no gun)
> 1 1/2-Squadron: HQ (1 × Vickers VIB)
>> 2 Troops, each: 2 × Vickers VIB
> 1 1/2-Squadron: HQ (1 × A-9)
>> 1 Troop: 2 × A-9
B Squadron: Sqdn HQ (1 × A-9 with no gun)
> 1 1/2-Squadron: HQ (1 × Vickers VIB)
>> 2 Troops, each: 2 × Vickers VIB
> 1 1/2-Squadron: HQ (1 × A-9 with no gun)
>> 1 Troop: 2 × A-9
C Squadron: Sqdn HQ (1 × A-9 with no gun)
> 1 1/2-Squadron: HQ (1 × Vickers VIB)

2 Troops, each: 2 × Vickers VIB
1 1/2-Squadron: HQ (1 × A-9 with no gun)
1 Troop: 3 × A-9
1 Medium Tank Group: 5 × Medium Mk.III

Actual 3rd Royal Tank Regiment, December 1939-February 1940

RHQ (3 × A-9, 2 recovery trucks, 2 × Vickers VIB)
A Squadron: Sqdn HQ (1 × A-9 with no gun)
1 1/2-Squadron: HQ (1 × Vickers VIB)
2 Troops, each: 3 × Vickers VIB
1 1/2-Squadron: HQ (1 × A-9)
1 Troop: 2 × A-9
B Squadron: Sqdn HQ (1 × A-9 with no gun)
1 1/2-Squadron: HQ (1 × Vickers VIB)
2 Troops, each: 3 × Vickers VIB
1 1/2-Squadron: HQ (1 × A-9 with no gun)
1 Troop: 2 × A-9
C Squadron: Sqdn HQ (1 × A-9 with no gun)
1 1/2-Squadron: HQ (1 × Vickers VIB)
2 Troops, each: 3 × Vickers VIB
1 1/2-Squadron: HQ (1 × A-9 with no gun)
1 Troop: 3 × A-9

Actual 3rd Royal Tank Regiment, March 1940

RHQ (2 × A-13 Mk.1, 2 × A-10 CS tanks, 3 recovery trucks)
A, B Squadrons, each: Sqdn HQ (2 × A-9, 1 × A-10CS Cruiser)
1 1/2-Squadron: HQ (1 × Vickers VIB)
2 Troops, each: 3 × Vickers VIB
1 1/2-Squadron: HQ (1 × A-9 Cruiser)
2 Troops, each: 2 × A-9
C Squadron: Sqdn HQ (1 × A-10CS, 1 × A-13 Mk.1)
1 1/2-Squadron: HQ (1 × Vickers VIB)
2 Troops, each: 3 × Vickers VIB
1 1/2-Squadron; HQ (1 × A-13 Mk.1)
2 Troops, each: 2 × A-13 Mk.1

Proposed Heavy Armoured Regiment

RHQ (2 × Vickers VIC, 2 × A-9 CS tanks)
3 Squadrons, each: Sqdn HQ (1 × Vickers VIC, 2 × A-9 CS tanks)
1 1/2-Squadron HQ (1 × A-10)
2 Troops, each: 2 × A-10
1 1/2-Squadron HQ (1 × A-13 Mk.1)
3 Troops, each: 2 × A-13 Mk.1

Divisional Motor Battalion

Btn HQ (2 trucks, 1 lorry, 2 rifle secs, 1 Boys, 1 LMG, 2 × Daimler Scout Car)
4 Companies, each: Coy HQ (1 (8 man) rifle sec, 1 Boys, 2 × 8cwt trucks, 1 × Scout Car)
3 platoons, each: 1 (4 man) rifle PHQ sec, 1 × 2", 1 truck, 3 (7 man) rifle secs, 3 Boys, 3 LMG, 3 trucks
1 platoon: Pl HQ (2 × Scout Carrier, 2 × Scout Cars)
3 Sections, each: 3 × Bren Carrier, 3 LMG, 3 Boys, 1 (6 man) rifle sec

Notes
1.   Radios were in all AFV and other Coy HQs, when working. Artillery is rated Assigned FC.
2.   Infantry sections had No.68 rifle A/T grenades or No.73 or No.74 A/T grenades.
3.   The division was in training in England and not committed to the BEF. The planned organisation of the Heavy Armoured Regiments is shown for comparison.
4.   Motor Battalion organisation was paper organisation, in practice Scout Cars were rare and usually replaced by staff cars.
5.   Actual examples of the 3rd Royal Tank Regiment are shown for comparison to the planned organisations.

1.2   BRITISH 1ST ARMOURED DIVISION, BRITAIN, AUGUST-OCTOBER 1940

The Division's main combat elements were:
2nd Armoured Brigade (Queen's Bays, 9th Lancers, 10th Hussars Armoured Regiments, 1st Btn Rifle Brigade Motor Battalion)
3rd Armoured Brigade (2nd, 3rd, 5th Royal Tank Regiments, 2nd KRRC Motor Battalion)
Troops are rated at poor training and average morale.

SUPPORT UNITS

Divisional Support

Included:
101st Mixed Anti-Tank/Anti-Aircraft Regiment:
2 Anti-Tank Batteries, each: Battery HQ (2 × Bedford OXA Anti-Tank Lorries or 1 truck)
3 Troops, each: 4 × Bedford OXA A/T lorries or 2 × 2pdr A/T guns, 2 trucks

2 AA Batteries, each: Battery HQ (1 rifle sec, 1 truck)
    3 platoons, each: 4 × 40mmL60 Bofors, 4 trucks
1st Field Engineer Squadron: Sqdn HQ (2 rifle secs, 1 lorry, 1 motorcycle)
    4 Troops, each: 4 (12 man) rifle/engineer secs, 3 LMG, 2 lorries
1st Engineer Park Squadron: (175 men)
    1 Workshop Section
    1 Bridging & Stores Section
11th Royal Horse Artillery Regiment: RHQ (4 rifle secs, 3 lorries, radio van, 4 AALMG, 1 Boys)
2 Batteries, each: Battery HQ (2 rifle secs, 4 trucks, 2 AALMG)
    2 Troops, each: 4 × 25pdr field guns, 4 trucks

Brigade Support
Armoured Brigade HQ (2 × A-13 Mk2, 2 staff cars, 3 × Daimler Scout Cars)

MAIN COMBAT ELEMENTS

Armoured Regiment
RHQ (Btn HQ): 3 × Vickers VIC, 2 × Daimler scout cars or field cars
3 Squadrons, each: Sqdn HQ (1 × A-13 Mk.2)
    2 Troops, each: 3 × A-13 Mk.2 Cruiser IV

Motor Rifle Battalion
Btn HQ (2 trucks, 1 lorry, 2 rifle secs, 2 LMG)
4 Companies, each: Coy HQ (1 rifle sec, 1 × 2", 1 Boys, 2 MMG, 2 trucks)
    3 platoons, each: 4 (6 man) rifle secs, 4 Boys, 1 × 2" mortar, 3 LMG, 4 trucks
    1 platoon: Pl HQ: 1 × Scout Carrier, 1 × staff car, 1 LMG
        2 sections, each: 3 × Bren Carrier, 3 LMG, 3 Boys, 1 (6 man) rifle sec
1 Battery: 2 × 3" mortars, 2 trucks

Notes
1. Radios were in all AFV and other Coy HQ, when working. Artillery is rated Assigned FC.
2. Infantry may have had No.68 A/T grenades or No.73 or No.74 A/T grenades.
3. The Division is rated average morale and poor training, due to rebuilding. It would have been used to counter-attack any German invasion of England if necessary.

1.3 BRITISH 1ST ARMOURED DIVISION, BRITAIN, OCTOBER 1940–MARCH 1941
The Division's main combat elements were:
    2nd Armoured Brigade (Queen's Bays, 9th Lancers, 10th Hussars Armoured Regiments, 1st Btn Rifle Brigade Motor Battalion)
    22nd Armoured Brigade (2nd Royal Gloucestershire Hussars, 3rd County of London Yeomanry, 4th County of London Yeomanry Armoured Regiments, 2nd KRRC Motor Battalion)
    Divisional Recce Regiment (12th Lancers) (November 1940+)
    Divisional Infantry Battalion (9th Battalion the Foresters) (February 1941+)
Troops are rated at average training and average morale.

SUPPORT UNITS

Divisional Support
Included:
11th Horse Artillery Regiment: RHQ (4 rifle secs, 3 lorries, radio van, 4 AALMG, 1 Boys)
3 Batteries, each: Battery HQ (2 rifle secs, 4 trucks, 2 AALMG)
    2 Troops, each: 4 × 25pdr field guns, 4 trucks, radio truck
61st Light AA Regiment:
    3 AA Batteries, each: Battery HQ (1 rifle sec, 1 truck) (November 1940+)
    3 platoons, each: 4 × 40mmL60 Bofors, 4 trucks
76th Anti-Tank Regiment:
    3 Anti-Tank Batteries, each: Battery HQ (1 rifle sec, 1 truck) (November 1940+)
    3 Troops, each: 3 × 2pdr A/T guns, 4 trucks, 1 LMG
1st, 7th Field Engineer Squadrons, each: Sqdn HQ (2 rifle secs, 1 lorry, 1 motorcycle)
    4 Troops, each: 4 (12 man) rifle/engineer secs, 3 LMG, 2 lorries
1st Engineer Park Squadron: (175 men)
    1 Workshop Section
    1 Bridging & Stores Section

Brigade Support
Armoured Brigade HQ (2 × A-13 Mk2, 2 staff cars, 3 × Daimler Scout Cars)

MAIN COMBAT ELEMENTS

Armoured Regiment, 2nd Armoured Brigade
RHQ (3 × Vickers VIC, 2 × Daimler scout cars or field cars)
3 Squadrons, each: Sqdn HQ (1 × A-13 Mk.2)
    2 Troops, each: 3 × A-13 Mk.2 Cruiser IV

2nd Royal Gloucestershire Hussars Armoured Regiment, 22nd Armoured Brigade
RHQ (3 × M36 Dutchman light tanks, 1 × Vickers VIB)
3 Squadrons, each: Sqdn HQ (3 × Vickers-Carden-Loyd M36 Dutchman)
    4 Troops, each: 3 × Vickers-Carden-Loyd M36 Dutchman

County of London Yeomanry Armoured Regiments, 22nd Armoured Brigade
RHQ (2 trucks, 1 × Vickers VIB)
3 Squadrons, each: Sqdn HQ (1 truck+ LMG, 1 car)
    4 Troops, each: 3 × light trucks with LMG, 3 (4 man) crew secs

Motor Rifle Battalion of Armoured Brigade
Btn HQ (2 trucks, 1 lorry, 2 rifle secs, 2 LMG)
4 Companies, each: Coy HQ (1 rifle sec, 1 × 2", 1 Boys, 2 MMG, 2 trucks)
    3 platoons, each: 4 (6 man) rifle secs, 4 Boys, 0–1 × 2" mortar, 3 LMG, 4 trucks
    1 platoon: Pl HQ: 1 × Scout Carrier, 1 × staff car, 1 LMG
      2 sections, each: 3 × Bren Carrier, 3 LMG, 3 Boys, 1 (6 man) rifle sec
0–1 Battery: 2 × 3" mortars, 2 trucks

9th Battalion the Foresters Divisional Motorised Infantry Battalion (February 1941+)
Btn HQ (2 rifle secs, 2 lorries, 1 LMG)
4 Companies, each: Coy HQ (1 rifle sec, 1 truck)
    3 platoons, each: 3 rifle secs, 1–3 LMG, 1 Boys, 1 lorry
1 Support Company: Coy HQ (1 rifle sec , 1 truck)
    1 platoon: 4 × 3" mortars, 2 lorries, 1 radio truck
    1 platoon: 2 rifle/engineer secs, 1 lorry, 2 LMG
    1 platoon: 2 AALMG, 2 trucks
    1 platoon: Pl HQ: 1 Bren Carrier, 1 × staff car, 1 LMG
      3 sections, each: 3 Bren Carrier, 3 LMG, 1 Boys, 1 (6 man) rifle sec

12th Lancers Divisional Armoured Recce Regiment (November 1940+)
RHQ (2–4 × Guy Mk1 or Rolls-Royce M1920)
Liaison/Communication Troop: 0–12 × staff cars &/or improvised armoured saloon cars
3 Squadrons, each: Sqdn HQ (3 × Guy Mk1 or Rolls-Royce M1920, 3 × staff cars)
    4 Troops, each: 3 × Guy Mk.1 or Rolls-Royce M1920 or Daimler Scout Cars?

Notes
1. Radios were in all AFV and other Coy HQ, when working.
2. Infantry may have had No.68 A/T grenades or No.73 or No.74 A/T grenades.
3. The 22nd Brigade had only the 2nd Royal Gloucestershire Hussars Armoured Regiment actually equipped with impounded Vickers tanks originally built for the Dutch East Indies, the other two regiments having trucks.
4. It is known that the 12th Lancers had some Guy Mk1 armoured cars at least, and had used Morris CS9 in France, so may have some of these. Also some Lanchesters and Rolls-Royce armoured cars were available in England at this time.

1.4   BRITISH 2ND ARMOURED DIVISION, BRITAIN, JUNE–SEPTEMBER 1940
The Division's main combat elements were:
    1st Light Armoured Brigade (King's Dragoons Guards, 4th Hussars, 3rd Hussars Armoured Regiments)
    22nd Armoured Brigade (2nd Royal Gloucestershire Hussars, 3rd and 4th County of London Yeomanry Armoured Regiments)
    2 Divisional Motor Battalions (1st Rangers, 1st Tower Hamlets Rifles)
Troops are rated at average training and average morale.

SUPPORT UNITS

Divisional Support
Included:
12th Royal Horse Artillery Regiment (up to July 1940)
    1 Battery: Battery HQ (2 rifle secs, 4 trucks, 2 AALMG)
      2 Troops, each: 4 × 18pdr Mk.IV field guns, 6 civilian trucks
    1 Battery: Battery HQ (2 rifle secs, 4 trucks, 2 AALMG)
      2 Troops, each: 4 × 4.5"L15 QF howitzers, 6 civilian trucks
    1 Battery: Battery HQ (2 rifle secs, 4 trucks, 2 AALMG)
      2 Troops, each: 4 × 75mm M1897 field guns, 6 civilian trucks
2nd Royal Horse Artillery Regiment: (from August 1940)
    RHQ (4 rifle secs, 3 lorries, radio van, 4 AALMG, 1 Boys)
    2 Batteries, each: BHQ (2 rifle secs, 4 trucks, 2 AALMG, 2 × Vickers VIA OP)
      2 Troops, each: 4 × 18pdr or 25pdr Mk.1, 4 trucks, radio truck
102nd Anti-Tank/Light AA Regiment:
    2 Anti-Tank Batteries, each: Battery HQ (2 × Bedford OXA Anti-Tank Lorries)
      3 Troops, each: 4 × Bedford OXA A/T lorries
    2 AA Batteries, each: Battery HQ (1 rifle sec, 1 truck)
      3 platoons, each: 4 × 40mm Bofors or 8 AALMG?, 4 trucks
3rd Field Engineer Squadron: Sqdn HQ (2 rifle secs, 1 lorry, 1 motorcycle)
    4 Troops, each: 4 (12 man) rifle/engineer secs, 3 LMG, 2 lorries

142nd Field Park Troop: Workshop, Stores Sections

Brigade Support
Armoured Brigade HQ (3 × Vickers VIc, 3 × A-10 Cruisers, 2 staff cars, 1 × Daimler S/C)

MAIN COMBAT ELEMENTS

Light Armoured Regiment, 1st Light Armoured Brigade
RHQ (4 × Vickers VIc)
2 Squadrons, each: Sqdn HQ (3 × Vickers VIB)
    4 Troops, each: 3 × Vickers VIB
1 Attached Squadron: Sqdn HQ (2 × A-9 or A-13 Mk.II or Universal Carriers)
    3 Troops, each: 3 × A-9 or A-13 Mk.II or Universal Carriers

2nd Gloucestershire Yeomanry Armoured Regiment, 22nd Armoured Brigade
RHQ(3 × M36 Dutchman, 1 × Vickers VIB)
3 Squadrons, each: Sqdn HQ (3 × Vickers-Carden-Loyd M36 Dutchman)
    4 Troops, each: 3 × Vickers-Carden-Loyd M36 Dutchman

3rd and 4th County of London Yeomanry Armoured Regiments, 22nd Armoured Brigade, each:
RHQ (2 trucks, 1 × Vickers VIB)
2 Squadrons, each: Sqdn HQ (1 truck+ LMG, 1 car)
    4 Troops, each: 3 × light trucks with LMG, 3 (4 man) crew secs
1 Squadron: Sqdn HQ (1 truck+ LMG, 1 car)
    3 Troops, each: 3 × Universal Carrier+ armoured roof, Boys or Bren

1st Rangers, 1st Tower Hamlets Rifles Divisional Motor Rifle Battalions, each:
Btn HQ (2 lorries, 2 rifle secs)
3 Companies, each: Coy HQ (1 rifle sec, 1 × 2" mortar, 1 Boys, 1 lorry)
    3 platoons, each: 3 (6 man) rifle secs, 2 LMG, 2 lorries
    1 platoon: Pl HQ: 1 × Bren Carrier
        2 sections, each: 3 × Bren Carrier, 1 LMG, 1 (6 man) rifle sec

Notes
1.   Radios are in all AFV Pl HQ and other CHQs, when working. Artillery is Assigned FC.
2.   Infantry secs had No.68 A/T grenades or No.73 or No.74 A/T grenades.
3.   At least one Regiment put armoured roofs on their Universal Carriers, but this reduced mobility severely, treat as speed 36kmh on road, 12kmh cross country.
4.   The 1st Light Armoured Brigade is known to have 150 Vickers VI, and 33 "Cruisers" available in June, probably from training units.

1.5 BRITISH 2ND ARMOURED DIVISION, BRITAIN, OCTOBER–DECEMBER 1940
The Division's main combat elements were:
    1st Armoured Brigade (King's Dragoons Guards, 4th Hussars, 3rd Hussars Armoured Regiments)
    3rd Armoured Brigade (2nd RTR, 3rd RTR, 5th RTR Armoured Regiments)
    2 Divisional Motor Battalions (1st Rangers, 1st Tower Hamlets Rifles)
Troops are rated at average training and average morale.

SUPPORT UNITS

Divisional Support
Included:
2nd Royal Horse Artillery Regiment: RHQ (4 rifle secs, 3 lorries, radio van, 4 AALMG, 1 Boys)
    2 Batteries, each: BHQ (2 rifle secs, 4 trucks, 2 AALMG, 2 × Vickers VIA OP)
        2 Troops, each: 4 × 18pdr or 25pdr Mk.1, 4 trucks, radio truck
102nd Anti-Tank/Light AA Regiment:
    2 Anti-Tank Batteries, each: Battery HQ (2 × Bedford OXA Anti-Tank Lorries or 2 trucks)
        3 Troops, each: 4 × Bedford OXA A/T lorries or 4 × 2pdr, 4 trucks
    2 AA Batteries, each: Battery HQ (1 rifle sec, 1 truck)
        3 platoons, each: 4 × 40mm Bofors or 16 AALMG?, 4 trucks
3rd Field Engineer Squadron: Sqdn HQ (2 rifle secs, 1 lorry, 1 motorcycle)
    4 Troops, each: 4 (12 man) rifle/engineer secs, 3 LMG, 2 lorries
142nd Field Engineer Park Troop: 1 Workshop Section, 1 Stores Section

Brigade Support
Armoured Brigade HQ: 3 × Vickers VIc, 7 × A-10 Cruisers, 2 staff cars, 1 × Daimler S/C

MAIN COMBAT ELEMENTS

Armoured Regiment, 1st Armoured Brigade
RHQ (4 × Vickers VIC)
3 Squadrons, each: Sqdn HQ (4 × Vickers VIB light tanks)
    4 Troops, each: 3 × Vickers VIB

2nd Royal Tank Regiment, 3rd Armoured Brigade
RHQ (4 × A-10, 0–6 × Daimler Scout Cars)
2 Squadrons, each: Sqdn HQ (2 × A-10 Cruisers, 2 × A-9 CS)
          5 Troops, each: 3 × A-10
1 Squadron: Sqdn HQ (2 × A-13 Mk.2, 2 × A-9 CS)
          5 Troops, each: 3 × A-13 Mk.2

3rd, 5th Royal Tank Regiments, 3rd Armoured Brigade, each:
RHQ (4 × A-13 Mk.2, 6–10 × Daimler Scout Cars)
1 Squadron: Sqdn HQ (2 × A-10, 2 × A-10 CS)
          5 Troops, each: 3 × A-10
2 Squadrons, each: Sqdn HQ (2 × A-13 Mk.2, 2 × A-10 CS)
          4 Troops, each: 3 × A-13 Mk.1/2

1st Rangers, 1st Tower Hamlets Rifles Divisional Motor Rifle Battalions, each:
Btn HQ (2 lorries, 2 rifle secs)
3 Companies, each: Coy HQ (1 rifle sec, 1 × 2" mortar, 1 Boys, 1 lorry)
          3 platoons, each: 3 (6 man) rifle secs, 2 LMG, 2 lorries
          1 platoon: Pl HQ: 1 × Universal Carrier, 1 LMG
                    3 sections, each: 3 × Universal Carrier, 3 LMG, 1 Boys, 1 rifle sec
0–1 Battery: 2 × 3" mortars, 2 trucks

Notes
1.   Radios were in all AFV Pl HQ and other CHQs, when working. Artillery is Assigned FC.
2.   Infantry secs had No.68 A/T grenades or No.73 or No.74 A/T grenades.
3.   At the end of 1940 the Division was en route to the Middle East.
4.   In July the 3rd RTR had some A-13 Mk.2 and 10 × Daimler Scout Cars.

1.6   BRITISH 6TH ARMOURED DIVISION, BRITAIN, MAY–SEPTEMBER 1940
The Division's main combat elements were:
          26th Armoured Brigade, in June 1940 renamed 1st Motorised Machine Gun Brigade (16th/5th Lancers, 17th/21st Lancers, 2nd Lothian & Border Horse Armoured Regiments)
          20th Armoured Brigade (1st Royal Gloucestershire Hussars, 1st and 2ndNorthamptonshire Yeomanry Armoured Regiments)
          Divisional Infantry Battalion (Queen's Own Rifles West Kent Regiment?)
The Division was in the process of formation and should be rated poor training and morale.

SUPPORT UNITS

Divisional Support
Included:
12th Royal Horse Artillery Regiment: from August 1940)
          1 Battery: Battery HQ (2 rifle secs, 4 trucks, 2 AALMG)
                    2 Troops, each: 4 × 18pdr Mk.IV field guns, 6 civilian trucks
          1 Battery: Battery HQ (2 rifle secs, 4 trucks, 2 AALMG)
                    2 Troops, each: 4 × 4.5"L15 QF howitzers, 6 civilian trucks
          1 Battery: Battery HQ (2 rifle secs, 4 trucks, 2 AALMG)
                    2 Troops, each: 4 × 75mm M1897 field guns, 6 civilian trucks
51st Light AA Regiment:
          3 Batteries, each: Battery HQ (1 rifle sec, 1 truck)
                    3 Troops, each: 4 × Lewis AAMG, 2 trucks
72nd Anti-Tank Regiment:
          3 Batteries, each: 1 Troop: 2–3 × 2pdr A/T guns, 4 trucks
5th Field Engineer Squadron: Sqdn HQ (1 rifle sec, 1 car)
          1 Troop: 4 rifle/engineer secs, 2 lorries, 1 LMG

Brigade Support
Armoured Brigade or Motorised MG Brigade HQ (4 rifle secs, 6 trucks, 2 cars)

MAIN COMBAT ELEMENTS

Armoured Regiment, 26th Armoured Brigade or 1st Motorised MG Brigade
RHQ (2 trucks, 4 (4 man) crew secs, 2 cars)
3 Squadrons, each: Sqdn HQ (2 trucks+ LMG, 2 (4 man) crew secs, 2 Boys)
          3 Troops, each: 6 cars or trucks, 2 MMG, 2 LMG, 2 Boys
          1 Troop: 2 × Matilda II (August 1940+)

Yeomanry Armoured Regiment, 20th Armoured Brigade
RHQ (2 trucks, 2 cars, 4 (4 man) crew secs)
1 Armoured Detachment: Sqdn HQ (1 × Guy Mk.1 armoured car)
          1 Troop: 3 × Guy Mk.1
          1–3 Troops, each: 3 × Bren Carriers, 3 LMG, 1 Boys
2 Squadrons, each: Sqdn HQ (2 trucks+ LMG)

3 Troops, each: 3–6 cars, 3–6 LMG, Boys, MMG

Divisional Infantry Battalion

Btn HQ (2 rifle secs, 1 staff car, 2 trucks, 5 motorcycles)
4 Companies, each: Coy HQ (1 (13 man) rifle squad)
        3 platoons, each: 1 (7 man) Pl HQ rifle sec, 1 × 2" mortar, 1 Boys, 3 (10 man) rifle secs, 3 LMG, 2 lorries
1 Support Company: Coy HQ (1 rifle sec, 1 truck)
        1 platoon: 2 × 3" mortars, 1 truck, radio truck
        1 platoon: 2 × AALMG on trucks
        1 platoon: 2 rifle/engineer secs, 1 lorry, 1 LMG
        1 platoon: Pl HQ: 1 × Carrier, 1 × Daimler S/C, 1 LMG
            1–3 sections, each: 3 × Bren Carrier, 3 LMG, 1 (6 man) rifle sec.

Notes
1. Radios were in all AFV and other CHQs when working.
2. Infantry had molotov cocktails if in defence.
3. Details were provisional.
4. By December 1940 each Armoured Regiment had about 15 Matilda II or Valentine I, and the divisional Infantry Battalion had been replaced by two Motor Battalions, the 2nd Btn Rangers and 2nd Btn Tower Hamlet Rifles.

1.7   BRITISH 9TH ARMOURED DIVISION, BRITAIN, JANUARY–MAY 1941

The Division's main combat elements were:
    27th Armoured Brigade (4th/7th Dragoon Guards, 13/18th Royal Hussars, 1st East Riding Yeomanry Armoured Regiments and 1st Btn Queen Victoria's Rifles Motor Battalion)
    28th Armoured Brigade later renamed 3rd Motor Machine Gun Brigade (5th Royal Inniskilling Dragoon Guards, 15th/19th King's Royal Hussars, 1st Fife & Forfar Yeomanry Motor Machine Gun Battalions and 2nd Btn Queen Victoria's Rifles Motor Battalion)
    Divisional Motorised Infantry Battalion (11th Worcestershire Regiment)
    Divisional Armoured Car Regiment (Inns of Court Armoured Car Regiment)
Troops are rated at poor training and average morale.

SUPPORT UNITS

Divisional Support

Included:
6th Royal Horse Artillery Regiment:
        3 Artillery Batteries, each: Battery HQ (4 rifle secs, 4 lorries, 1 AALMG)
            2 Troops, each: 4 × 25pdr, 4 trucks, radio truck, 1 AALMG, 1 Boys
74th Anti-Tank Regiment:
        3 Batteries, each: Battery HQ (1 rifle sec, 1 truck)
            3 Troops, each: 1–4 × 2pdr, 2 LMG, 4 trucks or Loyd Carriers
54th Light AA Regiment:
        3 Batteries, each: Battery HQ (rifle sec, 1 truck)
            3 Troops, each: 4 × 40mm Bofors, 4 trucks
10th, 11th Field Engineer Squadrons, each: Sqdn HQ (2 rifle secs, 1 lorry)
        4 Troops, each: 4 (12 man) rifle/engineer secs, 2 LMG, 2 lorries
146th Engineer Park Squadron:
    1 Workshop Section
    1 Bridging and Stores Section

Brigade Support

27th Armoured Brigade HQ (2 × Vickers VIB, 4 trucks+LMG, 2 rifle secs)
28th Armoured Brigade/3rd Motor Machine Gun Brigade HQ (6 trucks+ LMG, 2 cars+ MMG, 4 rifle secs)

MAIN COMBAT ELEMENTS

Armoured Regiment (27th Brigade)

RHQ (4 × Vickers VIB light tanks)
3 Squadrons, each: Sqdn HQ (2 × saloon cars, each: 1 MMG or Boys)
        3 Troops, each: 4 × saloon cars + Vickers MMG or Boys A/T rifle, 2 cars+ LMG
        2 Troops, each: 3 (8 man) rifle secs, 3 LMG or (March 1941+) 3 × Covenanter

5th Dragoons Guards (March 1941+)

RHQ (4 × Vickers VIB light tanks)
1 Armoured Squadron: Sqdn HQ (1 × Crusader I, 4 × Vickers VIB)
        2 Troops, each: 3 × Covenanter
        1 Troop: 4 × saloon cars+ Vickers MMG
        1 Troop: 1 × Vickers VIB, 2 × Vickers Commercial light tanks
2 Squadrons, each: Sqdn HQ (2 × saloon cars+ Vickers MMG or Boys)
        3 Troops, each: 4 × saloon cars+ Vickers MMG or Boys A/T rifle, 2 cars+ LMG
        2 Troops, each: 3 (8 man) rifle secs, 3 LMG or (May 1941+) 3 × Covenanter

Motor Machine Gun Battalion (28th Brigade)

Btn HQ (2 trucks, 2 LMG, 2 × Vickers VIB light tanks)
3 Squadrons, each: Sqdn HQ (2 trucks+ LMG)
        3 Troops, each: 6 × saloon cars, each: 1 MMG or Boys or LMG team
        2 Troops, each: 3 (8 man) rifle secs, 3 LMG

11th Worcestershire Regiment Divisional Motorised Battalion

Btn HQ (3 rifle secs, 1 lorry, 2 trucks, 1 LMG)
4 Companies, each: Coy HQ (1 rifle sec, 1 lorry)
        3 platoons, each: 1 (7 man) rifle Pl HQ sec, 1 × 2" mortar, 1 Boys, 3 (10 man) rifle secs, 3 LMG, 2 lorries
1 Support Company: Coy HQ (1 rifle sec, 1 truck)
        1 battery: 6 × 3" mortars, 6 trucks, radio truck, 2 Boys
        1 platoon: 4 trucks+ AALMG, 1 Boys
        1 platoon: 2 (7 man) rifle/engineer secs, 1 LMG, 1 lorry
        1 platoon: Pl HQ: 1 × Universal Carrier, 1 LMG, 1 × Daimler S/C
            4 sections, each: 3 × Universal Carriers, 3 LMG, 1 rifle sec, 1 × 2", 1 × Boys

Queen Victoria's Rifles Motor Rifle Battalion (of Armoured Brigades)

Btn HQ (2 rifle secs, 2 trucks, 1 lorry)
3 Companies, each: Coy HQ (1 rifle sec, 1 × 2" mortar, 1 Boys, 2 trucks)
        3 platoons, each: 4 (7 man) rifle secs, 3 LMG, 1 × 2", 4 Boys, 4 trucks
        1 platoon: Pl HQ: 1 × Universal Carrier, 1 LMG, 1 × Daimler S/C
            3 sections, each: 3 × Universal Carriers, 3 LMG, 1 rifle sec, 1 × 2", 1 × Boys

Inns of Court Divisional Armoured Car Regiment

RHQ (4 × Armoured Cars)
3 Squadrons, each: Sqdn HQ (2 × Armoured Cars)
        5 Troops, each: 2 × Armoured Cars, 2 × Scout Cars
1 Liaison/Communications Troop: 4 Sections, each: 3 × Scout Cars

Notes
1.   Radios were in all tanks and armoured cars, Carrier PHQs, and other CHQs.
2.   Infantry secs had No.74 A/T grenades or molotovs.
3.   The 28th Brigade was renamed the 3rd Motor Machine Gun Brigade to more reflect reality.
4.   Types of armoured cars are not known but could be Ironsides, Beaverettes and other Humber Light Recce Cars, or improvised armoured lorries.
5.   In April 1941 the Motor Battalions were renamed the 7th and 8th King's Royal Rifle Corps Motor Battalions.

1.8   BRITISH 9TH ARMOURED DIVISION, BRITAIN, JUNE 1941–JUNE 1942

The Division's main combat elements were:
        27th Armoured Brigade (4th/7th Dragoon Guards, 13/18th Royal Hussars, 1st East Riding Yeomanry Armoured Regiments and 7th KRRC Motor Battalion)
        28th Armoured Brigade (5th Royal Inniskilling Dragoon Guards, 15th/19th King's Royal Hussars, 1st Fife & Forfar Yeomanry Armoured Regiments and 8th KRRC Motor Battalion)
        Divisional Machine Gun Battalion (11th Worcestershire Regiment)
        Divisional Armoured Car Regiment (Inns of Court Armoured Car Regiment)
Troops are rated at average training and average morale.

SUPPORT UNITS

Divisional Support

Included:
6th Royal Horse Artillery Regiment:
        3 Artillery Batteries, each: Battery HQ (4 rifle secs, 4 lorries, 1 AALMG)
            2 Troops, each: 4 × 25pdr, 4 trucks, radio truck, 1 AALMG, 1 Boys
74th Anti-Tank Regiment:
        3 Batteries, each: Battery HQ (1 rifle sec, 1 truck)
            3 Troops, each: 4 × 2pdr, 2 LMG, 4 trucks or Loyd Carriers
54th Light AA Regiment:
        3 Batteries, each: Battery HQ (rifle sec, 1 truck)
            2 Troops, each: 4 × 40mm Bofors, 4 trucks
10th, 11th Field Engineer Squadrons, each: Sqdn HQ (2 rifle secs, 1 lorry)
        4 Troops, each: 4 (12 man) rifle/engineer secs, 2 LMG, 2 lorries
146th Engineer Park Squadron:
        1 Workshop Section
        1 Bridging and Stores Section
2 Airfield Defence Squadrons, each: Sqdn HQ (3 × Vickers VIB)
        4 Troops, each: 3 × Vickers VIB

Brigade Support

Armoured Brigade HQ: 8 × Covenanter, 1 × ACV, 1 × Vickers VI AA

MAIN COMBAT ELEMENTS

Armoured Regiment
RHQ (4 × Covenanter, 3 × Scammell Wreckers)
3 Squadrons, each: Sqdn HQ (2 × Covenanter, 2 × Covenanter CS)
    4 Troops, each: 3 × Covenanter

Motor Rifle Battalion (of Armoured Brigade)
Btn HQ (2 rifle secs, 2 trucks, 1 lorry)
3 Companies, each: Coy HQ (1 rifle sec, 1 × 2" mortar, 1 Boys, 2 trucks)
        3 platoons, each: 4 (8 man) rifle secs, 3 LMG, 1 × 2" mortar, 4 Boys, 4 trucks
        1 platoon: 2 × 3" mortars, 2 × Vickers MMG, 4 trucks (1942 only)
        1 platoon: Pl HQ: 1 × Universal Carrier, 1 LMG, 1 × Daimler S/C
            3 sections, each: 3 × Universal Carriers, 3 LMG, 1 rifle sec, 1 × 2" mortar, 1 × Boys

11th Worcestershire Regiment Divisional Machine Gun Battalion
Btn HQ (2 rifle secs, 2 trucks)
3 Companies, each: Coy HQ (1 rifle sec, 1 truck, 2 LMG)
        3 platoons, each: 4 × Vickers MMG, 2 trucks, 2 Boys

Inns of Court Divisional Armoured Car Regiment
RHQ (4 × Humber II or Daimler I armoured cars)
3 Squadrons, each: Sqdn HQ (2 × Armoured Cars)
        5 Troops, each: 2 × Armoured Cars, 2 × Scout Cars
    1 Liaison/Communications Troop: 4 Sections, each: 3 × Scout Cars
Notes
1.   Radios were in all tanks and armoured cars, Carrier PHQs, and other PHQs.
2.   Infantry secs had No.75 A/T grenades.
3.   2pdr fires AP only, in 1942 had APC and 25pdr had AP.
4.   Scout Cars were Daimler or Humber. Prior to late 1941 Armoured Cars were Beaverettes, Ironsides and Humber Light Recce Cars, after which Daimler I was available. Humber Armoured Cars became available in 1942.

1.9 BRITISH 9TH ARMOURED DIVISION, BRITAIN, JULY 1942–SEPTEMBER 1943
The Division's main combat elements were:
        28th Armoured Brigade (5th Royal Inniskilling Dragoon Guards, 15th/19th King's Royal Hussars, 1st Fife & Forfar Yeomanry Armoured Regiments and 8th KRRC Motor Battalion)
        7th Infantry Brigade (2nd Btn South Wales Borderers, 2nd/6th Btn East Sussex Regiment, 6th Btn Royal Sussex Regiment Infantry Battalions)
        Divisional Armoured Car Regiment (Inns of Court Armoured Car Regiment in 1942 only)
        Divisional Armoured Recce Regiment (1st Royal Gloucestershire Hussars from January 1943)
Troops are rated at average training and average morale.

SUPPORT UNITS

Divisional Support
Included:
6th Royal Horse Artillery Regiment, 141st Field Artillery Regiment, each:
        3 Artillery Batteries, each: Battery HQ (4 rifle secs, 4 lorries, 1 AALMG)
                2 Troops, each: 4 × 25pdr, 4 trucks, radio truck, 2 AALMG, OP Team
74th Anti-Tank Regiment:
        3 Batteries, each: Battery HQ (1 rifle sec, 1 truck)
                3 Troops, each: 4 × 2pdr or 6pdr or 17pdr, 2 LMG, 4 trucks
54th Light AA Regiment:
        3 Batteries, each: Battery HQ (1 rifle sec, 1 truck)
                3 Troops, each: 4–6 × 40mm Bofors, 4–6 trucks
10th, 11th Field Engineer Squadrons, each: Sqdn HQ (2 rifle secs, 1 lorry)
        4 Troops, each: 4 (12 man) rifle/engineer secs, 2 LMG, 2 lorries
146th Engineer Park Squadron:
        1 Workshop Section
        1 Bridging and Stores Section
3 Shadow Training/Defence Armoured Regiments (as Armoured Regiments, June 1943+)

Brigade Support
28th Armoured Brigade HQ (3 × Tanks, 1 × ACV, 3 × Daimler Scout Car, 6 × OP Tanks) with:
        1 AA Section: 3 × Vickers VI AA
        1 Defence Troop: 3 × Tanks
7th Infantry Brigade HQ (4 rifle secs, 6 lorries, 1 Scout Car) with:
        1 HQ Defence Troop: 1 (7 man) rifle Pl HQ sec, 1 Boys, 1 × 2" mortar, 1 lorry, 3 (10 man) rifle secs, 3 LMG

MAIN COMBAT ELEMENTS

Armoured Regiment
RHQ (4 × Tanks, 3 × Scammell Wreckers)

3 Squadrons, each: Sqdn HQ (2 × Tanks, 2 × CS Tanks)
      5 Troops, each: 3 × Tanks
1 Scout Troop: Troop HQ (2 × Daimler Scout Cars)
      3 Sections, each: 3 × Daimler Scout Cars
1 AA Troop: 4 × Vickers VI AA

Motor Rifle Battalion (of Armoured Brigade)

Btn HQ (2 rifle secs, 2 trucks, 1 lorry)
3 Companies, each: Coy HQ (1 rifle sec, 1 × 2" mortar, 2 trucks)
      3 platoons, each: 4 (8 man) rifle secs, 3 LMG, 1 × 2" mortar, 4 trucks
      1 platoon: 2 × 3" mortars, 2 × Universal Carriers
      1 platoon: 4 × Vickers MMG, 4 trucks or Carriers
      1 platoon: Pl HQ: 1 × Universal Carrier, 1 LMG, 1 × Daimler S/C
            3 sections, each: 3 × Carriers, 3 LMG, 1 rifle sec, 1 × 2", 1 × Boys
1 Anti-Tank Company: Coy HQ (1 rifle sec, 1 truck) (1943 only)
      4 platoons, each: 2 or 4 × 2pdr or 6pdr, trucks or Carriers

Motorised Infantry Battalion

Btn HQ (3 rifle secs, 2 trucks, 1 lorry, 1 LMG)
4 Companies, each: Coy HQ (2 rifle secs, 1 lorry)
      3 platoons, each: 1 (8 man) rifle Pl HQ sec, 1 × 2" mortar
            3 (10 man) rifle secs, 3 LMG, 2 lorries
1 Support Company: Coy HQ (1 rifle sec, 1 truck)
      1 platoon: 6 × 3" mortars, 6 trucks, radio truck
      1 platoon: 2 (8 man) rifle/engineer secs, 1 (5 man) rifle Pl HQ sec, 2 LMG, 1 lorry
      1 platoon: 4 × 2pdr A/T guns, 4 trucks or Carriers, 2 LMG
      1 platoon: Pl HQ: 1 × Universal Carrier, 1 Scout Car, 1 LMG
            4 Sections, each: 3 × Carrier, 3 LMG, 1 rifle sec, 1 × 2" mortar, 1 Boys

Inns of Court Divisional Armoured Car Regiment (1942)

RHQ (4 × Humber III or Daimler II armoured cars)
3 Squadrons, each: Sqdn HQ (2 × Armoured Cars)
      5 Troops, each: 2 × Armoured Cars, 2 × Scout Cars
1 Liaison/Communications Troop: 4 Sections, each: 3 × Scout Cars

1st Royal Gloucestershire Hussars Divisional Armoured Recce Regiment (1943)

RHQ (3 × Cromwell or Centaur, 2 × Universal Carriers)
1 AA Troop: 6 × Vickers VI AA
3 Squadrons, each: Sqdn HQ (2 × Cromwell or Centaur)
      3 Troops, each: 2 × Tanks, 1 × CS Tank
      1 Troop: Troop HQ: 1 × Universal Carrier, 1 LMG
            3 Sections, each: 3 × Carrier, 3 LMG or Boys, 1 × 2" mortar, 1 rifle sec

Notes
1. Radios were in all tanks and armoured cars, Carrier Pl HQs, and other Pl HQs.
2. Infantry secs had No.75 A/T grenades.
3. Tanks were Covenanter up to September 1942, at which time they were gradually replaced by Cavalier I, supplemented from December 1942 by Centaur I. From January 1943 Cromwell I–III became available in increasing numbers.
4. OP Tanks were Cavalier OP. CS Tanks were Covenanter CS if using Covenanter or Cavalier; Centaur IV if using Centaur or Cromwell.
5. By June 1943 the division had double the required number of tanks, hence the assumed Shadow training/ defence Armoured Regiments.
6. 2pdr had APC with one load of APCBC, 6pdr had APCBC. From 1943 2pdr had APCBC and HE, and 6pdr had AP with one load of APCBC.
7. 17pdr anti-tank guns were not available until 1943.
8. In January 1943 the Inns of Court divisional Armoured Car Regiment was replaced by the 1st Royal Gloucestershire Hussars Armoured Recce Regiment.

1.10 BRITISH 9TH ARMOURED DIVISION, UK, OCTOBER 1943–JULY 1944

The Division's main combat elements were:
      28th Armoured Brigade (5th Royal Inniskilling Dragoon Guards, 1st Fife & Forfar Yeomanry, 15th/19th Hussars Armoured Regiments, 8th KRRC Motor Battalion)
      7th Infantry Brigade (2nd Battalion/6th East Surrey Regiment, 6th Battalion Royal Sussex, 2nd South Wales Borderers Infantry Battalions)
      Divisional Armoured Recce Regiment (1st Royal Gloucestershire Hussars)
      From late 1943 the division was used as a reinforcement pool HQ for the Normandy invasion, and was disbanded by the end of July 1944.
      The 1st Fife & Forfar Yeomanry and 2nd South Wales Borderers left the Division in March 1944, and the 54th Light AA Regiment was replaced by the 150th Light AA Regiment.
Troops are rated average morale and training.

SUPPORT UNITS

Divisional Support

Included:

6th Royal Horse Artillery Regiment, 141st Field Artillery Regiment, each:
        3 Artillery Batteries, each: Battery HQ (4 rifle secs, 4 lorries, 1 AALMG)
                2 Troops, each: 4 × 25pdr, 4 trucks, radio truck, 2 AALMG, OP Team
92nd Anti-Tank Regiment:
        3 Batteries each: Battery HQ (1 rifle sec, 1 truck)
                3 Troops, each: 4 × 6pdr A/T guns 2 LMG, 4 trucks
        1 Battery: Battery HQ (1 rifle sec, 1 truck)
                3 Troops, each: 4 × 17pdr A/T guns, 2 LMG, 4 trucks
54th Light AA Regiment to March 1944, 150th Light AA Regiment to July 1944
        3 Batteries each: Battery HQ (1 rifle sec, 1 truck)
                3 Troops, each: 6 × 40mm Bofors, 4–6 trucks
10th, 611th Field Engineer Squadrons, each:
        Sqdn HQ (4 (11 man) rifle secs, 1 LMG, 1 PIAT, 4 lorries, 1 × Jeep)
        3 Troops, each: 1 (17 man) Pl HQ sec, 4 (12 man) rifle/engineer secs, 4 LMG, 4 lorries, 6 × Humber Light
                Recce S/C
146th Engineer Park Company: Coy HQ (3 rifle secs, 4 lorries)
        9th Bridge Troop: 1 × 40t 80' Bailey Bridge in 15 × 3-ton lorries, 51 men
        1 Stores Section: 12 assault boats, 3 bulldozers, 3 tractors, 29 men
        1 Workshop Section: 44 men, recovery lorries

Brigade Support

Armoured Brigade HQ(3 × Cromwell IV, 1 × ACV, 3 × Daimler Scout Car, 6 × OP Tanks, 2 lorries with:
        1 AA Section: 3 × Vickers VI AA or Crusader AA Mk.1 or Mk.2
        1 Defence Troop: 3 × Cromwell IV
        0–1 Bridge Troop: 3 × Valentine AVLB
Infantry Brigade HQ (4 rifle secs, 6 lorries, 1 Scout Car) with:
        1 Defence Troop: 4 rifle secs, 3 LMG, 1 PIAT, 1 × 2" mortar, 2 lorries

MAIN COMBAT ELEMENTS

5th Royal Inniskilling Dragoon Guards, 1st Fife & Forfar Yeomanry, 15th/19th Hussars Armoured Regiments (1943 only)

RHQ (4 × Cromwell I–III, 3 × Scammell Wreckers)
3 Squadrons, each: Sqdn HQ (2 × Tanks, 2 × CS Tanks)
        5 Troops, each: 3 × Tanks
1 Scout Troop: Troop HQ (2 × Daimler Scout Cars)
        3 Sections, each: 3 × Daimler Scout Cars
1 AA Troop: 4 × Vickers VI AA or Centuar AA Mk.1

5th Royal Inniskilling Dragoon Guards Armoured Regiment (May–July 1944 only)

RHQ (4 × Sherman V, 3 × Grant OP tanks, 3 × Grant ARV)
3 Squadrons, each: Sqdn HQ (4 × Sherman V)
        4 Troops, each: 3 × Sherman V, 1 × Firefly Vc
1 Scout Troop: Troop HQ (2 × Stuart III, 2 × Daimler Scout Cars)
        3 Sections, each: 3 × Stuart III, 3 × Daimler Scout Cars
1 AA Troop: 4 × Vickers VI AA or 6 × Crusader AA Mk.I or Mk.II

15th/19th Hussars Amphibious Armoured Regiment (January–August 1944 only)

RHQ (5 × Sherman V DD, 3 × Cromwell OP tanks, 3 × Sherman ARV)
3 Squadrons, each: Sqdn HQ (3 × Sherman V DD)
        5 Troops, each: 4 × Sherman V DD
1 Scout Troop: Troop HQ (1 × Stuart VI, 2 × Daimler Scout Cars)
        3 Sections, each: 1 × Stuart VI, 3 × Daimler Scout Cars

8th Battalion King's Royal Rifle Corps Motor Rifle Battalion (of 28th Armoured Brigade)

Btn HQ (3 rifle secs, 3 trucks, 1 lorry)
3 Companies each: Coy HQ (1 rifle sec, 1 × 2" mortar, 2 trucks)
        3 Platoons, each: 4 (8 man) rifle secs, 3 LMG, 1 × 2" mortar, 4 trucks, 1 PIAT
        1 Platoon: 2 × 3" mortars, 2 × Universal Carriers
        1 Platoon: Pl HQ: 1 × Universal Carrier, 1 LMG, 1 × Daimler S/C
                3 sections each: 3 × Carriers, 3 LMG, 1 rifle sec, 1 × 2" mortar, 1 PIAT
1 Support Company: Coy HQ (1 rifle sec, 1 truck)
        3 Platoons, each: 2 or 4 × 6pdr A/T guns, trucks or Carriers
        2 Platoons, each: 4 × Vickers MMG, 4 trucks or Carriers

2nd South Wales Borderers, 2nd Battalion/6th East Surrey Regiment, 6th Battalion Royal Sussex Infantry Battalions

Btn HQ (3 rifle secs, 2 trucks, 1 lorry, 1 LMG)
4 Companies each: Coy HQ (1 (13 man) rifle sec, 1 lorry)

3 Platoons, each: 1 (8 man) rifle Pl HQ sec, 1 × 2" mortar, 1 PIAT 3 (10 man) rifle secs, 3 LMG, 2 lorries
1 Support Company: Coy HQ (1 rifle sec, 1 truck)
    1 Platoon: 6 × 3" mortars, 6 trucks, radio truck, 2 PIAT
    1 Platoon: 3 (6 man) rifle/engineer secs, 2 LMG, 1 lorry
    1 Platoon: 6 × 6pdr A/T guns, 6 trucks or Carriers, 2 LMG
    1 Platoon: Pl HQ: 1 × Universal Carrier, 1 Scout Car, 1 LMG
        4 Sections, each: 3 × Carrier, 3 LMG, 1 rifle sec, 1 × 2" mortar, 1 PIAT

1st Royal Gloucestershire Hussars Divisional Armoured Recce Regiment
RHQ (3 × Cromwell IV, 2 × Universal Carriers)
1 AA Troop: 5 × Centaur AA Mk.1 or Crusader AA Mk.2
3 Squadrons each: Sqdn HQ (2 × Cromwell III or IV)
    3 Troops, each: 2 × Cromwell III or IV, 1 × Cromwell VICS
    1 Troop: Troop HQ (1 × Universal Carrier, 1 LMG)
        3 Sections, each: 3 × Carrier, 3 LMG or PIAT, 1 × 2" mortar, 1 rifle sec

Notes
1. Radios were in all tanks and armoured cars, Carrier PHQs, and other PHQs.
2. Infantry secs had No.75 A/T grenades.
3. Tanks were early Cromwell Mk.I–III and Centaur Mk.I & III.
4. OP Tanks were Centaur OP or Cromwell OP or Grant OP.
5. In 1944 the 15/19th Hussars Armoured Regiment was converted to a DD Regiment, and the 5th Royal Inniskilling Dragoon Guards Armoured Regiment was equipped with Shermans. The 1st Fife & Forfar Yeomanry Armoured Regiment left in early 1944.
6. Two OP per Artillery Regiment were in OP Tanks, rest were in trucks or Daimler S/C.
7. Shermans did not have .50" AAHMG. M3 H/T had .30" M1919A4 Browning MG.
8. Most Cromwells in the Recce Regiment were Mk.IV with 75mm, some were Mk.III with 6pdr gun.
9. It is possible that the 8th KRRC Motor Battalion had infantry in M3 halftracks or M3A1 White Scout Cars.
10. The Division in late 1943 had over 390 Cromwells and Centaurs, leaving around 160 spare for training and spare parts.

1.11 CANADIAN 5TH ARMOURED DIVISION, BRITAIN, AUGUST 1941–MARCH 1943
The Division's main combat elements were:
    1st Armoured Brigade (2nd, 6th, 10th Armoured Regiments, Westminster Regiment Motor Battalion)
    2nd Armoured Brigade (3rd, 5th, 9th Armoured Regiments, Perth Regiment Motor Battalion)
    Divisional Infantry Battalion (Cape Breton Highlanders)
    Divisional Armoured Car Regiment (Royal Canadian Dragoons)
Troops are rated good morale and poor training, until 1943 when they are average training and good morale.

SUPPORT UNITS

Divisional Support
Included:
17th Field Artillery Regiment:
    37th, 60th, 7th Batteries, each: Battery HQ (4 rifle secs, 4 lorries, 2 AALMG)
        2 Troops, each: 4 × 25pdr field guns, 6 trucks, AALMG
4th Anti-Tank Regiment:
    24th, 82nd, 98th Batteries, each: Battery HQ (1 rifle sec, 1 truck)
        1–3 Troops, each: 2–4 × 2pdr, 2 × LMG, 4 trucks.
5th Light AA Regiment:
    41st, 47th, 88th Batteries, each: Battery HQ (1 rifle sec, 1 truck)
        3 Troops, each: 4 × twin AALMG or (December 1942+) 4 × 40mmL60 Bofors, 4 trucks
1st, 10th Field Engineer Squadrons, each: Sqdn HQ (1 rifle sec, 1 truck)
    3 Troops, each: 4 (12 man) rifle/engineer secs, 2 LMG, 2 lorries
4th Engineer Park Squadron:
    Stores Troop, Bridging Troop, Workshop Troop

Brigade Support
Armoured Brigade HQ (6 × Tanks, 2 radio vans, 3 field or Scout Cars)

MAIN COMBAT ELEMENTS

Armoured Regiment (January–August 1942)
RHQ (2 × Stuart I, 2 trucks)
1 Squadron: Sqdn HQ (3 × Ram I (2pdr))
    2 Troops, each: 3 × Ram I
    1 Troop: 3 × Ram II (6pdr)
1 Squadron: Sqdn HQ (4 × Stuart I)
    3 Troops, each: 2–3 × Stuart I
    1 Troop: 2 × M2A4 light tank
0–1 Squadron: Sqdn HQ (1 × M3 Lee)(June 1942+)
    3 Troops, each: 2–3 × M3 Lee

Armoured Regiment(September 1942–March 1943)

RHQ (4 × Tanks, 1 × Ram ARV Mk.1)
3 Squadrons, each: Sqdn HQ (3 × Tanks)
   3–4 Troops, each: 3 × Tanks
1 Scout Troop: Troop HQ (2 × Otter I scout cars)
   3 Sections, each: 3 × Otter I scout cars

Motor Battalion

Btn HQ (2 rifle secs, 2 trucks)
3 Companies, each: Coy HQ (1 rifle sec, 1 truck, 1 Boys)
   1 platoon: 2 × 3" mortars, 2 trucks
   1 platoon: 4 Vickers MMG, 4 trucks
   3 platoons, each: 4 (8 man) rifle secs, 4 trucks, 4 Boys, 3 LMG
   1 platoon: Pl HQ: 1 × Universal Carrier, 1 LMG
      3 Sections, each: 3 × Carrier, 3 LMG, 1 rifle sec, 1 × 2" mortar, 1 Boys

Cape Breton Highlanders Divisional Infantry Battalion

Btn HQ (4 rifle secs, 2 lorries)
4 Companies, each: Coy HQ (1 rifle squad, 1 truck)
   3 platoons, each: 1 (7 man) rifle Pl HQ sec, 1 Boys, 1 × 2" mortar, 3 (10 man) rifle secs, 3 LMG, 2 lorries
1 Support Company: Coy HQ (rifle sec, 1 truck)
   1 platoon: 2 × 3" mortars, 2 trucks, Assigned FC
   1 platoon: 2 (6 man) rifle/engineer secs, 2 LMG, 1 truck
   1 platoon: 4 × twin Bren AALMG, 4 trucks
   1 platoon: Pl HQ: 1 × Universal Carrier, 1 LMG
      4 Sections, each: 3 × Carrier, 3 LMG, 1 × Boys, 1 × 2", 1 rifle sec

Royal Canadian Dragoons Divisional Armoured Car Regiment

RHQ (4 × Armoured Cars)
Communication Troop: Troop HQ (1–2 × Scout Cars)
   1–3 Sections, each: 3 × Scout Cars
3 Squadrons, each: Sqdn HQ (3 × Armoured Cars)
   5 Troops, each: 3 × Armoured Cars

Notes
1. Radios were in all tanks, armoured cars, Carrier Pl HQ and other Coy HQ.
2. Infantry secs had No.74 or No.75 A/T grenades.
3. No tanks were available in 1941 and were in short supply even up to mid 1942. Later in 1942 one Regiment per Brigade had Stuarts, one had M3 Lee and the other Ram II. By the end of 1942 Lees were replaced by Ram II, giving each Brigade two Ram Regiments and one Stuart Regiment.
4. Armoured Cars were either Humber II, Daimler II or Otter Mk.1, or even trucks+LMG earlier on. Scout Cars were probably Humber Light Recce Cars.
5. The 5th AA Regiment had very few Bofors before December 1942.
6. Artillery was rated Assigned FC until 1943 when Flexible FC was adopted, with one OP in truck or Scout Car per Artillery Troop.

1.12 CANADIAN 5TH ARMOURED DIVISION, BRITAIN, MAY–OCTOBER 1943

The Division's main combat elements were:
   5th Armoured Brigade (2nd, 5th, 9th Armoured Regiments, Westminster Regiment Motor Battalion)
   11th Infantry Brigade (Perth Regiment, Cape Breton Highlanders, Irish Regiment of Canada Infantry Battalions, Princess Louise's Fusiliers Brigade Support Group)
   Divisional Armoured Car Regiment (Governor General's Horse Guards)
Troops are rated good morale and average training.

SUPPORT UNITS

Divisional Support

Included:
17th Field Artillery Regiment:
   37th, 60th, 7th Batteries, each: Battery HQ (4 rifle secs, 4 lorries, 2 AALMG)
      2 Troops, each: 4 × 25pdr field guns, 6 trucks, AALMG
8th SP Artillery Regiment: (October 1943+)
   3 Batteries, each: Battery HQ (1 radio van, 2 trucks, 2 rifle secs, 4 AALMG)
      2 Troops, each: 4 × 25pdr Sexton, 1 radio van, 2 OP Teams
4th Anti-Tank Regiment:
   24th, 82nd, 98th Batteries, each: Battery HQ (1 rifle sec, 1 truck)
      3 Troops, each: 4 × 6pdr, 2 × LMG, 4 trucks or Carriers
   16th Battery: Battery HQ (1 rifle sec, 1 truck)
      3 Troops, each: 4 × 17pdr, 4 trucks, 2 LMG
5th Light AA Regiment:
   41st, 47th, 88th Batteries, each: Battery HQ (1 rifle sec, 1 truck)
      3 Troops, each: 6 × 40mmL60 Bofors, 6 trucks
1st, 10th Field Engineer Squadrons, each: Sqdn HQ (4 (11 man) rifle secs, 4 LMG, 2 lorries)

3 Troops, each: 1 (21 man) rifle/engineer Pl HQ sec, 1 LMG, 4 (12 man) rifle/engineer secs, 4 LMG, 2 lorries
4th Engineer Park Squadron: Sqdn HQ (4 (9 man) rifle secs, 2 lorries)
    Stores Troop: 5 LMG, 4 Boys, 4 rifle/crew secs, stores, tools, lorries
    Workshop Troop: 4 rifle/engineer secs, maintenance lorries
    Bridging Troop: pontoons, Bailey Bridge, 4 rifle/crew secs

Brigade Support

5th Armoured Brigade HQ (7 × Sherman V, 7 × Humber III Rear-Link, 6 × Ram OP, Air Liaison Team) with:
    1 Bridge Troop: 3 × Valentine AVLB
    1 Defence Troop: 3 × Sherman V
11th Infantry Brigade HQ (6 rifle secs, 6 trucks, 3 LMG) with:
1 Support Group: Coy HQ (1 rifle sec, 1 truck)
    3 platoons, each: 4 × Vickers MMG, 5 × Carrier
    2 platoons, each: 4 × 4.2" mortars, 6 × Carriers, OP Team in Carrier

MAIN COMBAT ELEMENTS

Armoured Regiment

RHQ (4 × Sherman V, 1 × Ram ARV Mk.2)
3 Squadrons, each: Sqdn HQ (4 × Sherman V)
    4 Troops, each: 3 × Sherman V
1 Scout Troop: Troop HQ (2 × Stuart I)
    3 Sections, each: 3 × Stuart I
1 Attached Motor Company: Coy HQ (1 rifle sec, 1 truck)
    1 platoon: 2 × 3" mortars, 2 trucks or Carriers
    3 platoons, each: 4 × M3A1 White S/C, 4 (7 man) rifle secs, 3 LMG, 1 × 2" mortar
    1 platoon: 2 × 6pdr A/T guns, 4 × Universal Carrier
    1 platoon: 4 × Vickers MMG, 4 × Carriers (in 2 Regiments only)
    1 platoon: Pl HQ: 1 × Universal Carrier, 1 LMG
        3 Sections, each: 3 × Carrier, 3 LMG, 1 Boys, 1 × 2", 1 rifle sec

Infantry Battalion

Btn HQ (4 rifle secs, 2 lorries)
4 Companies, each: Coy HQ (2 rifle secs, 1 lorry)
    3 platoons, each: 1 (7 man) rifle Pl HQ sec, 1 Boys, 1 × 2" mortar 3 (10 man) rifle secs, 3 LMG, 2 lorries
1 Support Company: Coy HQ (1 rifle sec, 1 truck)
    1 platoon: 6 × 3" mortars, 7 × Carrier
    1 platoon: 3 (6 man) rifle/engineer secs, 3 LMG, 3 × M3A1 White Scout Car
    1 platoon: 4 × 6pdr A/T guns, 4 × Carrier
    1 platoon: Pl HQ: 1 × Universal Carrier, 1 LMG
        4 Sections, each: 3 × Carrier, 3 LMG, 1 × Boys, 1 × 2" mortar, 1 rifle sec

Governor General's Horse Guards Divisional Armoured Recce Regiment

RHQ (4 × Sherman II)
3 Squadrons, each: Sqdn HQ (2 × Sherman II)
    5 Troops, each: 2 × Sherman II, 2 × Stuart I
1 Communications/Liaison Troop: Troop HQ (3 × Otter I)
    3 Sections, each: 3 × Otter I

Notes
1. Radios were in all tanks, armoured cars, Carrier Pl HQ and other Pl HQ.
2. Infantry secs had No.74 or No.75 A/T grenades. By October 1943 added one PIAT per platoon, replacing any Boys if present.
3. Artillery OP could be in Ram OP tanks. Humber III Rear Link had dummy guns.
4. In December 1943 the Division left all equipment in Britain and moved to Italy, taking over worn out equipment left by the British 7th Armoured Division.
5. 6pdr had APCBC with one load of APCR from October 1943. 75mm had APC. 37mm had APCBC.

1.13 CANADIAN 4TH ARMOURED DIVISION, BRITAIN, JULY 1942–DECEMBER 1942

The Division's main combat elements were:
    3rd Armoured Brigade (25th, 28th, 29th Armoured Regiments, Lake Superior Motor Btn)
    4th Armoured Brigade (21st, 22nd, 27th Armoured Regiments, Princess Louise's Fusiliers Motor Battalion)
    Divisional Infantry Battalion (Irish Regiment of Canada)
    Divisional Armoured Car Regiment (12th Manitoba Dragoons)
Troops are rated good morale and poor training.

SUPPORT UNITS

Divisional Support

Included:
15th Field Artillery Regiment:
    17th, 95th, 110th Batteries, each: Battery HQ (4 rifle secs, 4 lorries, 2 AALMG)
        2 Troops, each: 4 × 25pdr field guns, 6 trucks, AALMG

5th Anti-Tank Regiment:
        3rd, 65th, 96th Batteries, each: Battery HQ (1 rifle sec, 1 truck)
                1–3 Troops, each: 0–4 × 2pdr, 2 × LMG, trucks
8th Light AA Regiment:
        70th, 101st, 102nd Batteries, each: Battery HQ (1 rifle sec, 1 truck)
                3 Troops, each: 4 × wooden mock-up guns, 1 truck
8th, 9th Field Engineer Squadrons, each: Sqdn HQ (2 rifle secs, 2 lorries)
                3 Troops, each: 4 (12 man) rifle/engineer secs, 2 LMG, 2 lorries
6th Engineer Park Squadron:
        Stores Troop, Bridging Troop, Workshop Troop

Brigade Support

Armoured Brigade HQ (1 × Ram II, 4 trucks+ LMG, 2 radio vans, 3 staff cars)

MAIN COMBAT ELEMENTS

Armoured Regiment (June–September 1942)

RHQ (1 × Ram II (6pdr), 1 field car or truck)
3 Squadrons, each: Sqdn HQ (1 × Ram II)
        2 Troops, each: 2 × Ram I
        1 Troop: 1 × Valentine VI (2pdr)

Armoured Regiment(October–December 1942, UK)

RHQ (1 × Ram II, 1 × Ram ARV Mk.1)
3 Squadrons, each: Sqdn HQ (1 × Ram II)
        3 Troops, each: 2 × Ram II

Motor Battalion (of Armoured Brigade)

Btn HQ (2 rifle secs, 1 lorry)
3 Companies, each: Coy HQ (1 rifle sec, 1 truck)
        3 platoons, each: 4 (8 man) rifle secs, 4 trucks, 3 LMG, 1 Boys
        1 platoon: 2 × 3" mortars, 2 MMG, 4 trucks
        1 platoon: Pl HQ: 1 × Universal Carrier, 1 LMG
                3 Sections, each: 3 × Carrier, 3 LMG, 1 Boys, 1 × 2" mortar, 1 rifle sec

Irish Regiment of Canada Divisional Infantry Battalion

Btn HQ (4 rifle secs, 2 lorries)
4 Companies, each: Coy HQ (1 rifle sec, 1 truck)
        3 platoons, each: 1 (8 man) rifle Pl HQ sec, 1 Boys, 1 × 2" mortar 3 (10 man) rifle secs, 3 LMG, 2 lorries
1 Support Company: Coy HQ (1 rifle sec, 1 truck)
        1 platoon: 2 × 3" mortars, 2 trucks
        1 platoon: 2 (8 man) rifle/engineer secs, 2 LMG, 1 lorry
        1 platoon: 4 × twin AALMG, 4 trucks
        1 platoon: Pl HQ: 1 × Universal Carrier, 1 LMG
                4 Sections, each: 3 × Carrier, 3 LMG, 1 × Boys, 1 × 2" mortar, 1 rifle sec

12th Manitoba Dragoons Divisional Armoured Regiment

RHQ (4 × Armoured Cars)
3 Squadrons, each: Sqdn HQ (3 × Armoured Cars)
        5 Troops, each: 3 × Armoured Cars

Notes
1.   Radios were in all tanks, armoured cars, Carrier Pl HQ and other Coy HQ. Artillery was rated Assigned FC.
2.   Infantry secs had few No. 74 or No. 75 A/T grenades.
3.   The Division was poorly equipped during this time. It moved to Britain in September 1942.
4.   Armoured cars were likely to be a mix of Humber II, Otter I, trucks+ LMG, and field cars with 4-man rifle crew secs. Whilst in Canada it is likely to have had a few Otter I and trucks with machine guns at best.

1.14 CANADIAN 4TH ARMOURED DIVISION, BRITAIN, JANUARY–SEPTEMBER 1943

The Division's main combat elements were:
        4th Armoured Brigade Group (21st, 22nd, 27th Armoured Regiments, Lake Superior Motor Battalion)
        10th Infantry Brigade Group (29th Armoured Recce Regiment, Lincoln & Welland Regiment, Algonquin Regiment, Argyll & Sutherland Highlanders of Canada Infantry Battalions)
Troops are rated average morale and poor training.

SUPPORT UNITS

Divisional Support

Included:
5th Anti-tank Regiment:
        65th Anti-Tank Battery: Battery HQ (1 rifle sec, 1 truck)
                3 Troops, each: 4 × 6pdr or 17pdr, 4 trucks, 2 LMG
8th Light AA Regiment:
        3 AA Batteries, each: Battery HQ (1 rifle sec, 1 truck)

2 Troops, each: 6 × 40mmL60 Bofors, 6 trucks
6th Engineer Park Squadron:
Stores Troop, Bridging Troop, Workshop Troop

Brigade Support

4th Armoured Brigade HQ (3 × Ram II, 7 × Humber III Rear Link, 6 × Ram OP Tanks, Air Liaison Team) with:
14th Anti-Tank Battery: Battery HQ (1 rifle sec, 1 truck)
3 Troops, each: 4 × 6pdr, 4 trucks, 2 LMG
8th Field Engineer Squadron: Sqdn HQ (2 rifle secs, 1 lorry)
3 Troops, each: 4 (12 man) rifle/engineer secs, 2 LMG, 2 lorries
10th Infantry Brigade Group HQ (6 rifle secs, 6 trucks, 2 LMG) with:
15th Field Artillery Regiment:
17th, 95th, 110th Batteries, each: Battery HQ (4 rifle secs, 4 lorries, 2 LMG)
2 Troops, each: 4 × 25pdr, 6 trucks, 2 LMG, OP Team
3rd Anti-Tank Battery: Battery HQ (1 rifle sec, 1 truck)
3 Troops, each: 4 × 6pdr, 4 trucks, 2 LMG
9th Field Engineer Squadron: Sqdn HQ: 2 rifle secs, 1 lorry
3 Troops, each: 4 (12 man) rifle/engineer secs, 2 LMG, 2 lorries

MAIN COMBAT ELEMENTS

Armoured Regiment

RHQ (3 × Ram II (6pdr), 1 × Ram ARV Mk.1)
3 Squadrons, each: Sqdn HQ (4 × Ram II)
4 Troops, each: 2 × Ram II
1 Scout Troop: Troop HQ (1 × Otter I)
2–3 Troops, each: 2–3 × Otter I

Lake Superior Motor Battalion (of Armoured Brigade)

Btn HQ (2 rifle secs, 2 trucks)
3 Companies, each: Coy HQ (1 rifle sec, 1 truck, 1 Boys)
3 platoons, each: 4 (8 man) rifle secs, 4 trucks, 3 LMG, 4 Boys
1 platoon: 4 MMG, 4 trucks
1 platoon: 2 × 3" mortars, 2 trucks
1 platoon: 2 × 2pdr A/T guns, 2 × Universal Carrier
1 platoon: Pl HQ: 1 × Universal Carrier, 1 LMG
3 Sections, each: 3 × Carrier, 3 LMG, 1 Boys, 1 × 2" mortar, 1 rifle sec

29th Armoured Recce Regiment (South Alberta Regiment)

RHQ (3 × Ram II, 2 × Universal Carrier)
3 Squadrons, each: Sqdn HQ (2 × Ram II)
3 Troops, each: 3 × Ram II
1 Troop: THQ: 1 × Universal Carrier, 1 LMG
3 Sections, each: 3 × Carrier, 3 LMG, 1 Boys, 1 × 2" mortar, 1 rifle sec

Infantry Battalion

No troops effective, being formed in dribs and drabs from June–September 1943

Notes
1.   Radios were in all tanks, armoured cars, Carrier Pl HQ and other Pl HQ.
2.   Infantry secs had No.75 A/T grenades.
3.   In practice the Infantry Battalions were not available and arrived in small packets over the period June–September 1943.
4.   Artillery OP could be in Ram-OP tanks.

1.15 BRITISH GUARDS ARMOURED DIVISION, BRITAIN, 1942–OCTOBER 1943

The Division's main combat elements were:
5th Guards Armoured Brigade (2nd Btn Grenadier Guards, 1st Btn Coldstream Guards, 2nd Btn Irish Guards Armoured Regiments, 1st Btn Grenadier Guards Motor Battalion)
6th Guards Armoured Brigades (4th Btn Grenadier Guards, 3rd Btn Scots Guards, 2nd Btn Welsh Guards Armoured Regiments, 4th Btn Coldstream Guards Motor Btn)
Divisional Guards Infantry Battalion (up to June 1942) (1st Btn Welsh Guards)
32nd Guards Infantry Brigade (July 1942+) (5th Btn Coldstream Guards, 4th Btn Scots Guards, 1st Btn Welsh Guards Infantry Btns)
Divisional Recce Regiment (2nd Household Cavalry Regiment)
Troops are rated good morale and average training.

SUPPORT UNITS

Divisional Support

Included:
153rd Field Artillery Regiment:
3 Batteries, each: Battery HQ (4 rifle secs, 4 lorries, 2 AALMG)
2 Troops, each: 4 × 25pdr, 6 trucks, 2 AALMG

55th Field Artillery Regiment (July 1942+)
    3 Batteries, each: Battery HQ (4 rifle secs, 4 lorries, 2 AALMG)
        2 Troops, each: 4 × 25pdr, 6 trucks, 2 AALMG
21st Anti-Tank Regiment:
    3 Batteries, each: Battery HQ (1 rifle sec, 1 truck)
        3 Troops, each: 4 × 2pdr, 4 trucks, 2 LMG
94th Light AA Regiment:
    1 AA Troop: 6 × 40mmL60 Bofors, 6 trucks
14th, 15th Field Engineer Squadrons, each: Sqdn HQ (2 rifle secs, 2 trucks)
    4 Troops, each: 4 (12 man) rifle/engineer secs, 2 LMG, 2 lorries
148th Engineer Park Squadron:
    1 Bridging and Stores Section
    1 Workshop Troop
1 Armoured Division Support Company (October–December 1942): Coy HQ (1 rifle sec, 1 truck)
    4 platoons, each: 4 × Vickers MMG, 2 trucks

Brigade Support

5th, 6th Armoured Brigade HQs, each (8 × Covenanter, 2 × ACV, 3 × Scout Cars)
32nd Guards Infantry Brigade HQ (6 rifle secs, 2 LMG, 6 trucks) with:
    1 Support Company (October–December 1942): Coy HQ: 1 rifle sec, 1 truck
        4 platoons, each: 4 × Vickers MMG, 4 × Carriers or trucks

MAIN COMBAT ELEMENTS

Armoured Regiment (1942–March 1943)

RHQ (4 × Covenanter, 3 × Scammell Wrecker)
3 Squadrons, each: Sqdn HQ (2 × Covenanter, 2 × Covenanter-CS)
    4 Troops, each: 3 × Covenanter
    1 Training Troop: 3 × Universal Carrier
1 Recce Troop: Troop HQ (1 × Scout Car)
    3 Sections, each: 3 × Scout Car

Armoured Regiment (March 1943+)

RHQ (4 × Centaur I or M4A2 Sherman III, 3 × Centaur ARV) in Welsh Guards at least:
2 Squadrons, each: Sqdn HQ (2 × Centaur I, 2 × Covenanter-CS)
    1 Troop: 3 × Crusader III
    3 Troops, each: 3 × Centaur
1 Squadron: Sqdn HQ (4 × Stuart III)
    4 Troops, each: 3 × Stuart III

Or

(other Regiments)
3 Squadrons, each: Sqdn H (4 × Sherman III)
    4 Troops, each: 3 × Sherman III
1 AA Troop: 4 × Vickers VI AA
1 Bridge Troop: 3 × Covenanter AVLB
1 Scout Troop: Troop HQ (2 × Scout Cars)
    3 Sections, each: 3 × Scout Cars

2nd Household Cavalry Divisional Armoured Car Regiment

RHQ (4 × Armoured Cars)
3 Squadrons, each: Sqdn HQ (4 × Armoured Cars)
    5 Troops, each: 3 × Armoured Cars
1 Scout/Liaison Troop: Troop HQ (1 × Scout Car)
    3 Troops, each: 3 × Scout Cars

Motor Battalion (of Armoured Brigade)

Btn HQ (2 rifle secs, 2 trucks)
3 Companies, each: Coy HQ (1 rifle sec, 1 truck)
    1 battery: 2 × 3" mortars, 2 × Carriers
    3 platoons, each: 4 (7 man) rifle secs, 3 LMG, 4 Boys, 1 × 2" mortar, 4 trucks
    1 platoon: Pl HQ: 1 × Universal Carrier, 1 LMG
        3 sections, each: 3 × Carriers, 3 LMG, 1 rifle sec, 1 × Boys

Guards Infantry Battalion

Btn HQ (2 rifle secs, 2 trucks)
4 Companies, each: Coy HQ (1 rifle sec, 1 truck)
    3 platoons, each: 1 (6 man) rifle Pl HQ sec, 1 × 2" mortar, 1 Boys
        3 (9–10 man) rifle secs, 3 LMG, 2 lorries
1 Support Company: Coy HQ (1 rifle sec, 1 truck)
    1 battery: 6 × 3" mortars, 6 trucks or Carriers
    1 platoon: 2 (8 man) rifle/engineer secs, 1 (5 man) rifle Pl HQ sec, 2 lorries, 2 LMG
    1 platoon: 2 × Vickers MMG, 2 Carriers
    1 platoon: 4 × 2pdr or 6pdr A/T guns, 4 trucks, 2 LMG (1943 only)

1 platoon: Pl HQ: 1 × Universal Carrier, 1 LMG, 1 Scout car
4 Sections, each: 3 × Carrier, 3 LMG, 1 rifle sec, 1 Boys, 1 × 2" mortar

Notes
1. Radios were in all tanks and armoured cars, Carrier Pl HQs, and other Coy HQs.
2. Infantry secs had No.74 or Hawkins 75 A/T grenades.
3. From July 1942 the single Guards Infantry Battalion was amended to a full Brigade (32nd Guards Infantry Brigade) of three Battalions.
4. Shermans were available from March 1943.
5. Armoured Cars may have be Humber III or Daimler II. Scout cars were Daimler or Humber.
6. Artillery was rated Assigned FC in 1942, from 1943 used Flexible FC with OPs in Scout Cars or Centaur OP.

1.16 BRITISH 11TH ARMOURED DIVISION, BRITAIN, JULY–DECEMBER 1942

The Division's main combat elements were:
29th Armoured Brigade (23rd Hussars, 24th Lancers, 2nd Fife & Forfar Yeomanry Armoured Regiments, 8th Btn Rifle Brigade Motor Battalion)
159th Lorried Infantry Brigade (3rd Btn Monmouthshire Regiment, 4th Btn King's Shropshire Light Infantry, 1st Btn Herefordshire Regiment Infantry Battalions)
Divisional Recce Regiment (27th Lancers Armoured Car Regiment)
Troops are rated average morale and average training.

SUPPORT UNITS

Divisional Support

Included:
13th Royal Horse Artillery, 151st Field Artillery Regiments, each:
3 Artillery Batteries, each: Battery HQ (4 rifle secs, 4 lorries, 4 AALMG, 3 OP Teams)
2 Troops, each: 4 × 25pdr field guns, 4 trucks, radio truck, 2 AALMG
75th Anti-Tank Regiment:
3 Batteries, each: Battery HQ (1 rifle sec, 1 truck)
3 Troops, each: 4 × 2pdr or 6pdr, 2 LMG, 4 trucks
58th Light AA Regiment:
3 Batteries, each: Battery HQ (1 rifle sec, 1 truck)
3 Troops, each: 4 × 40mm Bofors, 6 trucks
12th, 13th Field Engineer Squadrons, each: Sqdn HQ (2 rifle secs, 1 lorry)
4 Troops, each: 4 (12 man) rifle/engineer secs, 2 LMG, 2 lorries
147th Engineer Park Squadron:
1 Workshop Section
1 Bridging and Stores Section

Brigade Support

29th Armoured Brigade HQ (x Valentine III, 2 × ACV, 1 × Vickers VI AA tank)
159th Infantry Brigade HQ (6 rifle secs, 2 LMG, 4 lorries)

MAIN COMBAT ELEMENTS

Armoured Regiment

RHQ (4 × Valentine III, 3 × Scammell Wrecker)
3 Squadrons, each: Sqdn HQ (2 × Crusader IICS, 2 × Valentine III)
2 Troops, each: 4 × Crusader II
2 Troops, each: 3 × Valentine VIII(6pdr), 1 × Valentine III(2pdr)
1 AA Troop: 2 × Vickers VI AA
1 Recce Troop: Troop HQ (1 × Humber S/C)
3 Sections, each: 3 × Humber Scout Car

Motorised Infantry Battalion

Btn HQ (2 rifle secs, 2 trucks)
4 Companies, each: Coy HQ (1 (13 man) rifle sec, 1 lorry)
3 platoons, each: 1 (7 man) rifle Pl HQ sec, 1 Boys, 1 × 2" mortar,
3 (10 man) rifle secs, 3 LMG, 2 lorries
1 Support Company: Coy HQ (1 rifle sec, 1 truck)
1 platoon: 6 × 2pdr anti-tank guns, 2 LMG, 6 trucks
1 platoon: 2 (8 man) rifle/engineer secs, 1 (5 man) Pl HQ sec, 2 LMG, 3 trucks
1 battery: 6 × 3" mortars, 7 × Universal Carriers, 3 Boys
1 platoon: Pl HQ: 1 × Universal Carrier, 1 LMG, 1 × Daimler S/C
4 sections, each: 3 × Carriers, 3 LMG, 1 rifle sec, 1 × 2", 1 × Boys

Motor Rifle Battalion (of Armoured Brigade)

Btn HQ (2 rifle secs, 2 trucks)
3 Companies, each: Coy HQ (1 rifle sec, 1 truck)
1 battery: 2 × 3" mortars, 2 trucks
3 platoons, each: 4 (8 man) rifle secs, 3 LMG, 1 × 2" mortar, 4 trucks
1 platoon: 4 × Vickers MMG, 4 trucks

1 platoon: Pl HQ: 1 × Universal Carrier, 1 LMG, 1 × Daimler S/C
    3 sections, each: 3 × Carriers, 3 LMG, 1 rifle sec, 1 × 2" mortar, 1 × Boys
0–1 Anti-Tank Company: Coy HQ (1 rifle sec, 1 truck) (September 1942+)
    3 platoons, each: 2 or 4 × 2pdr, 2–4 trucks, 2 LMG

27th Lancers Divisional Armoured Car Regiment

RHQ (4 × Armoured Cars, 2 × Scout Cars)
1 AA Troop: 4 × Humber AA
3 Squadrons, each: Sqdn HQ (4 × Armoured Cars)
    5 Troops, each: 3 × Armoured Cars
1 Liaison/Recce Troop: Troop HQ (2 × Humber Scout Cars)
    3 Sections, each: 3 × Humber Scout Cars

Notes
1. Radios were in all tanks and armoured cars, Carrier PHQs, and other CHQs.
2. Infantry secs had No.74 or Hawkins 75 A/T grenades.
3. 2pdr & 37mm had APCBC, 6pdr and 25pdr had AP, the 6pdr had one load of APCBC.
4. Armoured Cars were Humber III or Daimler II. Scout Cars were Humber or Daimler.
5. The Division was earmarked for North Africa. That resulted in the mixed Armoured Regiments until December 1942. In the event the Division did not leave the UK until D-Day.

1.17 BRITISH 11TH ARMOURED DIVISION, BRITAIN, JANUARY–SEPTEMBER 1943

The Division's main combat elements were:
    29th Armoured Brigade (23rd Hussars, 24th Lancers, 2nd Fife & Forfar Yeomanry Armoured Regiments, 8th Btn Rifle Brigade Motor Battalion)
    159th Lorried Infantry Brigade (3rd Btn Monmouthshire Regiment, 4th Btn King's Shropshire Light Infantry, 1st Btn Herefordshire Regiment Infantry Battalions)
    Divisional Armoured Recce Regiment (2nd Northamptonshire Yeomanry, April 1943+)
Troops are rated average morale and average training.

SUPPORT UNITS

Divisional Support

Included:
13th Royal Horse Artillery, 151st Field Artillery Regiments, each:
    3 Artillery Batteries, each: Battery HQ (4 rifle secs, 4 lorries, 4 AALMG, 3 OP Teams)
        2 Troops, each: 4 × 25pdr field guns, 4 trucks, radio truck, 2 AALMG
75th Anti-Tank Regiment:
    3 Batteries, each: Battery HQ (1 rifle sec, 1 truck)
        3 Troops, each: 4 × 6pdr, 2 LMG, 4 trucks
    1 Battery: Battery HQ (1 rifle sec, 1 truck)
        3 Troops, each: 4 × 6pdr or 17pdr, 4 trucks, 2 LMG
58th Light AA Regiment:
    3 Batteries, each: Battery HQ (1 rifle sec, 1 truck)
        3 Troops, each: 6 × 40mm Bofors, 6 trucks
13th, 612th Field Engineer Squadrons, each: Sqdn HQ (2 rifle secs, 1 lorry)
    4 Troops, each: 4 (12 man) rifle/engineer secs, 3 LMG, 2 lorries
147th Engineer Park Squadron:
    1 Workshop Section
    1 Bridging and Stores Section

Brigade Support

29th Armoured Brigade HQ (7 × Centaur or M4A1 Sherman II, 6 × Grant OP, 7 × Daimler S/C) with:
    1 Defence Troop: 3 × Centaur I or Sherman II
    1 Bridge Troop: 3 × Valentine AVLB
159th Infantry Brigade HQ (6 rifle secs, 2 LMG, 4 lorries)

MAIN COMBAT ELEMENTS

Armoured Regiment (January–March 1943)

RHQ (2 × Valentine III, 2 × Valentine VIII(6pdr), 3 × Scammell Wrecker)
3 Squadrons, each: Sqdn HQ (2 × Valentine III)
    2 Troops, each: 3 × Valentine III
    2 Troops, each: 2 × Valentine VIII(6pdr), 1 × Valentine III(2pdr)
1 Recce Troop: Troop HQ (2 × Daimler Scout Car)
    3 Sections, each: 3 × Daimler Scout Car

Armoured Regiment (April–September 1943)

RHQ (4 × M4A1 Sherman II, 3 × Cavalier ARV)
3 Squadrons, each: Sqdn HQ (4 × M4A1 Sherman II or Cavalier, or 2 × Centaur I, 2 × Centaur CS)
    5 Troops, each: 3 × Sherman II or Cavalier or Centaur I
1 Bridge Troop: 3 × Valentine AVLB
1 Recce Troop: Troop HQ (2 × Daimler Scout Car)

3 Sections, each: 3 × Daimler Scout Car

Motorised Infantry Battalion

Btn HQ (2 rifle secs, 1 lorry)
4 Companies, each: Coy HQ (1 rifle sec, 1 lorry)
        3 platoons, each: 1 (8 man) rifle Pl HQ sec, 1 × 2" mortar, 1 PIAT, 3 (10 man) rifle secs, 3 LMG, 2 lorries
1 Support Company: Coy HQ (1 rifle sec, 1 truck)
        1 platoon: 6 × 6pdr anti-tank guns, 2 LMG, 6 × Carriers
        1 platoon: 3 (6 man) rifle/engineer secs, 3 LMG, 3 trucks or M3A1 White Scout Car
        1 battery: 6 × 3" mortars, 7 × Universal Carriers
        1 platoon: Pl HQ: 1 × Universal Carrier, 1 LMG, 1 × Daimler S/C
            4 sections, each: 3 × Carriers, 3 LMG, 1 rifle sec, 1 × 2" mortar, 1 × Boys

Motor Rifle Battalion (of Armoured Brigade)

Btn HQ (2 rifle secs, 2 trucks)
3 Companies, each: Coy HQ (1 rifle sec, 1 truck or 2 × M3A1 White Scout Cars)
        1 battery: 2 × 3" mortars, 2 × Carriers
        3 platoons, each: 4 (7 man) rifle secs, 3 LMG, 1 × 2" mortar, 4 trucks or M3A1 White S/C
        1 platoon: 2 × 6pdr A/T guns, 2 × Carriers
        1 platoon: Pl HQ: 1 × Universal Carrier, 1 LMG, 1 × Daimler S/C
            3 sections, each: 3 × Carriers, 3 LMG, 1 rifle sec, 1 × 2" mortar, 1 × Boys
2 MG Platoons, each: 4 × Vickers MMG, 5 × Carriers
1 AA Platoon: 4 × 20mm cannon, 4 trucks

2nd Northamptonshire Yeomanry Divisional Armoured Recce Regiment (April 1943+)

RHQ (3 × Centaur I or Cavalier, 2 × Universal Carriers)
1 AA Troop: 6 × Centaur AA (on paper – none available)
3 Squadrons, each: Sqdn HQ (2 × Centaur I or Cavalier)
        3 Troops, each: 3 × Cavalier or 2 × Centaur I, 2 × Centaur CS
        1 Troop: Troop HQ: 1 × Universal Carrier, 1 LMG
            3 Sections, each: 3 × Carrier, 3 LMG, 1 Boys, 1 × 2" mortar, 1 rifle sec

Notes
1. Radios were in all tanks and armoured cars, Carrier PHQs, and other CHQs.
2. Infantry secs had No.74 or Hawkins 75 A/T grenades. May have had PIAT from July 1943, replacing Boys where appropriate.
3. 2pdr & 37mm had APCBC, 75mm, 6pdr and 25pdr had AP, the 6pdr had one load of APCBC.
4. By June 1943 the Division was over-strength in tanks, with enough spare for two more Armoured Regiments.

1.18 BRITISH 42ND ARMOURED DIVISION, BRITAIN, JULY 1942–OCTOBER 1943

The Division's main combat elements were:
    30th Armoured Brigade (22nd Dragoons, 1st Lothian & Border Horse, Westminster Dragoons Armoured Regiments, 12th Btn KRRC Motor Battalion)
    71st Motorised Brigade (1st Btn East Lancashire Regiment, 1st Btn Highland Light Infantry, 1st Oxfordshire & Buckinghamshire Light Infantry battalions)
    Divisional Recce Regiment (112th Regiment Royal Armoured Corps up to February 1943)
    Divisional Armoured Recce Regiment (1st Northamptonshire Yeomanry, April 1943+)
Troops are rated average morale and training.

SUPPORT UNITS

Divisional Support

Included:
Sufficient spare Covenanters for another Armoured Regiment
86th and 147th Field Artillery Regiments, each:
    3 Artillery Batteries, each: Battery HQ (4 rifle secs, 4 lorries, 4 AALMG, 3 OP Teams)
        2 Troops, each: 4 × 25pdr field guns, 4 trucks, radio truck, 2 AALMG
53rd Anti-Tank Regiment:
    3 Batteries, each: Battery HQ (1 rifle sec, 1 truck)
        3 Troops, each: 4 × 2pdr, 2 LMG, 4 trucks
93rd Light AA Regiment:
    3 Batteries, each: Battery HQ (1 rifle sec, 1 truck)
        1 Troop: 6 × 40mm Bofors, 6 trucks
16th, 17th Field Engineer Squadrons, each: Sqdn HQ (2 rifle secs, 1 lorry)
    4 Troops, each: 4 (12 man) rifle/engineer secs, 2 LMG, 2 lorries
149th Engineer Park Squadron:
    1 Workshop Section
    1 Bridging and Stores Section

Brigade Support

30th Armoured Brigade HQ (4 × Crusader II, 3 × Crusader III, 2 × ACV, 2 × Humber Scout Cars, 6 × Centaur OP tanks)
71st Motorised Brigade HQ (4 rifle secs, 2 LMG, 2 trucks, 2 lorries)

MAIN COMBAT ELEMENTS

Armoured Regiment (July–August 1942)
RHQ (4 × Covenanter, 3 × Scammell Wrecker)
1 Squadron: Sqdn HQ (1 × Crusader II, 1 × Covenanter, 2 × Covenanter-CS)
        3 Troops, each: 3 × Crusader II
        2 Troops, each: 3 × Covenanter
1 Squadron: Sqdn HQ (2 × Covenanter, 2 × Covenanter-CS)
        5 Troops, each: 3 × Covenanter
1 Squadron: Sqdn HQ (2 × Matilda IICS, 2 × Valentine II)
        3 Troops, each: 3 × Valentine II, II or V
        2 Troops, each: 3 × Crusader II
1 AA Troop: 2 × Vickers VI AA
1 Recce Troop: Troop HQ (1 × Humber S/C)
        3 Sections, each: 3 × Humber Scout Car

Armoured Regiment (September 1942–May 1943)
RHQ (4 × Covenanter, 3 × Scammell Wrecker)
3 Squadrons, each: Sqdn HQ (2 × Covenanter, 2 × Covenanter CS)
        5 Troops, each: 3 × Covenanter
1 AA Troop: 3 × Vickers VI AA
1 Recce Troop: Troop HQ (1 × Humber Scout Car)
        3 Sections, each: 3 × Humber Scout Car
1 Bridge Troop (1943 only): 3 × Covenanter AVLB

Armoured Regiment June–October 1943)
RHQ (1 × Crusader III, 2 × Cromwell I, 1 × Crusader II, 3 × Scammell Wrecker)
2 Squadrons, each: Sqdn HQ (2 × Covenanter, 2 × Covenanter CS)
        5 Troops, each: 3 × Covenanter
1 Squadron: Sqdn HQ (1 × Centaur, 2 × Covenanter CS)
        2 Troops, each: 3 × Centaur
        2 Troops, each: 3 × Covenanter
        1 Troop: 3 × Crusader II
1 AA Troop: 3 × Vickers VI AA
1 Recce Troop: Troop HQ (1 × Humber Scout Car)
        3 Sections, each: 3 × Humber Scout Car
1 Bridge Troop (1943 only): 3 × Covenanter AVLB

Motorised Infantry Battalion
Btn HQ (2 rifle secs, 2 trucks)
4 Companies, each: Coy HQ (1 (13 man) rifle sec, 1 lorry)
        3 platoons, each: 1 (7 man) rifle Pl HQ sec, 1 Boys, 1 × 2" mortar, 3 (10 man) rifle secs, 3 LMG, 2 lorries
1 Support Company: Coy HQ (1 rifle sec, 1 truck)
        2 platoons, each: 4 × 6pdr, 2 LMG, 4 trucks or Carriers
        1 platoon: 2 (8 man) rifle/engineer secs, 1 (5 man) Pl HQ sec, 2 LMG, 3 trucks
        1 battery: 6 × 3" mortars, 6 trucks, radio truck, 3 Boys
        1 platoon: Pl HQ: 1 × Universal Carrier, 1 LMG, 1 × Daimler S/C
            4 sections, each: 3 × Carriers, 3 LMG, 1 rifle sec, 1 × 2" mortar, 1 × Boys

12th Battalion King's Royal Rifle Corps Motor Battalion
Btn HQ (2 rifle secs, 2 trucks)
3 Companies, each: Coy HQ (1 rifle sec, 1 truck)
            1 section: 2 × 3" mortars, 2 × Universal Carriers
        3 platoons, each: 4 (8 man) rifle secs, 3 LMG, 1 × 2" mortar, 4 trucks
        1 platoon: 4 MMG, 4 trucks
        1 platoon: Pl HQ: 1 × Universal Carrier, 1 LMG, 1 × Daimler S/C
            3 sections, each: 3 × Carriers, 3 LMG, 1 rifle sec, 1 × 2" mortar, 1 × Boys
1 Anti-Tank Company: Coy HQ (1 rifle sec, 1 truck)
        3 platoons, each: 4 × 6pdr anti-tank guns, 4 trucks, 2 LMG

112th Regiment Royal Armoured Car Divisional Armoured Car Regiment (up to February 1943)
RHQ (4 × Humber III, 2 × Daimler Scout Cars)
3 Squadrons, each: Sqdn HQ (4 × Humber III armoured cars)
        5 Troops, each: 3 × Humber III
1 Liaison/Communication Troop: Troop HQ (2 × Scout Cars)
        3 Sections, each: 3 × Scout Cars

1st Northamptonshire Yeomanry Divisional Armoured Recce Regiment (April–October 1943)
RHQ (3 × Centaur I, 2 × Universal Carriers+ LMG)
3 Squadrons, each: Sqdn HQ (2 × Cromwell I)
        3 Troops, each: 2 × Centaur I, 1 × Covenanter CS

1 Troop: Troop HQ (1 × Universal Carrier, 1 LMG)
        3 Sections, each: 3 × Universal Carrier, 1 rifle sec, 1 Boys, 1 × 2" mortar, 3 LMG
1 Liaison/Recce Troop: Troop HQ (2 × Humber Scout Cars)
        3 Sections, each: 3 × Humber Scout Cars

Notes
1. Radios were in all tanks and armoured cars, Carrier PHQs, and other CHQs.
2. Infantry secs had No.74 or Hawkins 75 A/T grenades.
3. 2pdr & 37mm had APCBC, 6pdr and 25pdr had AP, the 6pdr had one load of APCBC.
4. Artillery OP could be in truck, Universal Carrier, or Daimler Scout Car or Covenanter OP tank.
5. In May 1943 the 86th Field Artillery Regiment was replaced by the 191st Field Artillery Regiment.
6. The 17th Field Engineer Squadron was re-numbered the 617th in March 1943.
7. The division was disbanded in October 1943.

1.19 BRITISH 79TH ARMOURED DIVISION, BRITAIN, OCTOBER 1942–MARCH 1943

The Division's main combat elements were:
    27th Armoured Brigade (4th/7th Dragoon Guards, 13th/18th Hussars, 1st East Riding Yeomanry Armoured Regiments, 7th KRRC Motor Battalion)
    185th Lorried Infantry Brigade (2nd Btn Royal Warwickshire Regiment, 2nd Btn Royal Norfolk Regiment, 2nd Btn King's Shropshire Light Infantry Regiment)
    Divisional Armoured Car Regiment (162nd Regiment Royal Armoured Corps to January 1943)
    Divisional Armoured Recce Regiment (2nd Northamptonshire Yeomanry (January 1943+)
Troops are rated average morale and average training.

SUPPORT UNITS

Divisional Support

Included:
142nd, 150th Field Artillery Regiments, each:
    3 Batteries, each: Battery HQ (4 rifle secs, 4 lorries, 2 AALMG)
        2 Troops, each: 4 × 25pdr field guns, 6 trucks, 2 LMG
55th Anti-Tank Regiment:
    3 Batteries, each: Battery HQ (1 rifle sec, 1 truck)
        3 Troops, each: 4 × 2pdr anti-tank guns, 4 trucks, 2 LMG
    1 Battery: Battery HQ (1 rifle sec, 1 truck)
        3 Troops, each: 4 × 6pdr anti-tank guns, 4 trucks, 2 LMG
119th Light Anti-Aircraft Regiment:
    3 Batteries, each: Battery HQ (1 rifle sec, 1 truck)
        1 Troop: 6 × 40mmL60 Bofors, 6 trucks
18th, 19th Field Engineer Squadrons, each: Sqdn HQ (2 rifle secs, 1 lorry)
    4 Troops, each: 4 (12 man) rifle/engineer secs, 2 LMG, 2 lorries
508th Engineer Field Park Squadron:
    1 Workshop Section
    1 Bridge & Stores Section

Brigade Support

27th Armoured Brigade HQ (8 × Covenanter, 1 × ACV, 2 × cars)
185th Infantry Brigade HQ (6 rifle secs, 6 trucks, 2 LMG)

MAIN COMBAT ELEMENTS

Armoured Regiment

RHQ (4 × Covenanter, 3 × Scammell Wrecker)
3 Squadrons, each: Sqdn HQ (2 × Covenanter, 2 × Covenanter-CS)
    3 Troops, each: 3 × Covenanter
1 Recce Troop: Troop HQ (2 × Daimler Scout Car)
    3 Sections, each: 3 × Daimler Scout Car

7th Battalion King's Royal Rifle Corps Motor Battalion

Btn HQ (2 rifle secs, 2 trucks)
3 Companies, each: Coy HQ (1 rifle sec, 1 truck, 1 × 2" mortar)
    1 section: 2 × 3" mortars, 2 × Universal Carriers, 2 MMG, 2 trucks
    3 platoons, each: 4 (8 man) rifle secs, 3 LMG, 1 × 2" mortar, 4 Boys, 4 trucks
    1 platoon: 4 × 6pdr anti-tank guns, 4 trucks, 2 LMG
    1 platoon: Pl HQ: 1 × Universal Carrier, 1 LMG
        3 sections, each: 3 × Carriers, 3 LMG, 1 rifle sec, 1 × 2" mortar, 1 Boys

162nd Regiment Royal Armoured Corps Divisional Armoured Car Regiment (up to January 1943)

RHQ (2 × Armoured Cars, 2 × Daimler Scout Cars)
3 Companies, each: Coy HQ (2 × Armoured Cars)
    3 Troops, each: 3 × Scout cars

2nd Northamptonshire Yeomanry Divisional Armoured Recce Regiment (January–March 1943)

RHQ (3 × Cavalier, 2 × Universal Carriers)
3 Squadrons, each: Sqdn HQ (2 × Cavalier)
        3 Troops, each: 3 × Cavalier
        1 Troop: Troop HQ: 1 × Universal Carrier, 1 LMG
                3 Sections, each: 3 × Carrier, 3 LMG, 1 Boys, 1 × 2" mortar, 1 rifle sec

Motorised Infantry Battalion

Btn HQ (2 rifle secs, 2 trucks)
4 Companies, each: Coy HQ (1 (13 man) rifle sec, 1 truck)
        3 platoons, each: 1 (7 man) rifle Pl HQ sec, 1 × 2" mortar, 1 Boys
                3 (10 man) rifle secs, 3 LMG, 2 lorries
1 Support Company: Coy HQ (1 rifle sec, 1 truck)
        2 platoons, each: 4 × 6pdr anti-tank guns, 4 trucks, 2 LMG
        1 platoon: 2 (8 man) rifle/engineer secs, 1 (5 man) Pl HQ sec, 2 LMG, 1 lorry
        1 platoon: 6 × 3" mortars, 6 × Carriers
        1 platoon: Pl HQ: 1 × Universal Carrier, 1 Scout Car, 1 LMG
                4 Sections, each: 3 × Carrier, 1 rifle sec, 1 × 2" mortar, 1 Boys, 3 LMG

Notes
1. Radios were in all tanks and armoured cars, Carrier PHQs, and other CHQs.
2. Infantry secs had No.74 or Hawkins 75 A/T grenades.
3. 2pdr had APCBC, 6pdr had AP with one load of APCBC. 25pdr had AP.
4. Armoured Cars were Humber III or Daimler II. Scout Cars were Humber or Daimler.
5. In April 1943 the Division became the HQ for the 'Funnies' specialised armoured engineer units.
6. In January 1943 the 162nd RAC was replaced by the 2nd Northamptonshire Yeomanry.

1.20 BRITISH 80TH ARMOURED DIVISION, BRITAIN, OCTOBER–DECEMBER 1942

The Division's main combat elements were:
        20th Armoured Brigade (1st Royal Gloucestershire Hussars, 1st Northamptonshire Yeomanry, 2nd Northampton-shire Yeomanry Armoured Regiments, 10th Btn KRRC Motor Battalion)
        Divisional Armoured Car Regiment (161st Royal Armoured Corps)
Troops are rated average morale and poor training.

SUPPORT UNITS

Brigade Support

20th Armoured Brigade HQ (8 × Valentine III, 2 × ACV, 3 × Scout Cars)

MAIN COMBAT ELEMENTS

Armoured Regiment

RHQ (4 × Valentine III, 3 × Scammell Wrecker)
3 Squadrons, each: Sqdn HQ (4 × Valentine III)
        3 Troops, each: 3 × Valentine III
1 Recce Troop: Troop HQ (2 × Daimler Scout Car)
        3 Sections, each: 3 × Daimler Scout Car
1 Training Troop: 2–6 × Crusader II

10th Battalion King's Royal Rifle Corps Motor Battalion

Btn HQ (2 rifle secs, 2 trucks)
3 Companies, each: Coy HQ (1 rifle sec, 1 truck)
        1 section: 2 × 3" mortars, 2 × Carriers
        3 platoons, each: 4 (7 man) rifle secs, 3 LMG, 1 Boys, 1 × 2" mortar, 4 trucks
        1 platoon: 4 × Vickers MMG, 4 trucks
        1 platoon: Pl HQ: 1 × Universal Carrier, 1 LMG
                3 sections, each: 3 × Carriers, 3 LMG, 1 rifle sec, 1 × 2" mortar

161st Royal Armoured Corps Divisional Armoured Car Regiment

RHQ (2 × Armoured Cars, 2 × Daimler Scout Cars)
3 Companies, each: Coy HQ (2 rifle secs, 1 lorry)
        2 platoons, each: 1 (7 man) rifle Pl HQ sec, 1 × 2" mortar, 1 Boys, 3 (10 man) rifle secs, 3 LMG, 4 trucks
        1 platoon: 4 × armoured cars
1 Scout Troop: Troop HQ: 1 × Universal Carrier, 1 LMG, 1 × Scout Car
        4 Sections, each: 3 × Universal Carrier, 3 LMG, 1 rifle squad, 1 × 2" mortar, 1 Boys
1 Battery: 4 × 3" mortars, 4 trucks, 2 Boys
1 Liaison/Communication Troop: Troop HQ (2 × Scout Cars)
        3 Sections, each: 3 × Scout Cars

Notes
1. Radios were in all tanks and armoured cars, Carrier PHQs, and other CHQs.
2. Infantry secs had No.74 or Hawkins 75 A/T grenades.
3. 2pdr & 37mm had APC.

4.   The Armoured Car Regiment was in the process of converting from an Infantry Battalion when the division was disbanded in December 1942.
5.   Armoured Cars may have be Humber III or Daimler II.

1.21 BRITISH MIXED DIVISION, BRITAIN, MID 1942–SEPTEMBER 1943

The Division's main combat elements were:
> Two Infantry Brigades (three Infantry Battalions)
> One Infantry Tank Brigade (one-three Infantry Tank Regiments)
> Divisional Recce Regiment

Troop were rated average morale with average training.

SUPPORT UNITS

Divisional Support

Included:
3 Field Artillery Regiments, each:
> 3 Artillery Batteries, each:
>> Battery HQ (4 rifle secs, 6 trucks, 4 AALMG, 2 Boys, 3 OP Teams)
>> 2 Troops, each: 4 × 25pdr field guns, 6 trucks, 1 Boys, 2 AALMG

1 Anti-Tank Regiment:
> 4 Anti-Tank Batteries, each: Battery HQ (1 rifle sec, 1 truck)
>> 3 platoons, each: 4 × 2pdr or 6pdr anti-tank guns, 5 trucks, 2 LMG

3 Field Engineer Companies, each: Coy HQ (2 rifle secs, 2 lorries)
> 3 platoons, each: 4 (12 man) rifle/engineer secs, 2 lorries, 3LMG

1 Field Park Company:
> 1 Workshop Section
> 1 Bridging Section
> 1 Stores Section

1 Light AA Regiment:
> 3 AA Batteries, each: Battery HQ (1 rifle sec,1 truck)
>> 3 platoons, each: 6 × 40mm Bofors, 6 trucks

1 Attached Medium Artillery Regiment: RHQ (8 rifle secs, 8 lorries, 4 AALMG)
> 4 batteries, each: 4 × 5.5" guns, 4 lorries, radio van, 2 LMG

1 Provost (Military Police) Company: 115 men, 25 trucks/cars, 79 LMG/SMG

1 Machine Gun Battalion (1st, 15th, 43rd Divisions only)
> 4 MG Companies, each: Coy HQ (1 rifle squad)
>> 4 platoons, each: 4 × Vickers MMG, 4 rifle crew secs

Brigade Support

Infantry Brigade HQ (6 rifle secs, 4 lorries, 1 staff car) with:
> 1 Defence Platoon: 1 (7 man) rifle Pl HQ sec, 1 × 2" mortar, 1 Boys or PIAT, 3 (10 man) rifle secs, 3 LMG

1 Support Group: Coy HQ (2 rifle secs, 2 trucks) (1943 only)
> 3 platoons, each: 4 × Vickers MMG, 4 trucks or Universal Carriers
> 2 platoons, each: 4 × 4.2" mortars, 9 × Loyd Carriers or 6 trucks

Tank Brigade HQ (7 × Tanks, 2 × ACV, 6 × Daimler Scout Cars, 3 × Vickers VI AA) with:
> 1 HQ Defence Troop: 3 × Tanks
> 1 Assault Gun Squadron: Sqdn HQ (1 × Churchill I/III) (1942–early 1943 only)
>> 3 Troops each 3 × Churchill 3" Gun Carrier SPG

MAIN COMBAT ELEMENTS

Infantry Battalion

Btn HQ (5 rifle secs, 1 LMG)
4 Companies, each: Coy HQ (1 (13 man) rifle sec)
> 3 platoons, each: 1 (7 man) rifle Pl HQ sec, 1 Boys, 1 × 2" mortar, 3 (10 man) rifle secs, 3 LMG

1 Support Company: Coy HQ (1 rifle sec)
> 1 platoon: 4 × twin AALMG, 4 Boys A/T Rifle in 2 rifle crew secs (1942 only)
> 1 platoon: 2 rifle/engineer secs, 1 stores truck
> 1 platoon: 6 × 2pdr or 6pdr anti-tank guns (1943 only)
> 1 battery: 6 × 3" mortars, 6 × Carriers, 1 Boys
> 1 platoon: Pl HQ: 1 × Universal Carrier, 1 × Daimler S/C, 1 LMG
>> 4 sections, each: 3 × Carrier, 3 LMG, 1 Boys, 1 × 2" mortar, 1 rifle sec

Infantry Tank Regiment

RHQ(2 × Tanks, 2 × CS Tanks)
3 Companies, each: Coy HQ (1–2 × Tanks, 2 × CS Tanks)
> 4–5 platoons, each: 3 × Tanks

1 AA Platoon: 2 Troops, each: 4 × Vickers VI AA
1 Recce Platoon: Pl HQ (1 × Daimler or Humber Scout Car)
> 3 sections, each: 3 × Scout Cars

Divisional Recce Regiment
RHQ (3 rifle secs, 3 LMG, 2 × Boys A/T Rifle, 3 trucks, staff cars)
3 Squadrons, each: Sqdn HQ (3 rifle secs, 1 LMG, 3 trucks)
        3 Troops, each: Troop HQ: 1 × Universal Carrier, 1 × A/C, 1 LMG, 1 Boys, 1 × 2" mortar
               2 sections, each: 2 × A/C or 1 × Armoured Car, 1 × Scout Car
               2 sections, each: 3 × Carrier, 1 rifle sec, 3 LMG, 1 Boys, 1 × 2" mortar
        1 Assault Troop: 4 (8 man) rifle secs, 1 Boys, 4 LMG, 5 trucks, 3 motorcycles

Notes
1. Radios were in all AFV and other Pl HQs.
2. Infantry may have had No.74 or No.75 A/T grenades.
3. In practice Boys A/T rifles were retired and not replaced by PIATs until late 1943.
4. Divisional artillery OP could be in Tank or Daimler Scout Car or Universal Carrier OP.
5. Tank was Valentine II–V or Churchill III or Matilda II. In the Brigade HQs Tanks may be Crusader II or Covenanter.
6. Close Support Tank was Matilda IICS or Churchill ICS or Churchill V.
7. Armoured Car (A/C) in Recce Regiment was Humber III or Daimler II.
8. This was an experimental formation that was not used in combat, other than 4th Division (see Vol.3).
9. Brigade Support Groups may not have been formed except in the 4th Division.
10. The Assault Gun Squadrons were experimental and never saw service.
11. Divisions formed were:
        1st Mixed Division (June–December 1942) (2nd, 3rd Infantry Brigades, 34th then 25th Tank Brigade, 1st Recce Regiment)
        3rd Mixed Division (June 1942–April 1943) (8th, 9th Infantry Brigades, 33rd Tank Brigade, 3rd Recce Regiment)
        4th Mixed Division (June–December 1943) (10th, 12th Infantry Brigades, 21st Tank Brigade, 4th Recce Regiment)
        15th Scottish Mixed Division (March–Sept 1943) (44th, 46th Infantry Bdes, 6th Guards Tank Brigade, 15th Recce Squadron)
        43rd Wessex Mixed Division (June 1942–Sept 1943) 129th, 130th Infantry Bdes, 25th Tank Brigade then 34th Tank Brigade, 43rd Recce Regiment)
        53rd Welsh Mixed Division (May 1942–October 1943) (158th, 160th Infantry Bdes, 31st Tank Brigade, 53rd Recce Regiment)

1.22 BRITISH INFANTRY TANK BRIGADES, BRITAIN, 1940–1943
The Brigade's main combat elements were:
    3 Infantry Tank Battalions
Troops are rated good morale and average training

SUPPORT UNITS

Brigade Support
Infantry Tank Brigade HQ (4 × Tanks, 2 × ACV, 6 × Daimler Scout Cars, recovery lorries) with:
        1 HQ Defence Troop: 3 × Tanks (1943 only)
        1 AA Section: 3 × Vickers VI AA tanks (1941+)
        1 Assault Gun Squadron: Sqdn HQ (1 × Churchill I/III) (1942–early 1943 only)
            3 Troops@ 3 × Churchill 3" Gun Carrier SPG

MAIN COMBAT ELEMENTS

Infantry Tank Battalion/Regiment
RHQ (2 × Tanks, 2 × CS Tanks)
3 Companies, each: Coy HQ (1–2 × Tanks, 2 × CS Tanks, 1 × Vickers VIC)
        4 platoons, each: 3 × Tanks
0–1 AA Platoon: 4 × Vickers VI AA (very rare in practice!)
0–1 Scout Platoon: Pl HQ: 1 × Scout Caror 2 × Universal Carrier (late 1942+)
        2–3 sections, each: 3 × Scout Car or Universal Carrier

Notes
1. Radios were in all AFV.
2. The Brigades when at full strength had 3 Battalions.
3. Tanks were Matilda II, Valentine II/III or Churchill I/II. In Valentine Regiments CS Tanks were Matilda IICS. Some Brigade HQs had Covenanters or Crusader IIs.
4. These brigades acted as Corps support assigned to Infantry Divisions.
5. Units formed were:
        1st Tank Brigade (July–Sept 1940) (4th RTR, 7th RTR, 8th RTR)
        (50 × Matilda II in 4th RTR, 50 × Matilda I in 8th RTR by Sept 1940)
        1st Tank Brigade (October–December 1940) (4th RTR, 8th RTR, 42nd RTR)
        (50 × Matilda II in 4th RTR, 50 × Matilda I in 8th RTR)
        1st Tank Brigade (January–March 1941) (8th RTR, 42nd RTR, 44th RTR)
        10th Tank Brigade (July 1942–November 1943) (108th, 109th, 143rd Regiments RAC)
        (81 × Churchill in Sept 1942, 141 × Sherman and Churchill by June 1943)
        11th Tank Brigade (Jul 1942–November 1943) (107th, 110th, 111th Regiments RAC) (105 × Churchill)
        21st Tank Brigade (March 1939–Sept 1940) (42nd RTR, 44th RTR, 48th RTR)
        (12 × Matilda II, 50?x Medium Mk.II)
        21st Tank Brigade (October 1940–April 1941) (42nd RTR, 43rd RTR, 48th RTR) (Valentine I)
        21st Tank Brigade (April–October 1941) (12th RTR, 48th RTR) (Matilda II, Valentine II, Churchill I)
        21st Tank Brigade (November 1941–June 1942) (12th RTR, 48th RTR, 145th Regiment RAC)
        (100 × Churchill, 4 × Covenanter in Bde HQ)
        25th Tank Brigade (1939–June 1940) (43rd RTR, 49th RTR, 51st RTR) (trucks + MG)
        25th Tank Brigade (June 1940–January 1941) (renamed 2nd Motor Machine Gun Brigade) (cars + MG)

25th Tank Brigade (February–March 1941) (11th RTR, 12th RTR, 51st RTR) (few Matilda II, Valentine I)
25th Tank Brigade (April–June 1941) (43rd RTR, 49th RTR, 51st RTR) (few Matilda II, Valentine II)
25th Tank Brigade (July–October 1941) (43rd RTR, 49th RR, 51st RTR)
(Matilda II, Churchill II, Valentine II)
25th Tank Brigade (November 1941–January 1942) (Churchill II, Churchill ICS)
25th Tank Brigade (February–December 1942) (North Irish Horse, 51st RTR, 142nd Regiment RAC) (fully equipped with Churchill III, ICS, 3 × Vickers VI AA, Universal Carriers, Daimler Scout Cars)
31st Tank Brigade (December 1941–April 1942) (9th RTR, 10th RTR, 141st Regiment RAC) (Churchill III)
31st Tank Brigade (December 1942–January 1943) (9th RTR, 10th RTR, 141st RAC) (Churchills)
31st Tank Brigade (February 1943–February 1944) (7th RTR, 9th RTR, 141st RAC) (Churchill III, IV)
34th Tank Brigade (December 1941–May 1942) (North Irish Horse, 147th RAC, 153rd RAC) (Churchill II)
35th Tank Brigade (December 1941–April 1943) (49th RTR, 152nd RAC, 155th RAC) (Churchill III)
36th Tank Brigade (January 1942–July 1943) (154th RAC, 156th RAC, 157th RAC) (Churchill III)

1.23 BRITISH INDEPENDENT ARMOURED UNITS, BRITAIN, JUNE–DECEMBER 1940

MAIN COMBAT ELEMENTS (CORPS SUPPORT)

7th RTR Tank Battalion (in June–July 1940)
Btn HQ (2 × Matilda II, 1 staff car, 1 recovery lorry)
2 'Squadrons', each: 3 × Matilda I
1 'Squadron': 3 × Matilda II

2 Armoured Car Squadrons, each:
Sqdn HQ (2 × Lanchester Mk.1 or Mk.II) (possibly in 12th Lancers)
3 Troops, each: 3 × Lanchester armoured cars

10 Factory Defence Units, each:
Coy HQ (1 Home Guard rifle sec) (poor training)
3 platoons, each: 3 × Leyland Beaver-Eel

15 Airfield Defence Platoons, each:
3 × Beaverette Mk.1 (poor training)

1 VIP Transport Unit:
3 × Guy Mk.1A, 1 × Lanchester 6x4 A/C converted to APC

3 Bovington Gate Guard Units, each:
3 × Mk.V Male WW1 tanks or Medium Mk.II as static pillboxes (poor training & poor morale)

3 Tank Training Companies, each:
Coy HQ (3 × Vickers Light Mk.III or Mk.IV or VIB)
3–4 platoons, each: 3 × tanks as above

2 Tank Training Companies, each:
Coy HQ (3 × Vickers 6-tonner Type B)
3–4 platoons, each: 3 × Vickers 6-tonner Type B)

3 Tank Training Companies, each:
Coy HQ (3 × Vickers Medium Mk.II) (up to 1941)
3 platoons, each: 3 × tanks as above, some unarmed

4 Tank Training Regiments, each: (December 1940+)
RHQ (3 × M1917 6-Tonner (American copy of FT-17)
3 Squadrons, each: Sqdn HQ (3 × M1917)
4 Troops, each: 3 × M1917

Notes
1.   Radios were in CHQs and above.
2.   These were the bulk of the independent armoured unit available had Britain been invaded in 1940.
3.   These units were generally rated as average morale with poor to average training.

1.24 CORPS ARMOURED RECCE REGIMENT, BRITAIN, 1942–1943

MAIN COMBAT ELEMENTS (CORPS SUPPORT)
RHQ (3 rifle secs, 3 LMG, 2 × Boys A/T Rifle, 3 trucks, staff cars)
3 Squadrons, each: Sqdn HQ (3 rifle secs, 1 LMG, 3 trucks)
3 Troops, each: THQ: 1 × Carrier, 1 × A/C, 1 (5 man) rifle sec, 1 LMG, 1 Boys, 1 × 2" mortar
2 sections, each: 2 × Armoured Car or 1 × Armoured Car, 1 × Scout Car
2 sections, each: 3 × Universal Carrier, 1 (12 man) rifle sec, 3 LMG, 1 Boys, 1 × 2"
1 Assault Troop: 4 rifle secs, 1 Boys, 4 LMG, 5 trucks, 3 motorcycles

Notes
1.   Radios were in all AFV.
2.   In practice the Boys A/T rifle was removed and replaced with PIATs in late 1943.
3.   Armoured Cars were Humber III or Daimler II. Scout Cars were Humber or Daimler.

1.25 AUSTRALIAN INFANTRY DIVISION, BRITAIN, OCTOBER 1940–1941

The Division's main combat elements were:
        18th Infantry Brigade (2/9th, 2/10th, 2/12th Infantry Battalions)
        25th Infantry Brigade (70th, 71st, 72nd Infantry Battalions)
Troops are rated good morale and average training

SUPPORT UNITS

Divisional Support

Included:
2nd/3rd Field Artillery Regiment:
        2 Artillery Batteries, each: Battery HQ (1 radio van, 4 trucks, 4 rifle secs, 2 Boys, 4 AALMG)
                2 Troops, each: 4 × 25pdr Mk.1 field guns, 5 trucks, radio van, 2 AALMG, 1 Boys
2nd/1st Australian Anti-tank Regiment:
        4 Anti-Tank Companies, each (Coy HQ: 1 rifle sec, 1 truck)
                3 Troops, each: 4 × 2pdr, 2 × LMG, 4 trucks
2nd/3rd Field Engineer Company: Coy HQ (1 rifle sec, 1 truck, 2 Boys, 2 LMG)
        3 platoons, each: 4 (12 man) rifle/engineer secs, 1 Boys, 1 LMG, 2 lorries
2nd/1st Engineer Park Company: explosives, tools, bridges

Brigade Support

Infantry Brigade HQ (4 rifle secs, 2 staff cars, 3 lorries) with up to:
        1 HQ Defence Platoon: 1 (7 man) rifle Pl HQ sec, 1 × 2" mortar, 1 Boys, 3 (10 man) rifle secs, 3 LMG 4
                                    trucks

MAIN COMBAT ELEMENTS

Australian Infantry Battalion

Btn HQ (4 rifle secs)
3 Companies, each: Coy HQ (1 (13 man) rifle sec, 1 lorry)
        3 platoons, each: 1 (7 man) Pl HQ rifle sec, 1 × 2" mortar, 1 Boys, 3 (10 man) rifle secs, 3 LMG, 2 lorries
1 Support Company: Coy HQ (1 rifle sec, 1 truck)
        1 platoon: 2 or 6 × 3" mortars, 2–3 trucks, radio truck
        1 platoon: 4 × Twin AALMG, 4 Boys, 4 trucks
        1 platoon: 2 rifle/engineer secs, 1 lorry
        1 platoon: Pl HQ: 1 × Carrier, 1 × Daimler S/C, 1 LMG
                2 sections, each: 3 × Bren Carrier, 3 LMG, 1 (6 man) rifle sec

Notes
1.   Radios were in all Coy HQ and AFV PHQs. All artillery was rated Assigned FC.
2.   Infantry secs had No.68 rifle A/T grenades.
3.   Battalion Carrier sections may in fact have been on motorcycles instead of Carriers.
4.   The Division was placed under the Aldershot Command.

1.26 NEW ZEALAND 2ND INFANTRY DIVISION, BRITAIN, OCTOBER 1940–1941

The Division's main combat elements were:
        5th Infantry Brigade (21st, 22nd, 23rd NZ Infantry Battalions)
        7th Brigade (28th Maori Infantry Battalion, 29th Composite Infantry Battalion)
        Attached Tank Regiment (8th RTR)
Troops are rated average training and good morale, with Maoris at excellent morale, and the Composite Battalion at average morale.

SUPPORT UNITS

Divisional Support

Included:
5th New Zealand Field Artillery Regiment:
        4 Batteries, each: Battery HQ (1 radio van, 4 trucks, 4 rifle secs, 2 Boys, 4 AALMG)
                2 Troops, each: 4 × 25pdr Mk.1 field guns, 5 trucks, radio van, 2 AALMG, 1 Boys
7th Field Engineer Company: Coy HQ (1 rifle sec, 1 truck, 2 Boys, 2 LMG)
        3 platoons, each: 4 (12 man) rifle/engineer secs, 1 Boys, 1 LMG, 2 lorries
1 Engineer Stores Platoon: explosives, tools, bridges
C Squadron, 2nd NZ Divisional Cavalry Regiment:
        Sqdn HQ (2 × Vickers VIB light tanks, 2 × Scout Carriers)
        2 Troops, each: 3 × Vickers VIB
        4 Troops, each: 3 × Scout Carriers, 1 rifle sec, 3 Boys, 3 LMG
157th NZ AA Battery: Battery HQ (1 rifle sec, 1 truck)
        3 platoons, each: 4 AAMMG, 4 trucks

Brigade Support

Infantry Brigade HQ (4 rifle secs, 2 staff cars, 3 lorries) with:
1 HQ Defence Platoon: 1 (7 man) rifle Pl HQ sec, 1 × 2" mortar, 1 Boys, 3 (10 man) rifle secs, 3 LMG 4 trucks

1 Anti-Tank Company: Coy HQ (1 rifle sec, 1 truck)
      3 platoons, each: 4 × 2pdr, 4 trucks

MAIN COMBAT ELEMENTS

New Zealand Infantry Battalion

Btn HQ (4 rifle secs)
4 Companies, each: Coy HQ ((13 man) rifle sec, 1 lorry)
      3 platoons, each: 1 (7 man) Pl HQ rifle sec, 1 × 2" mortar, 1 Boys, 3 (10 man) rifle secs, 3 LMG, 2 lorries
1 Support Company: Coy HQ (1 rifle sec, 1 truck)
      1 platoon: 2 or 6 × 3" mortars, 2–3 trucks, radio truck
      1 platoon: 4 × Twin AALMG, 4 Boys, 4 trucks
      1 platoon: 2 rifle/engineer secs, 1 lorry
      1 platoon: Pl HQ: 1 × Carrier, 1 × Daimler S/C, 1 LMG
          2 sections, each: 3 × Bren Carrier, 3 LMG, 1 (6 man) rifle sec

8th RTR British Army Tank Battalion

Btn HQ (2 × Matilda I, 4 × Vickers VIB)
3 Companies, each: Coy HQ (4 × Matilda I)
      4 platoons, each: 3 × Matilda I

Notes
1.   Radios were in all Coy HQ and AFV PHQs. All artillery is rated Assigned FC.
2.   Infantry secs had No.68 rifle A/T grenades.
3.   The Maori Battalion had machete type melee weapons.
4.   The 2nd Division, also known as the 2nd New Zealand Expeditionary Force, was under 12th Corps HQ in the Sussex area. It had the 8th RTR attached from the 1st Tank Brigade.

1.27 BRITISH INFANTRY DIVISION, BRITAIN, 1941–1943

The Division's main combat elements were:
      3 infantry brigades (each 3 Infantry Battalions, and in 1943, one Support Group Battalion)
      1 Divisional Recce Battalion or Recce Regiment or Recce Squadron
Troops are rated average morale and average training

SUPPORT UNITS

Divisional Support

Included:
3 Engineer Companies, each: Coy HQ (1 rifle sec, 1 truck)
      3 platoons, each: 4 (12 man) rifle/engineer secs, 3 LMG
or (1943+):
3 Engineer Companies: Coy HQ (4 (11 man) rifle secs, 1 LMG, 1 Boys, 2 lorries)
      3 platoons, each: 1 (17 man) rifle/engineer Pl HQ sec
          4 (12 man) rifle/engineer secs, 4 LMG, 2 lorries

1 Field Park Company: Coy HQ (3 rifle/engineer secs, 2 lorries)
      1 Workshop Platoon: 4 rifle/engineer secs, workshop lorries, gantry cranes
      1 Stores Platoon: 3 rifle/engineer secs, explosives, tools, etc
      1 Bridging Platoon: 5 rifle/engineer secs, pontoon bridges, etc
1 Light Anti-Aircraft Regiment:
      3 AA Batteries, each: Battery HQ (1 rifle sec, 1 truck)
      3 Troops, each: 4 or (1943+) 6 × 40mm Bofors, 6 trucks
1 Anti-Tank Regiment:
      4 Anti-Tank Batteries, each: Battery HQ (1 rifle sec, 1 truck)
          3 Troops, each: 4 × 2pdr or 6pdr, 4 truck portees, 2 LMG
3 Field Artillery Regiments, each:
      3 Batteries, each: Battery HQ (1 radio van, 5 trucks, 4 rifle secs, 2 Boys, 4 AALMG)
          2 Troops, each: 4 × 25pdr, 5 trucks, radio van, 1 Boys, 2 AALMG, OP Team
Divisional Machine Gun Battalion: 1941–1942
      4 MG Companies, each: Coy HQ (1 rifle sec)
          3 platoons, each: 4 MMG, 1 Boys A/T rifle, 1 LMG, 4 rifle crew secs
Proposed Divisional Support Battalion, 1943 (never implemented)
      Btn HQ (4 rifle secs, 2 lorries)
          1 Support Company: Coy HQ (2 rifle secs, 1 lorry)
             6 platoons, each: 4 × 20mm Oerlikon, 4 trucks
      3 Infantry Brigade HQ Support Companies, each: Coy HQ (2 rifle secs, 2 trucks)
          3 platoons, each: 4 × 20mm Oerlikon cannon, 4 trucks
          3 platoons, each: 4 × 4.2" mortars, 4 trucks, radio truck
1 Attached Medium Artillery Regiment: RHQ (8 rifle secs, 8 lorries, 4 AALMG, 2 Boys, 4 OP Teams)
      4 batteries, each: 4 × 5.5" BL guns, 4 lorries, radio van, 2 AALMG, 1 Boys
1 Provost Company (Military Police)

Brigade Support

Infantry Brigade HQ (6 rifle secs, 4 Lorries) with:
>> 1 HQ Defence Platoon: 1 (7 man) rifle Pl HQ sec, 1 × 2" mortar, 1 Boys, 3 (10 man) rifle secs, 3 LMG
>> 1 Support Group (Battalion):1943+
>>> 1 Mortar Company: Coy HQ (2 rifle secs, 2 trucks)
>>>> 2 platoons, each: 4 × 4.2" mortars, 8 × Universal or Loyd Carriers
>> 1 MG Company: Coy HQ (1 rifle sec, 1 truck, 4 LMG)
>>> 3 platoons, each: 4 × Vickers MMG, 5 × Universal Carrier
>> 1 AA Company: Coy HQ (1 rifle sec, 1 truck)
>>> 4 platoons, each: 4 × 20mm Oerlikon cannon, 4 trucks

MAIN COMBAT ELEMENTS

Infantry Battalion

Btn HQ (5 rifle secs, 1 LMG)
4 Companies, each: Coy HQ (1 (13 man) rifle sec)
>> 3 platoons, each: 1 (7 man) rifle Pl HQ sec, 1 × 2" mortar, 1 Boys, 3 (10 man) rifle secs, 3 LMG
1 Support Company: Coy HQ (1 rifle sec)
>> 1 platoon: 4 × twin AALMG, 4 Boys, in 2 rifle crew secs
>> 1 platoon: 4 or 6 × 3" mortars, 6 × Universal Carriers
>> 1 platoon: 2 rifle/engineer secs, 1 lorry
>> 1 platoon (1942+): 6 × 2pdr or 6pdr anti-tank guns, 6 × Universal Carriers, 3 LMG
>> 1 platoon: Pl HQ: 1 × Universal Carrier, 1 × Daimler S/C, 1 LMG
>>> 4 sections, each: 3 × Carrier, 3 LMG, 1 Boys, 1 × 2" mortar, 1 rifle sec

Divisional Recce Battalion (if present, 1941)

Btn HQ (4 rifle secs, 4 trucks, 3 LMG, 2 Boys)
1 AA Platoon: 4 × twin AALMG, 4 Boys, 4 trucks
1 Signals Platoon
1 Battery: 2 × 3" mortars, 2 trucks, Assigned FC
1 Anti-Tank Platoon: 8 × Boys in trucks or Bedford OXA anti-tank lorries
3 Companies, each: Coy HQ (3 rifle secs, 1 LMG, 3 trucks)
>> 3 platoons, each: Pl HQ: 1 × Universal Carrier, 1 LMG, 1 Boys, 1 × 2", 1 × Light Recce Car
>>> 2 Sections, each: 2 × Light Recce Cars
>>> 2 Sections, each: 3 × Universal Carrier, 1 × Boys, 3 LMG, 1 × 2", 1 rifle sec
>> 1 platoon: 4 (9 man) rifle secs, 4 trucks, 1 Boys, 4 LMG

Divisional Recce Regiment (if present, April 1942–1943)

RHQ (3 rifle secs, 3 LMG, 2 Boys, 3 × Light Recce Car)
3 Squadrons, each: Sqdn HQ (3 rifle secs, 1 LMG, 3 trucks, 1 Light Recce Car)
>> 3 Troops, each: Pl HQ: 1 × Carrier, 1 LMG, 1 Boys, 1 × 2" mortar, 1 × Light Recce Car
>>> 2 Sections, each: 2 × Light Recce Car OR 1 × A/C, 1 × Daimler S/C
>>> 2 Sections, each: 3 × Carrier, 1 × Boys, 3 LMG, 1 × 2" mortar, 1 rifle sec
>> 1 Troop: 4 rifle secs, 4 trucks, 1 Boys, 4 LMG
1 Mortar Battery: 6 × 3" mortars, 7 × Universal Carriers
1 A/T Platoon: 6 × 2pdr portees
1 AA Platoon: 4 × twin AALMG on trucks, 4 Boys

Divisional Recce Regiment (if present, August 1942–late 1943)

RHQ (3 rifle secs, 3 LMG, 3 × Light Recce Car)
1 Mortar Battery: 6 × 3" mortars, 7 × Universal Carriers, 1 Jeep
1 A/T Platoon: Pl HQ: 1 × Jeep, 4 × Loyd Carriers (for extra ammo)
>> 2–3 Troops, each: 4 × 2pdr or 6pdr A/T guns, 4 × Loyd Carriers
1 AA Platoon: 2 × twin AALMG on trucks
3 Squadrons, each: Sqdn HQ (3 rifle secs, 1 LMG, 3 trucks, 1 Light Recce Car, 1 Jeep)
>> 3 Troops, each: Pl HQ: 1 × Universal Carrier, 1 LMG, 1 Boys, 1 × 2" mortar
>>> 1 Section: 3 × Light Recce Car, 2 × Armoured Cars
>>> 2 Sections, each: 3 × Carrier, 1 × Boys, 3 LMG, 1 × 2" mortar, 1 rifle sec
>> 1 Troop: 4 rifle secs, 5 trucks, 4 LMG, 1 Jeep

Notes
1. Radios were in all Coy HQ and AFV. All artillery was rated Assigned FC up to July 1942. After that it was rated Flexible FC, with OP teams in truck or Daimler S/C.
2. Infantry secs had No.74 or No.75 Hawkins A/T grenades. Boys A/T Rifle could be replaced with PIATs from June 1943.
3. Divisional A/T Batteries do not have 6pdr until July 1942, with other units receiving them in 1943.
4. May have replaced Daimler S/C with Humber Light Recce Mk.II or III.
5. In 1942 25pdr could have AP. From May 1942 the 2pdr had APC, and APCBC from August 1942.
6. The Recce Regiment was not present in all divisions, in some divisions only a single Recce Company/ Squadron was held at divisional level.
7. Armoured Car was Humber III, was planned to have been Daimler II or Humber IV, but none materialised. Experimental units may havehad 8x8 T18E2 Boarhounds, of which 30 were received in the UK in late 1943. Light Recce Car was Beaverette I or II, or Humber Mk1 Ironsides from mid 1941. From 1942 could be Humber MK.II, III or IIIA, or Morris Light Recce Mk.I or Mk.II. The A/T Platoon could have 3 Troops in 1942 only.

8.   In 1941 some Infantry Divisions were on lower establishment of 3 Brigades, 2 Field Artillery Regiments, 2 Field Engineer Companies, 1 Field Park Platoon, no LAA Regiment, and the divisional Recce Battalion replaced by one Recce Company.

1.28 BRITISH COUNTY INFANTRY DIVISION, BRITAIN, FEBRUARY–DECEMBER 1941

The Division's main combat elements were:
        3 Brigades (each 4–5 Infantry Battalions)
Troops are rated as average to poor morale and poor training.

SUPPORT UNITS

Divisional Support

No units allocated

Brigade Support

Infantry Brigade HQ (4 rifle secs, 2 lorries, 1 car)

MAIN COMBAT ELEMENTS

County Infantry Battalion

Btn HQ (4 rifle secs)
4 Companies, each: Coy HQ (1 rifle sec, 1 × 2" mortar, 1–2 Boys)
        3 platoons, each: 1 (6 man) rifle Pl HQ sec, 3 (9–10 man) rifle secs, 1–3 LMG
1 Support Company: Coy HQ (1 rifle sec)
        0–1 platoon: 2 Lewis AAMG
        0–1 platoon: 2 × 3" mortars, 2 trucks
        0–1 platoon: 2 rifle/engineer secs, 1 lorry
        0–1 Scout platoon: Pl HQ: 1 × Universal Carrier or saloon car, 1 LMG
                3 sections, each: 3 × Universal Carrier or cars, 3 LMG, 1 rifle sec

Notes
1.   No radios were available.
2.   Infantry had molotovs for anti-tank use.
3.   The ten County Divisions formed for emergency home defence had 3 Brigades each of 4–5 Infantry Battalions and no other support at all. Most were disbanded by December 1941.

1.29 BRITISH CAVALRY UNITS, BRITAIN, 1938–1940

The Cavalry units available in Britain in September 1939 were:
        5th Cavalry Brigade (Nottinghamshire, Yorkshire Hussars, Yorkshire Dragoons Yeomanry Cavalry Regiments)
        6th Cavalry Brigade (Warwickshire, Staffordshire, Cheshire Yeomanry Cavalry Regiments)
12 Independent Regiments:
        Life Guards, Royal Horse Guards Guard Cavalry Regiments, Ayrshire Yeomanry, Duke of Lancaster's Own Yeomanry, Lanarkshire Yeomanry, Leicestershire Yeomanry, Lovat Scouts Regiment, Northumberland Hussars Yeomanry, North Somerset Yeomanry, Royal Wiltshire Yeomanry, Scottish Horse Scouts Regiment, Shropshire Yeomanry Cavalry Regiments
3 Training Regiments:
        Household Cavalry Reserve Regiment, Household Cavalry Training Regiment, 3rd Horse Cavalry Training Regiment, 2nd Remount Squadron
During late 1939–1940 were added:
        4th, 6th Horse Cavalry Training Regiments, 110th Cavalry Officer Training Unit
During late 1939–1940 the following were converted to artillery units:
        Ayrshire Yeomanry, Duke of Lancaster's Own Yeomanry, Lanarkshire Yeomanry, Shropshire Yeomanry, Leicestershire Yeomanry, Northumberland Hussars Yeomanry, Scottish Horse Scouts Regiment
In Palestine were: Royal Dragoons, Royal Scots Greys Guard Cavalry Regiments
Troops are rated average morale and training, with Guard Regiments as good morale and average training, and the Training Regiments as poor training and average morale.

SUPPORT UNITS

Brigade Support

Cavalry Brigade HQ (5 rifle secs, 8 trucks, 1 car)

MAIN COMBAT ELEMENTS

Cavalry Regiment

RHQ (10 rifle secs, 8 lorries)
3 Squadrons, each: Sqdn HQ (2 rifle secs, horses, sabres)
        3 Troops, each: 4 (8 man) rifle secs, horses, sabres
                1 (9 man) rifle Pl HQ sec, 2 Lewis LMG, 1 Boys, horses
1 MG Troop: 4 × Vickers MMG, pack horses
0–1 A/T Troop: 4 × Boys A/T rifles, horses
0–1 Scout Troop: 9 × saloon cars, 1 radio

Scout Cavalry Regiment (Scotland)

RHQ (10 rifle secs, 8 lorries)
2 Squadrons, each: Sqdn HQ (2 rifle secs, horses, sabres)
        3 Troops, each: 4 (8 man) rifle secs, horses, sabres
               1 (9 man) rifle Pl HQ sec, 2 Lewis LMG, 1 Boys, horses
2 Infantry Companies, each (Coy HQ: 1 rifle sec)
        3 platoons, each: 1 (7 man) rifle Pl HQ sec, 1 × 2" mortar, 1 Boys
               3 (10 man) rifle secs, 3 LMG, 2 lorries
1 MG Troop: 4 × Vickers MMG, pack horses
1 Battery: 4 × 3" mortars, pack horses
0–1 Scout Troop: 9 × saloon cars, 1 radio

Cavalry Training (Reserve) Regiment (poor training and average morale)

RHQ (6 rifle secs, 4 lorries, 4 cars)
1 Cavalry Squadron: Sqdn HQ (2 rifle secs, horses, sabres)
        3 Troops, each: 4 (8 man) rifle secs, horses, sabres
               1 (9 man) rifle Pl HQ sec, 2 Lewis LMG, 1 Boys, horses
3 Squadrons, each: Sqdn HQ (1 rifle sec, 1 truck)
        3 Troops, each: 4 (8 man) rifle secs, 4 trucks
               1 (9 man) rifle Pl HQ sec, 1 Hotchkiss LMG, 1 truck
1 Troop: 4 × Vickers MMG, 2 trucks

Notes
1.   Radios were in all Sqdn HQ and Scout Troop HQs.
2.   Infantry secs had no A/T grenades or molotovs.
3.   By 1940 a separate Cavalry Division was formed (see below) with eleven of the Cavalry Regiments. The rest converted to artillery units except the Lovat Scouts Cavalry Regiment, which formed part of the Iceland garrison.
4.   The number of Training Regiments increased to five before all were converted to other training battalions by the end of 1940.

1.30 BRITISH CAVALRY DIVISION NOVEMBER 1939–JANUARY 1940, BRITAIN

The Division's main combat elements were:
    4th Cavalry Brigade (1st Household Cavalry Regiment, Royal Wiltshire Regiment, North Somerset Yeomanry Regiment)
    5th Cavalry Brigade (Yorkshire Hussars, Nottinghamshire Yeomanry, Yorkshire Dragoons, Northumberland Hussars Cavalry Regiments)
    6th Cavalry Brigade (Warwickshire Yeomanry, Staffordshire Yeomanry, Cheshire Yeomanry Cavalry Regiments)
    Divisional Cavalry Regiment (1st Derbyshire Yeomanry)
Troops are rated as average morale and training.

SUPPORT UNITS

Divisional Support

Included:
104th, 106th, 107th Royal Horse Artillery Regiments, each: RHQ (4 rifle secs, horses and lorries)
        1 Battery: Battery HQ (4 rifle secs, 2 AALMG, horses, 2 trucks)
               2 Troops, each: 3–4 × 18pdr Mk.II, 4 trucks, 1 LMG, horses
        1 Battery: Battery HQ (4 rifle secs, 2 AALMG, horses, 2 trucks)
               2 Troops, each: 3–4 × 4.5" Mk.1 howitzers, 1 LMG, horses, 4 trucks
2nd Cheshire Field Engineer Squadron: Sqdn HQ (2 rifle secs, 1 lorry)
        4 Troops, each: 4 (12 man) rifle/engineer secs, 1 LMG, 2 lorries
141st Field Park Troop:
        1 Bridge Section: lorries
        1 Workshop Section: lorries
1st Remount Squadron
3 Field Ambulance Units (motorised)
3 Mobile Veterinary Sections (motorised)

Brigade Support

Cavalry Brigade HQ (5 rifle secs, 6 lorries)

MAIN COMBAT ELEMENTS

Cavalry Regiment

RHQ (10 rifle secs, 8 lorries)
3 Squadrons, each: Sqdn HQ (2 rifle secs, horses, sabres)
        3 Troops, each: 4 (8 man) rifle secs, horses, sabres
               1 (9 man) rifle Pl HQ sec, 1 Lewis LMG, 1 Boys
1 MG Troop: 4 × Vickers MMG, pack horses
1 Anti-Tank Troop: 4 × Boys A/T rifles, horses
1 Scout Troop: 9 × Austin 7 cars, 1 radio

Notes
1.   Radios were in all Sqdn HQ and artillery troops, and where noted.
2.   Infantry had no anti-tank grenades.

3.   The Division deployed to Palestine in early 1940, where it saw action in the counter-insurgency role against Arabs and Jews.

1.31 CANADIAN CORPS SUPPORT, BRITAIN, MAY 1940–1941

Troops are rated good morale and average training.

SUPPORT UNITS MAY–SEPTEMBER 1940

Included:
1st Canadian Infantry Division (see Volume 1, pg.7)
Royal Montreal Regiment, Toronto Scottish Regiment Machine Gun Battalions, each:
    4 Companies, each: Coy HQ (1 rifle sec)
        3 platoons, each: 4 MMG, 1 Boys A/T rifle, 1 LMG, 4 rifle crew secs
8th, 11th Field Artillery Regiments, each:
    2 Batteries, each: Battery HQ (1 radio van, 4 trucks, 4 rifle secs)
        2 Troops, each: 4 × 25pdr Mk.1, 5 trucks, radio van, 2 AALMG
1st Medium Artillery Regiment: RHQ (6 rifle secs, 4 lorries)
    4 batteries, each: 4 × 60pdr guns or 6" 26cwt howitzers?, 5 × lorries
12th Field Engineer Company: Coy HQ (1 rifle sec, 1 truck, 2 Boys, 2 LMG)
    3 platoons, each: 4 (12 man) rifle/engineer secs, 1 Boys, 1 LMG, 2 lorries
3rd Tunnelling Company
1st Corps Field Survey Company

CANADIAN 7TH CORPS SUPPORT UNITS OCTOBER 1940+

Included:
7th Corps HQ
1st Canadian Infantry Division (see Volume 1, pg.7)
2nd Canadian Infantry Division (see Volume 1, pg.8)
    4th Infantry Brigade (Royal Hamilton Light Infantry, Essex Scottish Regiment, Royal Regiment of Canada Infantry Btns)
    5th Infantry Brigade (1st Btn Black Watch of Canada, Le Regiment de Maisonneuve, Calgary Highlanders Infantry Btns)
    6th Infantry Brigade (Queen's Own Cameron Highlanders of Canada, South Saskatchewan Regiment, Les Fusiliers Mont-Royal Infantry Battalions)
    2nd A/T Regiment
    Toronto Scottish Regiment Machine Gun Battalion
    2nd, 7th Field Engineer Companies
    4th, 5th, 6th Field Artillery Regiments
    8th Recce Regiment
    3rd Light AA Regiment
Royal Montreal Regiment Machine Gun Battalion:
    4 Companies, each: Coy HQ (1 rifle sec)
        3 platoons, each: 4 MMG, 1 Boys A/T rifle, 1 LMG, 4 rifle crew secs
8th, 11th Field Artillery Regiments, each:
    3 Batteries, each: BHQ: 1 radio van, 4 trucks, 4 rifle secs
        2 Troops, each: 4 × 25pdr Mk.1, 5 trucks, radio van, 2 AALMG
1st Medium Artillery Regiment: RHQ (6 rifle secs, 4 lorries)
    4 batteries, each: 4 × 60pdr guns or 6" 26cwt howitzers, 5 × lorries
1 Survey Battery, 1st Canadian Survey Regiment
2 Super Heavy Artillery Batteries, each: 2 × 9.2" guns
12th, 13th Field Engineer Companies, each: Coy HQ (1 rifle sec, 1 truck, 2 Boys, 2 LMG)
    3 platoons, each: 4 (12 man) rifle/engineer secs, 1 Boys, 1 LMG, 2 lorries
3rd Tunnelling Company
1st Corps Field Survey Company
1st Field Park Company: stores, explosives, tools
1st, 2nd Pioneer Battalions, each: 4 Pioneer Companies

Notes
1.   Radios were in all Coy HQs and above. Artillery was rated Assigned FC.
2.   Infantry may have had No.68 rifle anti-tank grenades.
3.   Pioneers were probably organised as infantry companies, but only armed with rifles and shovels, and about 4 Boys and 4 Lewis MG per battalion. They should be rated average morale and poor training.

1.32 STURGES FORCE, ICELAND, MAY 1940

The initial force occupying Iceland in May 1940 was Sturges Force (2nd Royal Marine Battalion).
Troops are rated good morale and average training.

MAIN COMBAT ELEMENTS

2nd Royal Marine Battalion

Battalion HQ (1 rifle sec)
1 Firepower Platoon: 4 (7 man) rifle secs, 8 Bren LMG

4 Rifle Companies, each :Coy HQ (1 (8 man) rifle sec, 1 Boys)
       2 platoons, each: 4 (8 man) rifle secs, 1 × 2" mortar, 1 Boys, 2 Lewis MG
Y Battery, MNBDO1: 2 × 4" naval guns on semi-mobile mounts
1st Anti-MTB Battery, MNBDO1: 4 × 2pdr pom-pom coastal guns
1 Royal Navy Landing Battery: 2 × 3.7" pack howitzers

Notes
1. Radios were at Battalion HQ only. Telephone signals were available.
2. Infantry had no anti-tank grenades.
3. Sturges Force landed in Iceland on 10th May 1940 to pre-empt a German occupation. Iceland was part of Denmark at this time.
4. The Marine forces were part of the Marine Naval Base Defence Organisation No.1.
5. The Battalion used requisitioned civilian transport to become motorised, and left on May 21st 1940.
6. On May 19th the British 147th Infantry Brigade of the 49th Division reinforced this garrison.

1.33 ALABASTER FORCE, 49TH INFANTRY DIVISION, ICELAND, MAY–OCTOBER 1940

The Garrison's main combat elements were:
    Sturges Force (see above) (up to May 21st 1940)
    Alabaster Force, 49th Infantry Division:
    147th Infantry Brigade (landing on May 19th 1940) (1st/5th West Yorkshire Regiment, 1st/6th and 1st/7th Duke of Wellington's Regiment territorial infantry battalions)
    146th Brigade (landed on June 26th) (4th Battalion Lincolnshire Regiment, Hallamshire Battalion Yorks & Lancaster Regiment, 1st/4th King's Own Yorkshire Light Infantry infantry battalions)
Troops are rated average morale and poor training.

SUPPORT UNITS

Divisional Support (26th June 1940+)

Included:
Royal Marine Fortress Unit 1: (July–October 1940)
    HQ Company
    1 Landing Company
    1 Ship Unloading Company
    1 Gun Mounting Company: small tractors, dynamite, 18 × 3"–6" guns
    1 Boat Company: 1 MLC
    1 Transport & Workshop Company
No.1 Independent Company, 14th Battalion, Royal Fusiliers: (average morale and average training)
    Coy HQ (1 (13 man) rifle sec)
    3 platoons, each: 1 (7 man) rifle PHQ sec, 1 × 2" mortar
        3 (10 man) rifle/pioneer secs, 3 AALMG
4th Heavy AA Battery: Coy HQ (1 rifle sec, 1 lorry)(July 1940+)
    2 Troops, each: 4 × 3" 20cwt AA or 3.7" AA, 4 lorries
659th Royal Engineer General Construction Company
686th, 687th, 688th Royal Engineer Artisan Works Companies
19th Army Field Survey Company
3 Royal Engineer Road Construction Companies

Brigade Support

147th Infantry Brigade HQ (4 rifle secs, 2 staff cars, 3 lorries) with:
    69th Field Artillery Regiment:
    273rd, 274th Batteries, each: Battery HQ (1 radio van, 4 trucks, 4 rifle secs, 2 AALMG)
        2 Troops, each: 4 × 25pdr field guns, 6 trucks, 2 AALMG, 2 Boys
    294th Field Engineer Company: Coy HQ (1 rifle sec, 1 truck, 2 Boys, 2 LMG)
        3 Sections, each: 4 (12 man) rifle/engineer secs, 1 Boys, 1 LMG, 2 lorries
    Y Battery, MNBDO1: 2 × 4" Mk.IV naval guns on semi-mobile mounts (May 1940–Mar 1941)
    1st Anti-MTB Battery, MNBDO1: 4 × 2pdr pom-pom coastal guns (May–September 1940)
    1 Royal Navy Landing Battery: 2 × 3.7" pack howitzers (May 1940 only)
146th Infantry Brigade HQ (4 rifle secs, 2 staff cars, 3 lorries (June 26th 1940+)

MAIN COMBAT ELEMENTS

British Territorial Infantry Battalion, 147th Brigade (May 1940+)

Btn HQ (4 rifle secs, 1 LMG, staff car)
4 Companies, each: Coy HQ (2 rifle secs, 1 Boys)
    3 platoons, each: 1 (7 man) rifle PHQ sec, 0–1 × 2" mortar, 3 (10 man) rifle secs, 3 LMG

British Infantry Battalion, 146th Brigade (June 26th 1940+)

Btn HQ (2 rifle secs, 1 staff car, 2 trucks, 5 motorcycles)
4 Companies, each: Coy HQ (1 (13 man) rifle sec)
    3 platoons, each: 1 (7 man) rifle PHQ sec, 1 × 2" mortar, 1 Boys, 3 (10 man) rifle secs, 3 LMG
1 Support Company: Coy HQ (1 rifle sec, 1 truck)
    1 platoon: 4–6 × 3" mortars, 3 trucks, radio truck
    1 platoon: 4 × twin AALMG, 4 Boys, 4 trucks
    1 platoon: 2 (6 man) rifle/engineer secs, 1 stores truck

Notes
1.   Radios were at Battalion HQ only. Telephone signals were available.
2.   Infantry had no anti-tank grenades.
3.   Alabaster Force consisted of the 49th Infantry Division, starting with the 147th Infantry Brigade landing on May 19th 1940, joining existing Marine units.
4.   On June 26th the 146th Brigade landed with additional divisional support units.
5.   The Royal Engineer companies were about 150 men strong and armed with rifles only.
6.   The division was reinforced in October 1940 (see below).

1.34 ALABASTER FORCE, 49TH INFANTRY DIVISION, ICELAND, OCTOBER 1940–1942

The Garrison's main combat elements were:
    Alabaster Force consisted of the 49th Infantry Division:
        147th Infantry Brigade (1st/5th West Yorkshire Regiment, 1st/6th and 1st/7th Duke of Wellington's Regi
            ment infantry battalions)
        146th Brigade (4th Battalion Lincolnshire Regiment, Hallamshire Battalion Yorks & Lancaster Regiment,
            1st/4th King's Own Yorkshire Light Infantry infantry battalions)
        70th Brigade (1st Tyneside Scottish, 10th Battalion Durham Light Infantry and 11th Battalion Durham
            Light Infantry infantry battalions)
        Canadian Z-Brigade from 2nd Canadian Division (Royal Regiment of Canada, Les Fusiliers Mont-Royal
            infantry battalions, Cameron Highlanders of Ottawa Machine Gun Battalion)
Troops are rated average morale and average training.

SUPPORT UNITS

Divisional Support

Included:
No.1 Independent Company, 14th Battalion, Royal Fusiliers: Coy HQ (1 (13 man) rifle sec)
        3 platoons, each: 1 (7 man) rifle PHQ sec, 1 × 2" mortar
                3 (10 man) rifle/pioneer secs, 3 AALMG
4th Heavy AA Battery: Battery HQ (1 rifle sec, 1 lorry)(up to mid 1941)
        2 Troops, each: 4 × 3" 20cwt AA or 3.7" AA, 4 lorries
Naval Batteries (September 1940+):
        Hafnaafjord: 2 × 4.7" naval guns
        Reykjavik: 2 × 6" naval guns
        Hyalfjord: 2 × 12pdr naval guns
        Saurbuer: 2 × 6" naval guns
        2 other Batteries, each: 4 × 4" guns (April 1941+)
12th Heavy AA Regiment: (mid 1941+)
        3 Batteries, each Battery HQ (1 rifle sec, 1 lorry)
                2 Troops, each: 4 × 3.7" AA, 4 lorries
85th Light AA Regiment: (mid 1941+)
        3 Batteries, each: Battery HQ (1 rifle sec, 1 lorry)
                3 Troops, each: 4 × 40mmL60 Bofors, 6 trucks
659th Royal Engineer General Construction Company
686th, 687th, 688th Royal Engineer Artizan Works Companies
19th Army Field Survey Company
3 Royal Engineer Road Construction Companies
294th Divisional Field Engineer Company: Coy HQ (1 rifle sec, 1 truck, 2 Boys, 2 LMG)
        3 Sections, each: 4 (12 man) rifle/engineer secs, 1 Boys, 1 LMG, 2 lorries
69th Field Artillery Regiment:
        273rd, 274th Batteries, each: Battery HQ (1 radio van, 4 trucks, 4 rifle secs, 2 AALMG)
                2 Troops, each: 4 × 25pdr field guns, 6 trucks, 2 AALMG, 2 Boys
        + 366th Battery (April 1941+)
143rd Field Artillery Regiment:
        386th, 388th Batteries, each: Battery HQ (1 radio van, 4 trucks, 4 rifle secs, 2 AALMG)
                2 Troops, each: 4 × 25pdr field guns, 6 trucks, 2 AALMG, 2 Boys + 507th Battery (April 1941+)
Y Battery, MNBDO1: 2 × 4" Mk.IV naval guns on semi-mobile mounts (May 1940–March 1941)
Norwegian Company, Iceland (260 Norwegian volunteers – ski troops?) (July 1940–1943)
2nd Battalion, Kensington Regiment Machine Gun Battalion: (late 1941+)
        Btn HQ (4 rifle secs, 2 LMG, 2 lorries)
        3 MG Companies, each: Coy HQ (1 rifle sec, 1 LMG, 1 truck)
                3 platoons, each: 4 × Vickers MMG, 2 truck

Brigade Support

British Infantry Brigade HQ (4 rifle secs, 2 staff cars, 3 lorries) with:
        1 HQ Defence Platoon: 1 (8 man) rifle Pl HQ sec, 1 × 2" mortar, 3 (10 man) rifle secs, 3 LMG, 1 Boys
        147th Brigade Anti-tank Company (September 1940–April 1941, 147th Brigade only)
                Coy HQ (1 rifle sec, 1 truck, 1 car)
                3 platoons, each: 3 × 2pdr A/T guns or 25mm Hotchkiss, 3 trucks

MAIN COMBAT ELEMENTS

British Territorial Infantry Battalion, 147th Brigade (May 1940–April 1941) and 70th Brigade (October 1940–April 1941)

Btn HQ (4 rifle secs, 1 LMG, staff car)
4 Companies, each: Coy HQ (2 rifle secs, 1 Boys)
  3 platoons, each: 1 (7 man) rifle PHQ sec, 1 × 2" mortar, 3 (10 man) rifle secs, 3 LMG

British Infantry Battalion, 146th Brigade (June 26th 1940–1942)

British Territorial Infantry Battalion, 70th, 147th Brigades (April 1941+)

Btn HQ (2 rifle secs, 1 staff car, 2 trucks, 5 motorcycles)
4 Companies, each: Coy HQ (1 (13 man) rifle sec)
  3 platoons, each: 1 (7 man) rifle PHQ sec, 1 × 2" mortar, 1 Boys
    3 (10 man) rifle secs, 3 LMG
1 Support Company: Coy HQ (1 rifle sec, 1 truck)
  1 platoon: 4–6 × 3" mortars, 3 trucks, radio truck
  1 platoon: 4 × twin AALMG, 4 Boys, 4 trucks
  1 platoon: 2 (6 man) rifle/engineer secs, 1 stores truck
  1 platoon: Pl HQ: 1 × Universal Carrier, 1 LMG
    3–4 Sections, each: 3 × Carrier, 3 LMG, 3 Boys, 1 × 2" mortar, 1 rifle sec

Canadian Infantry Battalion (October–December 1940)

Btn HQ (4 rifle secs, 1 staff car, 2 lorries)
4 Companies@ CHQ (1 rifle squad)
  3 platoons, each: 1 (6 man) rifle Pl HQ sec, 4 (10 man) rifle secs, 2 × Lewis LMG
1 Support Company: Coy HQ (1 rifle sec)
  1 platoon: 2 × 3" mortars, 2 trucks, Assigned FC
  1 platoon: 2 (6 man) rifle/engineer secs, 1 truck
  1 platoon: 4 × Lewis AALMG, 4 trucks
  1 platoon: Pl HQ: 1 × Bren Carrier, 1 LMG
    3 sections, each: 3 × Bren Carrier, 2 LMG, 1 × Boys, 1 (6 man) rifle sec

Cameron Highlanders of Ottawa Canadian Machine Gun Battalion (October–December 1940)

Btn HQ (4 rifle secs, 2 LMG, 2 lorries)
3 MG Companies, each: Coy HQ (1 rifle sec, 1 LMG, 1 truck)
  3 platoons, each: 4 × Vickers MMG, 2 trucks, or pack horses

Notes
1. Radios were at CHQs and above only. Telephone signals were available.
2. Infantry had no anti-tank grenades.
3. The Canadian Brigade appears to have left by December 1940.
4. The Royal Engineer companies were about 150 men strong and armed with rifles only.
5. By April 1941 the Territorial Battalions of 147th and 70th Brigades were upgraded to first line equipment levels.
6. By late 1941 each infantry company had a ski platoon, with winter equipment.
7. The 70th Brigade left Iceland in December 1941, the 147th Brigade left in April 1942, and the 146th Brigade left in August 1942.
8. America took over garrisoning Iceland, with the 1st US Marine Brigade landing in July 1941, followed by the 10th Infantry Regiment in September 1941, then the rest of the US 5th Infantry Division in March 1942.
9. The Norwegian Company was formed from Norwegians in exile, becoming a Brigade Recce Company in 1944.

PART 2
MIDDLE EAST AND MEDITERRANEAN
THEATRES 1938–MAY 1945

2.1 BRITISH 1ST ARMOURED BRIGADE, GREECE, APRIL 1941

The Brigade's main combat elements were:
  4th Hussars Armoured Regiment
  3rd Royal Tank Regiment
  1st Battalion Rangers Motor Battalion
  Troops are rated good morale and average training

SUPPORT UNITS

Brigade Support

Armoured Brigade HQ (3 × Vickers VIB, 7 × A-10 or A-13 Mk.II, radio vans, 5 × Daimler S/C)
  102nd Anti-Tank Regiment:
    2 Batteries, each: Battery HQ (1 rifle sec, 1 truck)
      3 Troops, each: 4 × 2pdr anti-tank guns, 4 trucks or portees
  3rd Field Engineer Squadron: Sqdn HQ (2 rifle secs, 1 lorry)
      4 Troops, each: 4 (12 man) rifle/engineer secs, 2 lorries, 1 LMG
  142nd Field Park Troop: stores, bridges, explosives, lorries
  2nd Royal Horse Artillery Regiment:
    2 Batteries, each: Battery HQ (4 rifle secs, 3 lorries, radio van, 1 AALMG)
      2 Troops, each: 4 × 25pdr field guns, 6 trucks, 1 AALMG
  155th Light AA Battery: Battery HQ (2 rifle secs, 1 lorry)
      3 Troops, each: 4 × 40mmL60 Bofors, 4 trucks, 2 LMG

MAIN COMBAT ELEMENTS

3rd Royal Tank Regiment

RHQ (4 × A-10, 3 × Scammell Wreckers)
  3 Squadrons, each: Sqdn HQ (2 × A-10, 2 × A-9CS or A-10CS)
    4 Troops, each: 3 × A-10

4th Hussars Armoured Regiment

RHQ (4 × Vickers VIC, 3 recovery trucks)
  3 Squadrons, each: Sqdn HQ (4 × Vickers VIB)
    4 Troops, each: 3 × Vickers VIB

1st Battalion Rangers Motor Battalion

Btn HQ (2 rifle secs, 2 trucks, 1 lorry)
  3 Companies, each: Coy HQ (1 rifle sec, 1 × 2" mortar, 1 Boys, 2 trucks)
    3 Platoons, each: 4 (8 man) rifle secs, 4 Boys, 1 × 2" mortar, 3 LMG, 4 trucks
    1 Platoon: Pl HQ (1 × Universal Carrier, 1 × Daimler S/C, 1 LMG)
      3 Sections, each: 3 × Universal Carrier, 3 LMG, 1 Boys, 1 × 2" mortar, 1 rifle sec

Notes
1. Radios were in all tanks and other Coy HQs. Artillery was rated Assigned FC.
2. Infantry sections had no anti-tank grenades.
3. The Brigade was originally part of the 2nd Armoured Division. It was reduced to 2 or 3 tanks per Squadron by the time of evacuation from Greece. The Brigade left all guns and tanks behind on sailing to North Africa.

2.2 BRITISH 4TH ARMOURED BRIGADE, NORTH AFRICA, JUNE–JULY 1941

The Brigade's main combat elements were:
  4th Royal Tank Regiment
  7th Royal Tank Regiment

SUPPORT UNITS

Brigade Support

4th Armoured Brigade HQ (1 × ACV, 3 × Daimler S/C, 2 rifle secs, 2 trucks, 2 cars)
  31st Field Artillery Regiment:
    3 Batteries, each: Battery HQ (4 rifle secs, 3 lorries, radio van, 1 AALMG)
      2 Troops, each: 4 × 25pdr field guns, 5 trucks, radio van, 1 AALMG, 1 Boys
  A Squadron, 3rd Hussars: Sqdn HQ (2 × Vickers VIC, 2 × Vickers VIB)
    5 Troops, each: 3 × Vickers VIB
  1 Motor Company, 2nd Btn Rifle Brigade:

Coy HQ (1 rifle sec, 1 × 2" mortar, 1 Boys, 2 trucks)
3 Platoons, each: 4 (8 man) rifle secs, 4 Boys, 1 × 2" mortar, 3 LMG, 4 trucks
1 Platoon: 2 × 3" mortars, 2 × Vickers MMG, 4 trucks
1 Platoon: Pl HQ (1 × Universal Carrier, 1 × Daimler S/C, 1 LMG)
3 Sections, each: 3 × Universal Carrier, 3 LMG, 1 Boys, 1 × 2", 1 rifle sec
1 Indian Engineer Section: 1 (12 man) rifle/engineer sec, 1 × Wheeled Carrier IP, 1 LMG

MAIN COMBAT ELEMENTS

4th Royal Tank Regiment

RHQ (2 × Matilda II, 2 × A-10CS)
A, B Squadrons, each: Sqdn HQ (2 × Matilda II, 1 × Matilda IICS, 2 × Vickers VIB)
4 Troops, each: 3 × Matilda II
C Squadron: Sqdn HQ (2 × Matilda II, 1 × Matilda IICS, 2 × Vickers VIB)
3 Troops, each: 3 × Matilda II

7th Royal Tank Regiment

RHQ (2 × Matilda II, 2 × Matilda IICS, 2 × A-10CS)
2 Squadrons, each: Sqdn HQ (2 × Matilda II, 2 × Matilda IICS, 2 × Vickers VIB)
4 Troops, each: 3 × Matilda II
1 Squadron: Sqdn HQ (2 × Matilda II, 1 × Matilda IICS, 1 × Vickers VIB)
3 Troops, each: 3 × Matilda II

Notes
1. Radios were in all AFV and other Pl HQs. Artillery was rated Assigned FC.
2. Infantry secs had No.73 or No.74 or No.75 anti-tank grenades.
3. The Brigade was under command of the 7th Armoured Division (see Volume 1, List 2.5, pg.18), even though it was tasked to support the Indian 4th Infantry Division.
4. This list shows the Brigade's organisation for Operation Battleaxe in mid-June 1941.
5. By late June 1941 the Brigade was reduced to 28 Matildas and during July–August 1941 was in Egypt refitting.

2.3   BRITISH 9TH ARMOURED BRIGADE, ITALY, MAY 1944–SEPTEMBER 1944

The Brigade's main combat elements were:
3rd King's Own Hussars Armoured Regiment
Royal Wiltshire Yeomanry Armoured Regiment
Warwickshire Yeomanry Armoured Regiment
1st Battalion King's Royal Rifle Corps Motor Battalion
Troops are rated average morale and average training

SUPPORT UNITS

Brigade Support

9th Armoured Brigade HQ (7 × Sherman III, 2 × Sherman II-OP, 2 × Sherman ARV, 7 × Humber S/C)
1 AA Troop: 2 × Humber AA
1 Defence Troop: 3 × Sherman II
1 Engineer Troop, 3rd Field Squadron: 1 (17 man) rifle/engineer Pl HQ sec, 1 PIAT, 1 LMG, 4 (12 man)
rifle/engineer secs, LMG, 4 lorries
1st Royal Horse Artillery Regiment:
3 Batteries, each: Battery HQ (2 rifle secs, 4 lorries, 2 AALMG, 3 OP Teams)
2 Troops, each: 4 × 25pdr Sexton, 1 radio van, 2 AALMG

MAIN COMBAT ELEMENTS

Armoured Regiment

RHQ (4 × Sherman, 2 × Sherman OP, 3 × Sherman ARV)
3 Squadrons, each: Sqdn HQ (4 × Sherman)
4 Troops, each: 3 × Sherman
1 Recce Troop: Troop HQ (1 × Stuart III Recce, 2 × Humber Scout Cars)
3 Sections, each: 3 × Stuart III Recce, 3 × Humber Scout Cars

1st KRRC Motor Battalion

Btn HQ (3 trucks, 1 staff car, 2 rifle secs)
3 Companies, each: Coy HQ (1 rifle sec, 1 truck, 1 × 2" mortar, 1 PIAT)
1 Section: 2 × 3" mortars, 2 × Universal Carriers
3 Platoons, each: 4 (8 man) rifle secs, 4 LMG, 4 PIAT, 1 × 2" mortar, 4 trucks
1 Platoon: Pl HQ: 1 × Universal Carrier, 1 LMG
3 Sections, each: 3 × Carrier, 3 LMG, 1 rifle sec, 1 × 2" mortar, 1 PIAT
1 Support Company: Coy HQ (1 rifle sec, 1 truck, 1 Jeep)
3 Platoons, each: 4 × 6pdr A/T guns, 4 × Carriers, 2 LMG
2 Platoons, each: 4 × Vickers MMG, 5 × Universal Carriers

Notes
1. Radios were in all tanks and other Pl HQs.
2. Infantry had Hawkins 75 anti-tank grenades.

3.   The 3rd Hussars had Sherman III in July, Sherman V later. The Wiltshire Yeomanry had Sherman III, and the Warwickshire Yeomanry probably had Sherman III.

4.   During September 1944 the 1st KRRC returned to 2nd Armoured Brigade, the 3rd Hussars were withdrawn to retrain on DD tanks. The Wiltshire and Warwickshire Yeomanry Regiments returned to England.

2.4 BRITISH MOBILE DIVISION, EGYPT, 1938–FEBRUARY 1940

The Division's main combat elements were:

Heavy Armoured Brigade (1st RTR, 6th RTR Armoured Regiments)
Light Armoured Brigade (7th Hussars, 8th Hussars Armoured Regiments, 11th Hussars Armoured Car Regiment)
Divisional Motor Battalion (1st King's Royal Rifle Corps)

Troops are rated good morale and average training

SUPPORT UNITS

Divisional Support

Included:

3rd Royal Horse Artillery Regiment (1938): RHQ (4 rifle secs, 3 lorries, AALMG, radio van)
    3 Batteries, each: 1 Troop: 4 × 3.7" howitzers, 4 × Light Dragon III, radio truck
or 3rd Royal Horse Artillery Regiment (1939+): RHQ (4 rifle secs, 3 lorries, AALMG, radio van)
    1 Battery: Battery HQ (4 rifle secs, 3 lorries, 1 AALMG, radio van)
        2 Troops, each: 4 × 25pdr Mk.1, 4 trucks, radio truck, AALMG
    2 Anti-Tank Batteries, each: Battery HQ (1 rifle sec, 1 truck)
        3 Troops, each: 4 × 37mm Bofors portees on 3-ton lorries, 1 LMG
F Battery, 4th Royal Horse Artillery Regiment (1939+):
    Battery HQ (4 rifle secs, 3 lorries, 1 AALMG, radio van)
        2 Troops, each: 4 × 25pdr Mk.1, 4 trucks, radio truck, AALMG

Brigade Support

Heavy Armoured Brigade HQ (2 rifle secs, 1 radio van, 4 trucks)
Light Armoured Brigade HQ (2 rifle secs, 1 radio van, 4 trucks)

MAIN COMBAT ELEMENTS

1st Royal Tank Regiment

RHQ (4 × Vickers VIB)
3 Squadrons, each: Sqdn HQ (3 × Vickers Light Mk.VIB)
    5 Troops, each: 3 × Vickers VIB

6th Royal Tank Regiment (in September 1939)

RHQ (4 × Vickers VIB)
1 Squadron: Sqdn HQ (4 × Medium Mk.II)
    4 Troops, each: 3 × Vickers Medium Mk.II
1 Squadron: Sqdn HQ (2 × Vickers VIB, 2 × A-9 CS)
    2 Troops, each: 3 × A-9
    1 Troop, 3 × Vickers VIB
1 Squadron: Sqdn HQ (3 × "armoured cars")
    3 Troops, each: 3 × "armoured cars" – type unknown, probably 15cwt trucks + AALMG

6th Royal Tank Regiment (1940)

RHQ (4 × Vickers VIB)
1 Squadron: Sqdn HQ (1 × Medium Mk.II)
    3 Troops, each: 3 × Vickers Medium Mk.II
1 Squadron: Sqdn HQ (1 × A-9, 1 × A-9CS)
    3 Troops, each: 3 × A-9
1 Squadron: Sqdn HQ (3 × Vickers Light Mk.VIB)
    5 Troops, each: 3 × Vickers VIB

11th Hussars Recce Regiment "Cherry Pickers" (1938) (good morale and training)

RHQ (2 × Crossley 6x6 armoured cars + radio)
3 Squadrons, each: Sqdn HQ (1 × Rolls-Royce M1924, 1 × Crossley 6x6 + radio)
    3 Troops, each: 3 × Rolls-Royce M1924

11th Hussars Recce Regiment "Cherry Pickers" (1939+) (good morale and training)

RHQ (2 × Morris CS9 armoured cars)
3 Squadrons, each: Sqdn HQ (1 × Morris CS9, 1 × Rolls-Royce M1924)
    5 Troops, each: 2 × Rolls-Royce M1924, 1 × Morris CS9

1st KRRC Motor Rifle Battalion

Btn HQ (2 rifle secs, 2 trucks, 1 radio van)
4 Companies, each: Coy HQ (1 rifle sec, 2 × MMG, 2 trucks)
    3 platoons, each: 4 (6 man) rifle secs, 3 LMG, 4 trucks
    1 platoon: Pl HQ: 1 × Bren Carrier, 1 staff car

3 sections, each: 3 × Bren Carriers, 3 LMG

7th Hussars Light Armoured Regiment
RHQ (4 × Vickers VIB)
2 Squadrons, each: Sqdn HQ (4 × Vickers Mk.IIB or Mk.III or Mk.VIB) (1938)
    4 Troops, each: 3 × Vickers Light Mk.IIB or Mk.III or Mk.VIA
or   3 Squadrons, each: Sqdn HQ (4 × Vickers VIB) (mid 1939+)
    4 Troops, each: 3 × Vickers VIB

8th Hussars Light Armoured Regiment
RHQ (4 × Vickers VIB)
B, C Squadrons, each: Sqdn HQ (2 × Ford 15cwt trucks + Vickers-Berthier AALMG) 3 Troops, each: 4 × Ford 15cwt trucks + AALMG, 2 rifle secs
A Squadron: Sqdn HQ (2 × Vickers Mk.III, 1 × Vickers Mk.VIB) (early 1939+)
    2 Troops, each: 3 × Vickers Light Mk.VIB
    3 Troops, each: 3 × Vickers Light Mk.III

Notes
1. Radios were in all tanks and Morris CS9 and other CHQs. Artillery was Assigned FC.
2. Infantry secs had no A/T grenades. May have had Boys A/T rifle in 1939, at one per platoon.
3. Later in February 1940 the Mobile Division became the 7th Armoured Division (see Vol.1 pg.14 and Vol. 3 Sect)

2.5 BRITISH 6TH ARMOURED DIVISION, NORTH AFRICA, JUNE–AUGUST 1943
The Division's main combat elements were:
    26th Armoured Brigade (16th/5th Lancers, 17th/21st Lancers, 2nd Lothian & Border Horse Armoured Regiments, 10th Btn Rifle Brigade Motor Battalion)
    1st Guards Infantry Brigade (3rd Btn Grenadier Guards, 2nd Btn Coldstream Guards, 3rd Btn Welsh Guards Infantry Battalions)
    Divisional Armoured Recce Regiment. (1st Derbyshire Yeomanry)
Troops are rated average morale with average training, with Guards Btns at good morale.

SUPPORT UNITS

Divisional Support
included:
5th, 8th Field Engineer Squadrons, each: Sqdn HQ (2 rifle secs, 1 lorry)
    4 Troops, each: 4 (12 man) rifle/engineer secs, 3 LMG, 2 lorries
144th Engineer Park Company: (175 men)
    1 Workshop Section
    1 Bridging & Stores Section
152nd Field Artillery Regiment:
    3 Artillery Batteries, each: Battery HQ (4 rifle secs, 4 lorries, 4 AALMG, 3 OP Teams)
    2 Troops, each: 4 × 25pdr field guns, 4 trucks, radio truck, 2 AALMG
12th Royal Horse Artillery Regiment:
    3 Batteries, each: Battery HQ (1 × ACV, 3 lorries, 4 rifle secs, 4 AALMG, 2 OP Teams)
    2 Troops, each: 4 × 105mm M7 Priest, 1 radio van, 2 AALMG
72nd Anti-Tank Regiment:
    3 Anti-Tank Batteries, each: Battery HQ (1 rifle sec, 1 truck)
    3 Troops, each: 4 × 6pdr anti-tank guns, 2 LMG, 4 trucks
    1 Anti-Tank Battery, each: Battery HQ (1 rifle sec, 1 truck)
    3 platoons, each: 4 × 17pdr A/T guns, 2 LMG, 4 trucks
51st Light AA Regiment:
    2 AA Batteries, each: Battery HQ (1 rifle sec, 1 truck)
    3 Troops, each: 6 × 40mm Bofors, 6 trucks
1 Provost Company (Military Police)

Brigade Support
26th Armoured Brigade HQ (3 × Sherman III, 2 × ACV, 1 × Vickers I AA)
1st Guards Infantry Brigade HQ (4 rifle secs, 2 LMG, 2 trucks, 2 lorries) with:
    1 HQ Defence Platoon: 1 (6 man) rifle Pl HQ sec, 1 × 2" mortar, 3 (10 man) rifle secs, 3 LMG, 2 lorries
    1 MG Company: Coy HQ (1 rifle sec, 1 truck)
    3 platoons, each: 4 Vickers MMG, 4 trucks
    1 battery: 4 × 4.2" mortars, 5 trucks, radio truck

MAIN COMBAT ELEMENTS

Armoured Regiment
RHQ (4 × Sherman III)
3 Squadrons, each: Sqdn HQ (4 × Sherman III)
    5 Troops, each: 3 × Sherman III
1 AA Troop: 4 × Vickers VI AA
1 Recce Troop: Troop HQ (2 × Stuart I)
    3 Sections@3 × Stuart I

10th Battalion, Rifle Brigade Motor Battalion

Btn HQ (2 rifle secs, 2 trucks)
3 Companies, each: Coy HQ (1 rifle sec, 1 × 2" mortar, 2 trucks)
        2 platoons, each: 4 (8 man) rifle secs, 3 LMG, 1 × 2" mortar, 4 trucks
        1 platoon: 2 × 3" mortars, 3 × Universal Carriers
        1 platoon: 4 MMG, 5 × Universal Carriers
        1 platoon: Pl HQ: 2 × Universal Carrier, 1 LMG, 1 × Daimler S/C
            3 sections, each: 3 × Universal Carriers, 3 LMG, 1 rifle sec, 1 × 2" mortar, 1 × Boys
1 Anti-Tank Company: Coy HQ (1 rifle sec, 1 truck)
        3 platoons, each: 4 × 6pdr, portéed or truck tows, 2 LMG

Guards Infantry Battalion

Btn HQ (2 rifle secs, 2 trucks)
4 Companies, each: Coy HQ (1 (13 man) rifle sec, 1 lorry)
        3 platoons, each: 1 (6 man) rifle Pl HQ sec, 1 × 2" mortar
                3 (10 man) rifle secs, 3 LMG, 2 lorries
1 Support Company: Coy HQ (1 rifle sec, 1 truck)
        1 platoon: 4 × 6pdr anti-tank guns, 2 LMG, 4 trucks or Carriers
        1 platoon: 3 rifle/engineer secs, 1 lorry
        1 battery: 6 × 3" mortars, 7 × Universal Carriers
        1 platoon: Pl HQ: 1 × Universal Carrier, 1 LMG, 1 × Daimler S/C
            4 sections, each: 3 × Carriers, 3 LMG, 1 rifle sec, 1 × 2" mortar, 0–1 × Boys

1st Derbyshire Yeomanry Divisional Armoured Recce Regiment

RHQ (4 × Sherman III)
1 Scout/Liaison Troop: Troop HQ (3 × Daimler Scout Cars)
        3 Sections, each: 3 × Daimler Scout Cars
3 Squadrons, each: Sqdn HQ (4 × Sherman III)
        5 Troops, each: 2 × Sherman III, 2 × Stuart I

Notes
1.   Radios were in all tanks and armoured cars, Carrier PHQs, and other CHQs.
2.   Infantry secs had No.74 or Hawkins 75 A/T grenades.
3.   2pdr, 6pdr & 37mm had APCBC and HE, 75mm and 25pdr had AP.
4.   Artillery OP could be in truck, Daimler Scout car, Sherman or Auster AOP.
5.   The Division was in reserve in North Africa until sent to Italy in September 1943 (see Vol.3 Section 3.3)

2.6   BRITISH 7TH ARMOURED DIVISION, TUNISIA, LATE FEBRUARY 1943

The Division's main combat elements were:
        131st Queen's Infantry Brigade (1st/5th, 1st/6th, 1st/7th Infantry Battalions)
        22nd Armoured Brigade (1st RTR, 5th RTR, 4th County of London Yeomanry Armoured Regiments, 1st Battalion Rifle Brigade Motor Battalion)
        Divisional Armoured Car Regiment (12th Lancers)
Troops are rated good morale and average training.

SUPPORT UNITS

Divisional Support

included:
3rd, 5th Royal Horse Artillery Regiments, 146th Field Artillery Regiments, each:
        3 Artillery Batteries, each: Battery HQ (2 rifle secs, 2 trucks, radio van, 4 AALMG)
        2 Troops, each: 4 × 25pdr field guns, 4 trucks, radio truck, 2 AALMG, OP Team
15th Light AA Regiment:
        4 Batteries, each: Battery HQ (1 rifle sec, 1 truck)
            3 Troops, each: 4 × 40mmL60 Bofors, 4 trucks
65th Anti-Tank Regiment:
        1 Battery: Battery HQ (1 rifle sec, 2 × Universal Carriers)
            4 Troops, each: 4 × Deacon, 1 × Deacon Cargo
        3 Batteries, each: Battery HQ (1 rifle sec, 1 truck)
            4 Troops, each: 4 × 6pdr, 4 trucks, 2 LMG
4th, 21st Field Engineer Squadrons, each: Sqdn HQ (2 rifle secs, 1 lorry, 1 × Jeep)
        3 Troops, each: 4 (8 man) rifle/engineer secs, 3 LMG, 2 lorries
143rd Engineer Park Company:
        1 Workshop Section
        1 Bridging/Stores Section
        Water pumping/purification set

Brigade Support

22nd Armoured Brigade HQ (3 × Sherman III, 1 × ACV, 2 × Daimler S/C)
131st Infantry Brigade HQ (4 rifle secs, 2 LMG, 2 trucks, 2 lorries)

MAIN COMBAT ELEMENTS

1st RTR, 5th RTR, 4th County of London Yeomanry Armoured Regiments (22nd Armoured Brigade)

RHQ (1 × Crusader III, 3 × Sherman III)
1 Squadron: Sqdn HQ (1 × Grant I)
      3 Troops, each: 3 × Grant I
1 Squadron: Sqdn HQ (3 × Sherman II)
      3 Troops, each: 3 × Sherman II
1 Squadron: Sqdn HQ (4 × Crusader III)
      5 Troops, each: 3 × Crusader III
1 Recce Troop: Troop HQ (1 × Daimler S/C)
      3 Sections, each: 3 × Daimler Scout Car

1st Battalion Rifle Brigade Motor Battalion (22nd Armoured Brigade)

Btn HQ (2 rifle secs, 2 trucks)
3 Companies, each: Coy HQ (1 rifle sec, 1 × 2" mortar, 2 trucks)
      1 battery: 2 × 3" mortars, 2 × Universal Carriers
      2 platoons, each: 4 (8 man) rifle secs, 3 LMG, 1 × 2" mortar, 4 trucks
      1 platoon: 4 × Vickers MMG, 4 × Universal Carriers or trucks
      1 platoon: Pl HQ: 1 × Universal Carrier, 1 LMG, 1 × Daimler S/C
         3 sections, each: 3 × Carriers, 3 LMG, 1 rifle sec, 1 × 2" mortar, 1 × Boys
1 Anti-Tank Company: Coy HQ (1 rifle sec, 1 truck)
      4 platoons, each: 4 × 6pdr portees, 2 LMG

Infantry Battalion (131st Queen's Infantry Brigade)

Btn HQ (2 rifle secs, 2 trucks)
4 Companies, each: Coy HQ (1 (10 man) rifle sec, 1 lorry)
      3 platoons, each: 1 (6 man) rifle Pl HQ sec, 1 × 2" mortar, 3 (8–10 man) rifle secs, 3 LMG, 2 lorries
1 Support Company: Coy HQ (1 rifle sec, 1 truck)
      2 platoons, each: 4 × 2pdr or 6pdr, 2 LMG, 4 trucks or Universal Carriers
      1 platoon: 2 (6 man) rifle/engineer secs, 1 (3 man) PHQ sec, 1 lorry, 2 LMG
      1 battery: 6 × 3" mortars, 7 × Universal Carriers or 6 trucks, radio truck
      1 platoon: PHQ: 1 × Universal Carrier, 1 LMG, 1 × Daimler S/C
         4 sections, each: 3 × Carriers, 3 LMG, 1 rifle sec, 1 × 2" mortar

12th Lancers Divisional Armoured Car Regiment

RHQ (4 × Humber III)
3 Squadrons, each: Sqdn HQ (2 × Humber III, 2 × Daimler II)
      4 Troops, each: 2 × Humber III, 1 × Daimler II

Notes
1. Radios were in all tanks and armoured cars, and other PHQs.
2. Infantry secs may have had Hawkins 75 A/T grenades.
3. This list shows the division's approximate strength from 15th–28th February 1943, during which it was more or less halted regrouping in front of the Mareth Line in southern Tunisia.
4. Artillery OP was in Universal Carrier, truck, Daimler Scout Car, or Stuart III tank.
5. Issue of Deacons was not certain, may have been replaced by towed equivalent.

2.7   BRITISH 7TH ARMOURED DIVISION, TUNISIA, EARLY MARCH 1943

The Division's main combat elements were:
      31st Queen's Infantry Brigade (1st/5th, 1st/6th, 1st/7th Infantry Battalions)
      22nd Armoured Brigade (1st RTR, 5th RTR, 4th County of London Yeomanry Armoured Regiments, 1st Battalion Rifle Brigade Motor Battalion)
      8th Armoured Brigade (3rd RTR, Sherwood Rangers, Staffordshire Yeomanry Armoured Regiments, 1st Buffs Motor Battalion)
      Divisional Armoured Car Regiment (11th Hussars)
Troops are rated good morale and average training.

SUPPORT UNITS

Divisional Support

included:
3rd, 5th Royal Horse Artillery Regiments, 146th Field Artillery Regiments, each:
      3 Artillery Batteries, each: Battery HQ (2 rifle secs, 2 trucks, radio van, 4 AALMG)
         2 Troops, each: 4 × 25pdr field guns, 4 trucks, radio truck, 2 AALMG, OP Team
15th Light AA Regiment:
      4 Batteries, each: Battery HQ (1 rifle sec, 1 truck)
         3 Troops, each: 4 × 40mmL60 Bofors, 4 trucks
65th Anti-Tank Regiment:
      1 Battery: Battery HQ (1 rifle sec, 2 × Universal Carriers)
         4 Troops, each: 4 × Deacon, 1 × Deacon Cargo
      3 Batteries, each: Battery HQ (1 rifle sec, 1 truck)

4 Troops, each: 4 × 6pdr, 4 trucks, 2 LMG
4th, 21st Field Engineer Squadrons, each: Sqdn HQ (2 rifle secs, 1 lorry, 1 × Jeep)
3 Troops, each: 4 (8 man) rifle/engineer secs, 3 LMG, 2 lorries, 1 bulldozer
143rd Engineer Park Company:
1 Workshop Section
1 Bridging/Stores Section
Water pumping/purification set

Brigade Support

22nd Armoured Brigade HQ (3 × Sherman III, 1 × ACV, 2 × Daimler S/C)
8th Armoured Brigade HQ (2 × Stuart-HQ, 3 × Sherman III, 2 × Marmon-Herrington II)
131st Infantry Brigade HQ (4 rifle secs, 2 LMG, 2 trucks, 2 lorries)

MAIN COMBAT ELEMENTS

1st RTR, 5th RTR, 4th County of London Yeomanry Armoured Regiments (22nd Armoured Brigade)

RHQ (1 × Crusader III, 3 × Sherman III)
1 Squadron: Sqdn HQ (1 × Grant I)
3 Troops, each: 3 × Grant I
1 Squadron: Sqdn HQ (3 × Sherman II)
3 Troops, each: 3 × Sherman II
1 Squadron: Sqdn HQ (4 × Crusader III)
5 Troops, each: 3 × Crusader III
1 Recce Troop: Troop HQ (1 × Daimler Scout Car)
3 Sections, each: 3 × Daimler Scout Car

3rd RTR, Sherwood Rangers, Staffordshire Yeomanry Armoured Regiments (8th Armoured Bde)

RHQ (3 × Sherman II, 1 × Crusader II)
A Squadron: Sqdn HQ (2 × Crusader II)
5 Troops, each: 3 × Crusader III
B Squadron: Sqdn HQ (1 × M3 Lee, 3 × Sherman II)
4 Troops, each: 3 × Sherman II
C Squadron: Sqdn HQ (4 × Sherman III)
3 Troops, each: 3 × Sherman II
Recce Troop: 3 Sections, each: 2–3 × Marmon-Herrington II (MG turret)

1st Battalion Rifle Brigade Motor Battalion (22nd Armoured Brigade)

1st Buffs Motor Battalion (8th Armoured Brigade)

Btn HQ (2 rifle secs, 2 trucks)
3 Companies, each: Coy HQ (1 rifle sec, 1 × 2" mortar, 2 trucks)
1 battery: 2 × 3" mortars, 2 × Universal Carriers
2 platoons, each: 4 (8 man) rifle secs, 3 LMG, 1 × 2" mortar, 4 trucks
1 platoon: 4 × Vickers MMG, 4 × Carriers or trucks
1 platoon: Pl HQ: 1 × Universal Carrier, 1 LMG, 1 × Daimler S/C
3 sections, each: 3 × Carriers, 3 LMG, 1 rifle sec, 1 × 2" mortar, 1 × Boys
1 Anti-Tank Company: Coy HQ (1 rifle sec, 1 truck)
4 platoons, each: 4 × 6pdr portees, 2 LMG

11th Hussars Divisional Armoured Car Regiment

RHQ (4 × M3A1 White Scout Cars, 4 (5 man) rifle/SMG secs, 6 Jeeps)
3 Squadrons, each: Sqdn HQ (4 × Daimler II)
4 Troops, each: 2 × Daimler II armoured cars, 2 × Daimler Scout Car
1 Jeep Troop: 2–6?x Jeeps
0–1 Assault Troop: 4 × M3A1 White S/C, 4 (6 man) rifle secs, 3 LMG, 1 × 2"mortar

Infantry Battalion (131st Queen's Infantry Brigade)

Btn HQ (2 rifle secs, 2 trucks)
4 Companies, each: Coy HQ (1 (10 man) rifle sec, 1 lorry)
3 platoons, each: 1 (6 man) rifle Pl HQ sec, 1 × 2" mortar
3 (8–10 man) rifle secs, 3 LMG, 2 lorries
1 Support Company: Coy HQ (1 rifle sec, 1 truck)
2 platoons, each: 4 × 2pdr or 6pdr, 2 LMG, 4 trucks or Universal Carriers
1 platoon: 2 (6 man) rifle/engineer secs, 1 (3 man) PHQ sec, 1 lorry, 2 LMG
1 battery: 6 × 3" mortars, 7 × Universal Carriers or 6 trucks, radio truck
1 platoon: Pl HQ: 1 × Universal Carrier, 1 LMG, 1 × Daimler S/C
4 sections, each: 3 × Carriers, 3 LMG, 1 rifle sec, 1 × 2" mortar

Notes
1.   Radios were in all tanks and armoured cars, and other PHQs.
2.   Infantry secs may have had Hawkins 75 A/T grenades.

3.   This list shows the division's approximate strength from 3rd–15th March 1943 during which it took part in the battle of Medenine in front of the Mareth Line.
4.   Artillery OP was in Universal Carrier, truck, Daimler Scout Car, or Stuart III tank.
5.   Issue of Deacons was not certain, may have been replaced by towed equivalent.
6.   Marmon-Herringtons in poor condition, probably only MG armed.

2.8 BRITISH 7TH ARMOURED DIVISION, TUNISIA, MARCH–MAY 1943

The Division's main combat elements were:
>   131st Queen's Infantry Brigade (1st/5th, 1st/6th, 1st/7th Infantry Battalions)
>   22nd Armoured Brigade (1st RTR, 5th RTR, 4th County of London Yeomanry Armoured Regiments, 1st Battalion Rifle Brigade Motor Battalion)
>   Divisional Armoured Car Regiment (11th Hussars)

Troops are rated good morale and average training.

SUPPORT UNITS

Divisional Support

included:
3rd, 5th Royal Horse Artillery Regiments, 146th Field Artillery Regiments, each:
>   3 Artillery Batteries, each: Battery HQ (2 rifle secs, 2 trucks, radio van, 4 AALMG)
>   2 Troops, each: 4 × 25pdr field guns, 4 trucks, radio truck, 2 AALMG, OP Team
15th Light AA Regiment:
>   4 Batteries, each: Battery HQ (1 rifle sec, 1 truck)
>   3 Troops, each: 4 × 40mmL60 Bofors, 4 trucks
65th Anti-Tank Regiment:
>   1 Battery: Battery HQ (1 rifle sec, 2 × Universal Carriers)
>   4 Troops, each: 4 × Deacon, 1 × Deacon Cargo
>   3 Batteries, each: Battery HQ (1 rifle sec, 1 truck)
>   4 Troops, each: 4 × 6pdr, 4 trucks, 2 LMG
4th, 21st Field Engineer Squadrons, each: Sqdn HQ (2 rifle secs, 1 lorry, 1 × Jeep)
>   3 Troops, each: 4 (8 man) rifle/engineer secs, 3 LMG, 2 lorries, 1 bulldozer
143rd Engineer Park Company:
>   1 Workshop Section
>   1 Bridging/Stores Section
>   Water pumping/purification set

Brigade Support

22nd Armoured Brigade HQ (3 × Sherman III, 1 × ACV, 2 × Daimler S/C)
131st Infantry Brigade HQ (4 rifle secs, 2 LMG, 2 trucks, 2 lorries)

MAIN COMBAT ELEMENTS

1st RTR, 5th RTR, 4th County of London Yeomanry Armoured Regiments (22nd Armoured Brigade)

RHQ (2 × Crusader III, 2 × Sherman III)
1 Squadron: Sqdn HQ (1 × Grant I)
>   2 Troops, each: 3 × Grant I
>   2 Troops, each: 3 × Sherman II
1 Squadron: Sqdn HQ (3 × Sherman II)
>   4 Troops, each: 3 × Sherman II
1 Light Squadron: Sqdn HQ (3 × Crusader III)
>   4 Troops, each: 3 × Crusader III
1 Recce Troop: Troop HQ (1 × Daimler Scout Car)
>   3 Sections, each: 3 × Daimler Scout Car

1st Battalion Rifle Brigade Motor Battalion (22nd Armoured Brigade)

Btn HQ (2 rifle secs, 2 trucks)
3 Companies, each: Coy HQ (1 rifle sec, 1 × 2" mortar, 2 trucks)
>   1 battery: 2 × 3" mortars, 2 × Universal Carriers
>   2 platoons, each: 4 (8 man) rifle secs, 3 LMG, 1 × 2" mortar, 4 trucks
>   1 platoon: 4 × Vickers MMG, 4 × Carriers or trucks
>   1 platoon: Pl HQ: 1 × Universal Carrier, 1 LMG, 1 × Daimler S/C
>   3 sections, each: 3 × Carriers, 3 LMG, 1 rifle sec, 1 × 2" mortar, 1 × Boys
1 Anti-Tank Company: Coy HQ (1 rifle sec, 1 truck)
>   4 platoons, each: 4 × 6pdr portees, 2 LMG

11th Hussars Divisional Armoured Car Regiment

RHQ (4 × M3A1 White Scout Cars, 4 (5 man) rifle/SMG secs, 6 Jeeps)
3 Squadrons, each: Sqdn HQ (4 × Daimler II)
>   4 Troops, each: 2 × Daimler II, 2 × Daimler Scout Cars
>   1 Jeep Troop: 3 × Jeeps
0–1 Assault Troop: 4 × M3A1 White S/C, 4 (6 man) rifle secs, 3 LMG, 1 × 2" mortar

Infantry Battalion (131st Queen's Infantry Brigade)

Btn HQ (2 rifle secs, 2 trucks)
4 Companies, each: Coy HQ (1 (10 man) rifle sec, 1 lorry)
        3 platoons, each: 1 (6 man) rifle Pl HQ sec, 1 × 2" mortar
                3 (7–10 man) rifle secs, 3 LMG, 2 lorries
1 Support Company: Coy HQ (1 rifle sec, 1 truck)
        2 platoons, each: 4 × 6pdr anti-tank guns, 2 LMG, 4 trucks or Universal Carriers
        1 platoon: 2 (6 man) rifle/engineer secs, 1 (3 man) PHQ sec, 1 lorry, 2 LMG
        1 battery: 6 × 3" mortars, 7 × Universal Carriers or 6 trucks, radio truck
        1 platoon: Pl HQ: 1 × Universal Carrier, 1 LMG, 1 × Daimler S/C
                4 sections, each: 3 × Carriers, 3 LMG, 1 rifle sec, 1 × 2" mortar

Notes
1.   Radios were in all tanks and armoured cars, and other PHQs.
2.   Infantry secs may have had Hawkins 75 A/T grenades.
3.   This list shows the division's approximate strength from 16th–30th March 1943 during which time it saw little action in front of the Mareth Line, to the final advance into Tunis in early May 1943.
4.   Artillery OP was in Universal Carrier, truck, Daimler Scout Car, or Stuart III tank.
5.   Issue of Deacons was not certain, may have been replaced by towed equivalent.

2.9   BRITISH 7TH ARMOURED DIVISION, TUNISIA, JUNE–AUGUST 1943

The Division's main combat elements were:
    131st Queen's Infantry Brigade (1st/5th, 1st/6th, 1st/7th Infantry Battalions)
    22nd Armoured Brigade (1st RTR, 5th RTR, 4th County of London Yeomanry Armoured Regiments, 1st Battalion Rifle Brigade Motor Battalion)
    Divisional Armoured Car Regiment (11th Hussars)
Troops are rated good morale and average training.

SUPPORT UNITS

Divisional Support

3rd Royal Horse Artillery Regiment, 146th Field Artillery Regiment:
    3 Artillery Batteries, each: Battery HQ (4 rifle secs, 4 lorries, 4 AALMG, 3 OP Teams)
        2 Troops, each: 4 × 25pdr field guns, 4 trucks, radio truck, 2 AALMG
5th Royal Horse Artillery Regiment:
    3 Batteries, each: Battery HQ (1 × ACV, 3 lorries, 4 rifle secs, 4 AALMG, 2 OP Teams)
        2 Troops, each: 4 × 105mm M7 Priest, radio van, 2 AALMG
65th Norfolk Yeomanry Anti-Tank Regiment:
    3 Anti-Tank Batteries, each: Battery HQ (1 rifle sec, 1 truck)
        3 Troops, each: 4 × 6pdr, 2 LMG, 4 trucks
        1 Troop: 4 × 6pdr or 17pdr, 2 LMG, 4 trucks
    1 Anti-Tank Battery: Battery HQ (2 × Universal Carriers, 1 rifle sec)
        2–3 platoons, each: 4 × M10 Wolverine
15th Light AA Regiment:
    3 AA Batteries, each: Battery HQ (1 rifle sec, 1 truck)
        3 platoons, each: 6 × 40mmL60 Bofors, 6 trucks
4th, 621st Field Engineer Squadrons, each: Sqdn HQ (2 rifle secs, 1 lorry)
        4 Troops, each: 4 (12 man) rifle/engineer secs, 2 LMG, 2 lorries
143rd Engineer Park Squadron:
    1 Bridge Troop: 1 × 40t 80' Bailey Bridge in 15 × 3-ton lorries, 1+x Valentine AVLB
    1 Stores Section: 24 assault boats, 1 large bulldozer, 1 small bulldozer
    1 Workshop Section

Brigade Support

22nd Armoured Brigade HQ (1 × Sherman III, 5 × Grant I, 2 × ACV, 2 × Humber AA, 3 × Stuart I OP)
131st Infantry Brigade HQ (4 rifle secs, 2 LMG, 2 trucks, 2 lorries) with:
    C Company, 1st Cheshire MG Regiment: Coy HQ (1 rifle sec, 1 truck)
        4 platoons, each: 4 × Vickers MMG, 2 trucks
        1 platoon: 4 × 4.2" mortars, 8 × Loyd Carriers or 4 trucks, radio truck

MAIN COMBAT ELEMENTS

1st RTR, 5th RTR, 4th County of London Yeomanry Armoured Regiments (22nd Armoured Brigade)

RHQ (4 × M4A2 Sherman III)
3 Squadrons, each: Sqdn HQ (4 × Sherman III)
        4 Troops, each: 3 × Sherman III
1 Recce Troop: Troop HQ (2 × Daimler S/C)
        3 Sections, each: 3 × Daimler Scout Car

1st Battalion Rifle Brigade Motor Battalion (22nd Armoured Brigade)

Btn HQ (2 rifle secs, 2 trucks)

3 Companies, each: Coy HQ (1 rifle sec, 1 × 2" mortar, 2 trucks)
   1 battery: 2 × 3" mortars, 3 × Universal Carriers
   2 platoons, each: 4 (8 man) rifle secs, 3 LMG, 1 × 2", 0–4 Boys, 4 trucks
   1 platoon: 4 MMG, 5 × Universal Carriers
   1 platoon: Pl HQ: 1 × Universal Carrier, 1 LMG, 1 × Daimler S/C
     3 sections, each: 3 × Carriers, 3 LMG, 1 rifle sec, 1 × 2" mortar, 1 × Boys
1 Anti-Tank Company: Coy HQ (1 rifle sec, 1 truck)
   4 platoons, each: 4 × 6pdr portees on 3-ton lorries, 2 LMG

Infantry Battalion (131st Queen's Infantry Brigade)
Btn HQ (2 rifle secs, 2 trucks)
4 Companies, each: Coy HQ (1 rifle sec, 1 lorry)
   3 platoons, each: 1 (8 man) rifle Pl HQ sec, 0–1 Boys, 1 × 2" mortar, 2 lorries
     3 (10 man) rifle secs, 3 LMG
1 Support Company: Coy HQ (1 rifle sec, 2 lorries)
   2 platoons, each: 4 × 2pdr anti-tank guns, 2 LMG, 4 trucks or Carriers
   1 platoon: 2 (8 man) rifle/engineer secs, 1 (5 man) rifle Pl HQ sec, 2 LMG
   1 battery: 6 × 3" mortars, 7 × Universal Carriers or 6 trucks, radio truck
   1 platoon: Pl HQ: 1 × Universal Carrier, 1 LMG, 1 × Daimler S/C
     4 sections, each: 3 × Carriers, 3 LMG, 1 rifle sec, 1 × 2" mortar, 0–1 × Boys

11th Hussars Divisional Recce Regiment
RHQ (4 × M3A1 White Scout Cars, 4 (6 man) rifle secs)
3 Squadrons, each: Sqdn HQ (4 × Daimler II armoured cars)
   4 Troops, each: 2 × Daimler II, 2 × Daimler Scout Cars
   1 Troop: 2 × M3 GMC halftrack with 75mm gun
   1 Assault Troop: 4 × M3A1 White S/C, 4 (6 man) rifle secs, 3 LMG, 1 × 2" mortar, 1 PIAT

Notes
1. Radios were in all tanks and armoured cars, Carrier PHQs, and other CHQs.
2. Infantry secs had No.74 or Hawkins 75 A/T grenades. A few PIATs may have been available for training from July 1943. Most units will have dropped the Boys A/T rifle by this time.
3. 2pdr, 37mm, 6pdr, 75mm had APCBC and HE. 17pdr had APCBC only.
4. Artillery OP could be in truck, Carrier, Daimler S/C, Auster AOP, turretless Marmon-Herrington, or Stuart III tank.
5. The Division was resting and reorganising in Tunisia during June–August 1943.

2.10 BRITISH 7TH ARMOURED DIVISION, ITALY, SEPTEMBER–DECEMBER 1943
The Division's main combat elements were:
  22nd Armoured Brigade (1st RTR, 5th RTR, 4th County of London Yeomanry Armoured Regiments, 1st Battalion Rifle Brigade Motor Battalion)
  131st Queen's Motorised Brigade (1st/5th, 1st/6th, 1st/7th Infantry battalions)
  Divisional Recce Regiment (11th Hussars)
Troops are rated average morale and training.

SUPPORT UNITS
Divisional Support
Included:
3rd Royal Horse Artillery Regiment, 146th Field Artillery Regiment, each:
   3 Artillery Batteries each: Battery HQ (4 rifle secs, 4 lorries, 4 AALMG, 3 OP Teams)
     2 Troops, each: 4 × 25pdr, 4 trucks, radio truck, 2 AALMG
5th Royal Horse Artillery Regiment:
   3 Batteries each: Battery HQ (1 × ACV, 3 lorries, 4 rifle secs, 4 AALMG, 2 OP Teams)
     2 Troops, each: 4 × 105mm M7 Priest, radio van, 2 AALMG
65th Norfolk Yeomanry Anti-Tank Regiment:
   3 Anti-Tank Batteries, each: Battery HQ (1 rifle sec, 1 truck)
     3 Troops, each: 4 × 6pdr A/T guns, 2 LMG, 6 Jeeps
     1 Troop: 4 × 6pdr or 17pdr A/T guns, 2 LMG, 4 trucks
   1 Anti-Tank Battery: Battery HQ (2 × Carriers, 1 rifle sec)
     2–3 Platoons, each: 4 × M10 Wolverine, 1 × Universal Carrier Pl HQ
15th Light AA Regiment:
   3 AA Batteries each: Battery HQ (1 rifle sec, 1 truck)
     3 Platoons, each: 6 × 40mm Bofors, 6 trucks
4th, 621st Engineer Squadrons, each: Sqdn HQ (2 rifle secs, 1 lorry)
   4 Troops, each: 4 (12 man) rifle/engineer secs, 2 LMG, 2 lorries
143rd Engineer Park Squadron:
   1 Bridge Troop: 1 × 40t 80' Bailey Bridge in 15 × 3-ton lorries, 1–3 × Valentine AVLB
   1 Stores Section: 24 assault boats, 1 large bulldozer, 1 small bulldozer
   1 Workshop Section: 44 men, recovery lorries

Brigade Support
22nd Armoured Brigade HQ (1 × Sherman III, 5 × Grant 1, 2 × ACV, 2 × Humber AA, 3 × Stuart I)
131st Queen's Motorised Brigade HQ (4 rifle secs, 2 LMG, 2 trucks, 2 lorries) with:

C Company, 1st Cheshire MG Regiment: Coy HQ (1 rifle sec, 1 truck)
4 Platoons, each: 4 × Vickers MMG, 2 trucks
1 mortar Platoon: 4 × 4.2" mortars, 8 × Loyd Carriers or 4 trucks

MAIN COMBAT ELEMENTS

1st RTR, 5th RTR, 4th County of London Yeomanry Armoured Regiments

RHQ (4 × M4A2 Sherman III)
3 Squadrons each: Sqdn HQ (4 × Sherman III)
4 Troops, each: 3 × Sherman III
1 Recce Troop: Troop HQ (2 × Daimler S/C)
3 Sections, each: 3 × Daimler Scout Car

1st Battalion, Rifle Brigade Motor Battalion (of 22nd Armoured Brigade)

Btn HQ (2 rifle secs, 2 trucks)
3 Companies each: Coy HQ (1 rifle sec, 1 × 2" mortar, 2 trucks)
1 battery: 2 × 3" mortars, 3 × Carriers
2 Platoons, each: 4 (8 man) rifle secs, 3 LMG, 1 × 2" mortar, 4 PIAT, 4 trucks
1 Platoon: 4 × Vickers MMG, 5 × Universal Carriers
1 Platoon: Pl HQ: 1 × Universal Carrier, 1 LMG, 1 × Daimler S/C
3 sections each: 3 × Carriers, 3 LMG, 1 rifle sec, 1 × 2" mortar, 1 × PIAT
1 Anti-Tank Company: Coy HQ (1 rifle sec, 1 truck)
4 Platoons, each: 4 × 6pdr A/T gun portees on 3-ton lorries, 2 LMG

1st/5th, 1st/6th, 1st/7th Queen's Royal Regiment Motorised Infantry Battalions, each:

Btn HQ (2 rifle secs, 2 trucks)
4 Companies, each: Coy HQ (1 rifle sec, 1 lorry)
3 Platoons, each: 1 (8 man) rifle Pl HQ sec, 1 PIAT, 1 × 2" mortar, 2 lorries
3 (10 man) rifle secs, 3 LMG
1 Support Company: Coy HQ (1 rifle sec, 2 lorries)
2 Platoons, each: 4 × 2pdr anti-tank guns, 2 LMG, 4 trucks or Carriers
1 Platoon: 2 (8 man) rifle/engineer secs, 1 (5 man) rifle Pl HQ sec, 2 LMG
1 battery: 6 × 3" mortars, 7 × Universal Carriers or 6 trucks, radio truck
1 Platoon: Pl HQ: 1 × Universal Carrier, 1 LMG, 1 × Daimler S/C
4 sections each: 3 × Carriers, 3 LMG, 1 rifle sec, 1 × 2" mortar, 1 × PIAT

11th Hussars Divisional Recce Regiment

RHQ (4 × M3A1 White Scout Cars, 4 (6 man) rifle secs)
3 Squadrons each: Sqdn HQ (4 × Daimler II armoured cars)
4 Troops, each: 2 × Daimler II, 2 × Daimler Scout Cars
1 Troop: 2 × M3 GMC halftrack with 75mm gun
1 Assault Troop: 4 × M3A1 White S/C, 4 (6 man) rifle secs, 3 LMG, 1 × 2" mortar, 1 PIAT

Notes
1.   Radios were in all tanks and armoured cars, Carrier PHQs, and other CHQs.
2.   Infantry secs had No.74 or Hawkins 75 A/T grenades.
3.   2pdr, 37mm, 6pdr A/T gun, 75mm had APCBC and HE. 17pdr had APCBC only.
4.   Artillery OP could be in truck, Carrier, Daimler S/C, turretless Marmon-Herrington, or Stuart III tank.
5.   In December the division left all its equipment behind for the 5th Canadian Armoured Division and sailed to England.
6.   During September 27th to early October the 23rd Armoured Brigade and the 69th Medium Artillery Regiment (16 × 5.5" guns) were attached.

2.11 SOUTH AFRICAN 6TH ARMOURED DIVISION, EGYPT, JULY 1943–MARCH 1944

The Division's main combat elements were:
11th Armoured Brigade (Pretoria, Special Service Battalion, Prince Alfred's Guard Armoured Regiments, and Imperial Light Horse Motor Battalion)
12th Motorised Brigade (Royal Natal Carabiniers, First City/Capetown Highlanders, Witwatersrand Rifles infantry battalions)
Divisional Armoured Recce Regiment (Natal Mounted Rifles)
Troops are rated good morale and average training.

SUPPORT UNITS

Divisional Support

Included:
1st/6th Field Artillery Regiment:
3 Batteries, each: Battery HQ (4 rifle secs, 2 AALMG, 4 lorries)
2 Troops, each: 4 × 25pdr field guns, 6 trucks, 2 AALMG, OP Team
4/22nd Field SP Artillery Regiment:
3 Batteries, each: Battery HQ (4 rifle secs, 2 AALMG, 4 lorries, 1 PIAT)
2 Troops, each: 4 × 105mm M7 Priest, radio truck, 2 AALMG, 1 PIAT
7th/23rd Medium Artillery Regiment:
Regiment HQ (6 rifle secs, 4AALMG, 1 PIAT, 8 lorries, 4 OP Teams)

       2 Batteries, each: (4 rifle secs, 2 AALMG, 4 lorries)
               2 Troops, each: 4 × 5.5" guns, 4 lorries, radio van, 2 AALMG
1st/11th Anti-Tank Regiment:
       4 (1 Rhodesian) Batteries, each: Battery HQ (1 rifle sec, 1 truck)
               3 Troops, each: 4 × 2pdr or 6pdr A/T guns, 4 trucks, 2 LMG
1st/12th Light AA Regiment, South African Air Force:
       3 Batteries, each: Battery HQ (1 rifle sec,1 truck)
               3 Troops, each 6 × 40mmL60 Bofors, 6 trucks
8th, 12th Field Engineer Squadrons each Sqdn HQ (2 rifle secs, 1 lorry)
       3 Troops, each: 4 (12 man) rifle/engineer secs, 2 lorries, 4 LMG
17th Field Park Squadron:
       Bridging & Stores Troop
       Workshop Troop

Brigade Support

11th Armoured Brigade HQ (7 × Sherman V, 6 × Crusader OP, 7 × Daimler Scout Cars)
12th Motorised Brigade HQ (6 rifle secs, 6 trucks, 2 LMG) with:
       1 Support Battalion (Royal Durban Light Infantry)
           Btn HQ (2 rifle secs, 2 lorries)
           2 Companies, each: Coy HQ (1 rifle sec, 1 truck)
               3 Platoons, each: 6 × Vickers MMG, 4 (8 man) crew secs, 6 × Carriers
           2 Companies, each: Coy HQ (1 rifle sec, 1 truck)
               2 Platoons, each: 6 × 4.2" mortars, 4 (8 man) crew secs, 12 × Carriers

MAIN COMBAT ELEMENTS

Pretoria Regiment, Special Service Battalion Armoured Regiments, each:

RHQ (4 × Sherman II or V, 3 × Crusader OP, 1 × Sherman ARV Mk.1)
A, B Squadrons, each: Sqdn HQ (4 × Sherman II or V)
       4 Troops, each: 3 × Sherman II or V
C Rhodesian Squadron: Sqdn HQ (4 × Sherman II or V)
       4 Troops, each: 3 × Sherman II or V
D Reserve Squadron: spare tanks and spare crews
1 Scout Troop: Troop HQ (2 × Stuart IV)
       3 Sections, each: 3 × Stuart IV

Prince Alfred's Guard Armoured Regiment

RHQ (4 × Sherman II or V, 3 × Crusader OP, 1 × Sherman ARV Mk.1)
A, B Squadrons each: Sqdn HQ (4 × Sherman II or V)
       4 Troops, each: 3 × Sherman II or V
B Rhodesian Squadron: Sqdn HQ (4 × Sherman II or V)
       4 Troops, each: 3 × Sherman II or V
1 Scout Troop: Troop HQ (1 × Crusader III)
       3 Sections, each: 3 × Crusader III
D Reserve Squadron: Sqdn HQ (4 × Crusader II or III)
       5 Troops, each 3 × Crusader II or III

Royal Natal Carabiniers, First City/Capetown Highlanders, Witwatersrand Rifles Infantry Battalions, each:

Btn HQ (3 rifle secs, 1 LMG, 2 lorries)
3 Companies, each: Coy HQ (1 rifle sec, 1 truck)
       3 Platoons, each: 1 (6 man) rifle Pl HQ sec, 1 × 2" mortar, 1 PIAT
           3 (8 man) rifle secs, 3 LMG, 2 lorries
1 Support Company: Coy HQ (1 rifle sec, 1 truck)
       1 battery: 6 × 3" mortars, 7 × Universal Carriers
       1 Platoon: 6 × 6pdr A/T guns, 6 × Carriers, 3 LMG
       1 Platoon: 3 (5 man) rifle/engineer secs, 3 LMG, 3 trucks
       1 Platoon: Pl HQ: 1 × Universal Carrier, 1 LMG, 1 × Daimler Scout Car
           4 Sections, each: 3 × Carrier, 3 LMG, 1 × 2", 1 Boys,1 (6 man) rifle sec

Imperial Light Horse/Kimberley Motor Battalion (of Armoured Brigade)

Btn HQ (2 rifle secs, 4 trucks, 2 LMG)
3 Companies, each: Coy HQ (1 × Stuart III Kangaroo, 1 (6 man) rifle sec, 1 LMG, 1 PIAT)
       3 Platoons, each: 1 × Stuart III Kangaroo Pl HQ, 3 trucks, 4 (6 man) rifle secs
           4 LMG, 1 × 2" mortar, 1 PIAT
       1 Platoon: Pl HQ: 1 × Stuart III Kangaroo, 1 LMG
           3 Sections, each: 3 × Carrier, 3 LMG, 1 Boys, 1 × 2" mortar, 1 (5 man) rifle sec
       1 Platoon: 2 × 6pdr A/T guns, 2 trucks or Carriers, 1 LMG
       1 Platoon: 2 MMG, 2 × 3" mortars, 4 trucks or Carriers

Natal Mounted Rifles Divisional Armoured Recce Regiment

RHQ (4 × Sherman II, 1 × Sherman ARV)
3 Squadrons, each: Sqdn HQ (4 × Sherman II)

5 Troops, each: 2 × Sherman II, 2 × Stuart III
1 Scout/Liaison Troop: Troop HQ (3 × Daimler Scout Cars)
3 Sections, each: 3 × Daimler Scout Cars

Notes
1. Radios were in all AFV, Carrier PHQs and other PHQs.
2. Infantry had Hawkins No.75 anti-tank grenades.
3. The division was in training in Egypt during this period.
4. Stuart 'Kangaroo' were turretless Stuart III seized and used as HQ APCs.
5. The Durban Light Infantry Support Battalion had only sufficient crews to man four weapons per Platoon at any one time.

2.12 SOUTH AFRICAN 6TH ARMOURED DIVISION, ITALY, MAY–JULY 1944

The Division's main combat elements were:
11th Armoured Brigade (Pretoria, Special Service Battalion, Prince Alfred's Guard Armoured Regiments, Imperial Light Horse Motor Battalion)
12th Motorised Brigade (Royal Natal Carabiniers, First City/Capetown Highlanders, Witwatersrand Rifles infantry battalions)
British 24th Guards Infantry Brigade (5th Btn Grenadier Guards, 3rd Btn Coldstream Guards, 1st Btn Scots Guards)
Divisional Armoured Recce Regiment (Natal Mounted Rifles)
Troops are rated good morale and average training.

SUPPORT UNITS

Divisional Support

Included:
1st/6th Field Artillery Regiment:
3 Batteries, each: Battery HQ (4 rifle secs, 2 AALMG, 4 lorries)
2 Troops, each: 4 × 25pdr field guns, 6 trucks, 2 AALMG, OP Team
4/22nd Field SP Artillery Regiment:
3 Batteries, each: Battery HQ (4 rifle secs, 2 AALMG, 4 lorries, 1 PIAT)
2 Troops, each: 4 × 105mm M7 Priest, radio truck, 2 AALMG, 1 PIAT
7th/23rd Medium Artillery Regiment:
Regiment HQ (6 rifle secs, 4AALMG, 1 PIAT, 8 lorries, 4 OP Teams)
2 Batteries, each: (4 rifle secs, 2 AALMG, 4 lorries)
2 Troops, each: 4 × 5.5" guns, 4 lorries, radio van, 2 AALMG
1st/11th Anti-Tank Regiment:
1 Rhodesian Battery: Battery HQ (1 rifle sec, 1 truck)
3 Troops, each: 4 × 17pdr A/T guns, 4 trucks, 2 LMG
1 Battery: Battery HQ (1 rifle sec, 1 truck)
2 Troops, each: 4 × 17pdr A/T guns, 4 trucks, 2 LMG
2 Batteries, each: Battery HQ (1 rifle sec, 2 × M3 halftrack)
3 Troops, each: 4 × M10 Wolverine, 1 × Universal Carrier Pl HQ
1st/12th Light AA Regiment, South African Air Force:
3 Batteries, each: Battery HQ (1 rifle sec,1 truck)
3 Troops, each 6 × 40mmL60 Bofors, 6 trucks
8th, 12th Field Engineer Squadrons, each:
Sqdn HQ (4 (11 man) rifle secs, 4 LMG, 2 PIAT, 3 lorries)
3 Troops, each: 1 (21 man) rifle/engineer Pl HQ sec, 1 LMG, 2 PIAT, 6 × Humber Scout Cars
4 (12 man) rifle/engineer secs, 4 LMG, 4 lorries
17th Field Park Squadron: Sqdn HQ (3 (12 man) rifle secs, 4 lorries, 5 LMG, 4 PIAT)
1 Bridge Troop: 1 × 40t 80' Bailey Bridges in 15 × 3-ton lorries, 51 men
1 Stores Section: 12 assault boats, 3 bulldozers, 3 tractors, 29 men
1 Workshop Section: 44 men, recovery lorries

Brigade Support

11th Armoured Brigade HQ (7 × Sherman V-HQ, 6 × Crusader OP, 7 × Daimler Scout Cars) with:
1 Defence Troop: 4 × Sherman V
12th Motorised Brigade HQ (6 rifle secs, 6 trucks, 2 LMG) with:
1 Support Battalion (Royal Durban Light Infantry)
Btn HQ (2 rifle secs, 2 lorries)
2 Companies, each: Coy HQ (1 rifle sec, 1 truck)
3 Platoons, each: 6 × Vickers MMG, 4 (8 man) crew secs, 6 × Carriers
2 Companies, each: Coy HQ (1 rifle sec, 1 truck)
2 Platoons, each: 6 × 4.2" mortars, 4 (8 man) crew secs, 12 × Carriers
24th British Guards Brigade HQ (6 rifle secs, 4 lorries, Air Liaison Team, 2 LMG) with:
23rd Field Artillery Regiment
3 Batteries, each: Battery HQ (4 rifle secs, 2 AALMG, 4 lorries)
2 Troops, each: 4 × 25pdr field guns, 6 trucks, 2 AALMG, OP Team

MAIN COMBAT ELEMENTS

Pretoria Regiment, Special Service Battalion Armoured Regiments, each:
RHQ (4 × Sherman II or V, 3 × Crusader OP, 1 × Sherman ARV Mk.1)
A, B Squadrons, each: Sqdn HQ (4 × Sherman II or V)
    4 Troops, each: 3 × Sherman II or V
C Rhodesian Squadron: Sqdn HQ (4 × Sherman II or V)
    4 Troops, each: 3 × Sherman II or V
D Reserve Squadron: spare tanks and spare crews
1 Scout Troop: Troop HQ (2 × Stuart IV)
    3 Sections, each: 3 × Stuart IV, 3 × Daimler Scout Car

Prince Alfred's Guard Armoured Regiment
RHQ (4 × Sherman II or V, 3 × Crusader OP, 1 × Sherman ARV Mk.1)
A, B Squadrons each: Sqdn HQ (4 × Sherman II or V)
    4 Troops, each: 3 × Sherman II or V
B Rhodesian Squadron: Sqdn HQ (4 × Sherman II or V)
    4 Troops, each: 3 × Sherman II or V
1 Scout Troop: Troop HQ (2 × Crusader III or Stuart IV)
    3 Sections, each: 3 × Crusader III or Stuart IV
D Reserve Squadron: Sqdn HQ (4 × Crusader II or III or Sherman II)
    5 Troops, each 3 × Crusader II or Crusader III or Sherman II

Royal Natal Carabiniers, First City/Capetown Highlanders, Witwatersrand Rifles Infantry Battalions, each:
Btn HQ (3 rifle secs, 1 LMG, 2 lorries)
4 Companies, each: Coy HQ (1 rifle sec, 1 truck)
    3 Platoons, each: 1 (6 man) rifle Pl HQ sec, 1 × 2" mortar, 1 PIAT, 3 (8 man) rifle secs, 3 LMG, 2 lorries
1 Support Company: Coy HQ (1 rifle sec, 1 truck)
    1 battery: 6 × 3" mortars, 7 × Universal Carriers
    1 Platoon: 6 × 6pdr A/T guns, 6 × Carriers, 3 LMG
    1 Platoon: 3 (5 man) rifle/engineer secs, 3 LMG, 3 trucks
    1 Platoon: Pl HQ:1 × Universal Carrier, 1 LMG, 1 × Daimler Scout Car
        4 Sections, each: 3 × Carrier, 3 LMG, 1 × 2", 1 Boys,1 (6 man) rifle sec

5th Btn Grenadier Guards, 3rd Btn Coldstream Guards, 1st Btn Scots Guards Infantry Battalions, each:
Btn HQ (4 rifle secs, 1 LMG, 2 lorries)
4 Companies, each: Coy HQ (1 (13 man) rifle sec, 1 truck)
    3 Platoons, each: 1 (7 man) rifle Pl HQ sec, 1 × 2" mortar, 1 PIAT
        3 (10 man) rifle secs, 3 LMG, 2 lorries
1 Support Company: Coy HQ (1 rifle sec, 1 truck)
    1 battery: 6 × 3" mortars, 7 × Universal Carriers, 2 PIAT
    1 Platoon: 6 × 6pdr A/T guns, 6 × Carriers, 3 LMG
    1 Platoon: 2 (10 man) rifle/engineer secs, 2 LMG, 3 trucks
    1 Platoon: 4 × Vickers MMG, 5 × Universal Carriers, 5 LMG, 1 × 2" mortar, 1 PIAT
    1 Platoon: Pl HQ: 1 × Universal Carrier, 1 LMG, 1 × Daimler Scout Car
        2 Sections, each: 3 × Carrier, 3 LMG, 1 × 2", 1 Boys,1 (6 man) rifle sec

Imperial Light Horse/Kimberley Motor Battalion (of Armoured Brigade)
Btn HQ (2 rifle secs, 4 trucks, 2 LMG)
3 Companies, each: Coy HQ (1 × Stuart III Kangaroo, 1 (6 man) rifle sec, 1 LMG, 1 PIAT)
    1 Section: 2 × 3" mortars, 2 × Universal Carriers
    3 Platoons, each: 1 × Stuart III Kangaroo Pl HQ, 3 trucks, 4 (6 man) rifle secs, 4 LMG, 1 × 2" mortar, 1 PIAT
    1 Platoon: Pl HQ: 1 × Stuart III Kangaroo, 1 LMG
        3 Sections, each: 3 × Carrier, 3 LMG, 1 Boys, 1 × 2" mortar, 1 (5 man) rifle sec
1 Support Company: Coy HQ (1 rifle sec, 1 truck, 1 × Universal Carrier)
    3 Platoons, each: 2 × 6pdr A/T guns, 2 trucks or Carriers, 1 LMG
    2 MG Platoons, each: 2 MMG, 2 × Universal Carriers

Natal Mounted Rifles Divisional Armoured Recce Regiment
RHQ (4 × Sherman II, 1 × Sherman ARV)
3 Squadrons, each: Sqdn HQ (4 × Sherman II)
    5 Troops, each: 2 × Sherman II, 2 × Stuart III
1 Scout/Liaison Troop: Troop HQ (3 × Daimler Scout Cars)
    3 Sections, each: 3 × Daimler Scout Cars

Notes
1. Radios were in all AFV, Carrier PHQs and other PHQs.
2. Infantry had Hawkins No.75 anti-tank grenades.
3. Stuart 'Kangaroo' were turretless Stuart III seized and used as HQ APCs.
4. The Durban Light Infantry Support Battalion had only sufficient crews to man four weapons per Platoon at any one time.
5. It is likely that the Crusaders were soon replaced by Shermans and Stuarts.

2.13 SOUTH 6TH AFRICAN ARMOURED DIVISION, ITALY, AUGUST–OCTOBER 1944

The Division's main combat elements were:

11th Armoured Brigade (Pretoria, Special Service Battalion, Prince Alfred's Guard Armoured Regiments, Imperial Light Horse Motor Battalion)

12th Motorised Brigade (Royal Natal Carabiniers, First City/Capetown Highlanders, Witwatersrand Rifles, 4th/13th Indian Frontier Force infantry battalions)

British 24th Guards Infantry Brigade (5th Btn Grenadier Guards, 3rd Btn Coldstream Guards, 1st Btn Scots Guards)

Divisional Armoured Recce Regiment (Natal Mounted Rifles)

Troops are rated good morale and average training, with ex-South African Air Force personnel acting as infantry, rated as average morale and average training. In practice the Division formed mixed brigades by cross-attaching one armoured regiment to each Infantry Brigade Group, leaving the Armoured Brigade Group with one Armoured Regiment and the Motor Battalion.

SUPPORT UNITS

Divisional Support

Included:

7th/23rd Medium Artillery Regiment:
> Regiment HQ (6 rifle secs, 4AALMG, 1 PIAT, 8 lorries, 4 OP Teams)
> 2 Batteries, each: (4 rifle secs, 2 AALMG, 4 lorries)
>> 2 Troops, each: 4 × 5.5" guns, 4 lorries, radio van, 2 AALMG

1st/11th Anti-Tank Regiment:
> 1 Battery: Battery HQ (1 rifle sec, 1 truck)
>> 2 Troops, each: 4 × 17pdr A/T guns, 4 trucks, 2 LMG

1st/12th Light AA Regiment, South African Air Force:
> 2 Batteries, each: Battery HQ (1 rifle sec, 1 truck)
>> 3 Troops, each 6 × 40mmL60 Bofors, 6 trucks

17th Field Park Squadron: Sqdn HQ (3 (12 man) rifle secs, 4 lorries, 5 LMG, 4 PIAT)
> 1 Bridge Troop: 1 × 40t 80' Bailey Bridges in 15 × 3-ton lorries, 51 men
> 1 Stores Section: 12 assault boats, 3 bulldozers, 3 tractors, 29 men
> 1 Workshop Section: 44 men, recovery lorries

Attached Corps Support

178th South African Medium Artillery Regiment:
> Regiment HQ (6 rifle secs, 4AALMG, 1 PIAT, 8 lorries, 4 OP Teams)
> 2 Batteries, each: (4 rifle secs, 2 AALMG, 4 lorries)
>> 2 Troops, each: 4 × 5.5" guns, 4 lorries, radio van, 2 AALMG

76th South African Heavy AA Regiment:
> 3 Batteries, each: Battery HQ (2 rifle secs, 4 trucks)
>> 2 Troops, each: 4 × 3.7" AA guns, 6 lorries

Brigade Support

11th Armoured Brigade Group HQ (7 × Sherman V-HQ, 6 × Crusader OP, 7 × Daimler S/C) with:
> 1 Defence Troop: 4 × Sherman V
> 1 Mortar Platoon, Royal Durban Light Infantry: 4 × 4.2" mortars, 8 × Universal Carrier, 4 LMG
> 1 A/T Battery, 1st/11th A/T Regiment: Battery HQ (1 rifle sec, 2 × M3 halftrack)
>> 3 Troops, each: 4 × M10 Wolverine, 1 × Universal Carrier Pl HQ
> 12th Field Engineer Squadron: Sqdn HQ (4 (11 man) rifle secs, 4 LMG, 2 PIAT, 3 lorries)
>> 3 Troops, each: 1 (21 man) rifle/engineer
>> Pl HQ sec, 1 LMG, 2 PIAT, 6 × Humber Scout Car, 4 (12 man) rifle/engineer secs, 4 LMG, 4 lorries

4/22nd Field SP Artillery Regiment:
> 3 Batteries, each: Battery HQ (4 rifle secs, 2 AALMG, 4 lorries, 1 PIAT)
>> 1 Troop: 4 × 105mm M7 Priest, radio truck, 2 AALMG, 1 PIAT
>> 1 Troop: 3 × 105mm M7 Priest, radio truck, 2 AALMG, 1 PIAT

12th Motorised Brigade Group HQ (6 rifle secs, 6 trucks, 2 LMG) with:
> 1 A/T Battery

1st/11th A/T Regiment: Battery HQ (1 rifle sec, 2 × M3 halftrack)
>> 3 Troops, each: 4 × M10 Wolverine, 1 × Universal Carrier Pl HQ
> Group A, Royal Durban Light Infantry
>> Btn HQ (2 rifle secs, 2 lorries)
>> 1 MG Company: Coy HQ (1 rifle sec, 1 truck)
>>> 3 Platoons, each: 4 × Vickers MMG, 5 × Universal Carrier
>> 1 Mortar Platoon: 4 × 4.2" mortars, 8 × Universal Carrier
> 8th Field Engineer Squadron: Sqdn HQ (4 (11 man) rifle secs, 4 LMG, 2 PIAT, 3 lorries)
>> 3 Troops, each: 1 (21 man) rifle/engineer Pl HQ sec, 1 LMG, 2 PIAT, 6 × Humber Scout Cars, 4 (12 man) rifle/engineer secs, 4 LMG, 4 lorries

1st/6th Field Artillery Regiment:
> 3 Batteries, each: Battery HQ (4 rifle secs, 2 AALMG, 4 lorries)
>> 2 Troops, each: 4 × 25pdr field guns, 6 trucks, 2 AALMG, OP Team

24th British Guards Brigade Group HQ (6 rifle secs, 4 lorries, Air Liaison Team, 2 LMG) with:
> 1 A/T Battery, 1st/11th A/T Regiment: Battery HQ (1 rifle sec, 1 truck)

3 Troops, each: 4 × 17pdr A/T guns, 4 trucks, 2 LMG
Group B, Royal Durban Light Infantry
Btn HQ (2 rifle secs, 2 lorries)
1 MG Company: Coy HQ (1 rifle sec, 1 truck)
3 Platoons, each: 4 × Vickers MMG, 5 × Universal Carrier
1 Mortar Platoon: 4 × 4.2" mortars, 8 × Universal Carrier
166th Newfoundland Field Artillery Regiment
3 Batteries, each: Battery HQ (4 rifle secs, 2 AALMG, 4 lorries)
2 Troops, each: 4 × 25pdr field guns, 6 trucks, 2 AALMG, OP Team
8th British Field Engineer Squadron:
Sqdn HQ (4 (11 man) rifle secs, 4 LMG, 2 PIAT, 3 lorries)
3 Troops, each: 1 (21 man) rifle/engineer Pl HQ sec, 1 LMG, 2 PIAT, 6 × Humber Scout Car, 4 (12 man) rifle/engineer secs, 4 LMG, 4 lorries

MAIN COMBAT ELEMENTS

Pretoria Regiment, Special Service Battalion Armoured Regiments, each:
RHQ (4 × Sherman II or V, 3 × Crusader OP, 1 × Sherman ARV Mk.1)
A, B Squadrons, each: Sqdn HQ (4 × Sherman II or V)
4 Troops, each: 3 × Sherman II or V
C Rhodesian Squadron: Sqdn HQ (4 × Sherman II or V)
4 Troops, each: 3 × Sherman II or V
D Reserve Squadron: spare tanks and spare crews
1 Scout Troop: Troop HQ (2 × Stuart IV)
3 Sections, each: 3 × Stuart IV, 3 × Daimler Scout Car

Prince Alfred's Guard Armoured Regiment
RHQ (4 × Sherman II or V, 3 × Crusader OP, 1 × Sherman ARV Mk.1)
A, B Squadrons each: Sqdn HQ (4 × Sherman II or V)
4 Troops, each: 3 × Sherman II or V
B Rhodesian Squadron: Sqdn HQ (4 × Sherman II or V)
4 Troops, each: 3 × Sherman II or V
1 Scout Troop: Troop HQ (2 × Stuart IV)
3 Sections, each: 3 × Stuart IV
D Reserve Squadron: Sqdn HQ (4 × Sherman II)
5 Troops, each 3 × Sherman II

Royal Natal Carabiniers, First City/Capetown Highlanders, Witwatersrand Rifles Infantry Battalions, each:
Btn HQ (3 rifle secs, 1 LMG, 2 lorries)
3 Companies, each: Coy HQ (1 rifle sec, 1 truck)
3 Platoons, each: 1 (5 man) rifle Pl HQ sec, 1 × 2" mortar, 1 PIAT
3 (6–8 man) rifle secs, 3 LMG, 2 lorries
1 Reserve Company, ex-SAAF personnel: Coy HQ (1 rifle sec, 1 truck)
3 Platoons, each: 4 (7 man) rifle secs, 4 LMG, 1 × 2" mortar, 1 PIAT, 2 lorries
1 Support Company: Coy HQ (1 rifle sec, 1 truck)
1 battery: 6 × 3" mortars, 7 × Universal Carriers
1 Platoon: 6 × 6pdr A/T guns, 6 × Carriers, 3 LMG
1 Platoon: 3 (5 man) rifle/engineer secs, 3 LMG, 3 trucks
1 Platoon: Pl HQ: 1 × Universal Carrier, 1 LMG, 1 × Daimler Scout Car
4 Sections, each: 3 × Carrier, 3 LMG, 1 × 2", 1 Boys, 1 (4 man) rifle sec

5th Btn Grenadier Guards, 3rd Btn Coldstream Guards, 1st Btn Scots Guards Infantry Battalions, each:
Btn HQ (4 rifle secs, 1 (8 man) sniper sec, 1 LMG, 2 lorries)
3 Companies, each: Coy HQ (1 (13 man) rifle sec, 1 truck)
3 Platoons, each: 1 (7 man) rifle Pl HQ sec, 1 × 2" mortar, 1 PIAT
3 (10 man) rifle secs, 3 LMG, 2 lorries
1 Support Company: Coy HQ (1 rifle sec, 1 truck)
1 battery: 6 × 3" mortars, 7 × Universal Carriers, 3 PIAT
1 Platoon: 3 (10 man) rifle secs, 1 (6 man) Pl HQ sec, 3–4 LMG, 1 PIAT, 1 × 2" mortar
1 Platoon: 2 (8 man) rifle/engineer secs, 1 (5 man) Pl HQ Sec, 3 LMG, 3 trucks
1 Platoon: 4 × Vickers MMG, 5 × Universal Carriers, 5 LMG, 1 × 2" mortar, 1 PIAT
1 Platoon: Pl HQ:1 × Universal Carrier, 1 LMG, 1 × Daimler Scout Car
3 Sections, each: 3 × Carrier, 3 LMG, 1 × 2" mortar, 1 PIAT,1 (6 man) rifle sec

Imperial Light Horse/Kimberley Motor Battalion (of Armoured Brigade)
Btn HQ (2 rifle secs, 4 trucks, 2 LMG)
3 Companies, each: Coy HQ (1 × Stuart III Kangaroo, 1 (6 man) rifle sec, 1 LMG, 1 PIAT)
1 Section: 2 × 3" mortars, 2 × Universal Carriers
2 Platoons, each: 1 × Stuart III Kangaroo Pl HQ, 3 trucks, 4 (6 man) rifle secs, 4 LMG, 1 × 2" mortar, 1 PIAT

1 Platoon: Pl HQ: 1 × Stuart III Kangaroo, 1 LMG
   3 Sections, each: 3 × Carrier, 3 LMG, 1 PIAT, 1 × 2" mortar, 1 (5 man) rifle sec
1 Platoon: 3 (8 man) rifle secs, 3 LMG, 1 PIAT, 1 × 2" mortar, 3 trucks (ex-SAAF personnel)
1 Support Company: Coy HQ (1 rifle sec, 1 truck, 1 × Universal Carrier)
   3 Platoons, each: 2 × 6pdr A/T guns, 2 trucks or Carriers, 1 LMG
   2 MG Platoons, each: 2 MMG, 2 × Universal Carriers

4th/13th Indian Frontier Force Infantry Battalion

Btn HQ (4 rifle secs, 1 LMG, 2 lorries)
4 Companies, each: Coy HQ (1 (13 man) rifle sec, 1 truck)
   3 Platoons, each: 1 (7 man) rifle Pl HQ sec, 1 × 2" mortar, 1 PIAT
     3 (10 man) rifle secs, 3 LMG, 2 lorries
1 Support Company: Coy HQ (1 rifle sec, 1 truck)
   1 battery: 6 × 3" mortars, 7 × Universal Carriers, 3 PIAT
   1 Platoon: 3 (10 man) rifle secs, 1 (6 man) Pl HQ sec, 3–4 LMG, 1 PIAT, 1 × 2" mortar
   1 Platoon: 2 (8 man) rifle/engineer secs, 1 (5 man) Pl HQ Sec, 3 LMG, 3 trucks
   1 Platoon: 4 × Vickers MMG, 5 × Universal Carriers, 5 LMG, 1 × 2" mortar, 1 PIAT
   1 Platoon: Pl HQ: 1 × Universal Carrier, 1 LMG, 1 × Daimler Scout Car
     3 Sections, each: 3 × Carrier, 3 LMG, 1 × 2", 1 PIAT, 1 (6 man) rifle sec

Natal Mounted Rifles Divisional Armoured Recce Regiment

RHQ (4 × Sherman II, 1 × Sherman ARV)
3 Squadrons, each: Sqdn HQ (4 × Sherman II)
   5 Troops, each: 2 × Sherman II, 2 × Stuart III
   1 Platoon: 4 (8 man) rifle secs, 2 lorries, 4 LMG, 1 × 2" mortar, 1 PIAT
1 Scout/Liaison Troop: Troop HQ (3 × Daimler Scout Cars)
   3 Sections, each: 3 × Daimler Scout Cars
1 AA Troop: 5 × Crusader II
1 attached Mortar Platoon, Royal Durban Light Infantry: 4 × 4.2" mortars, 8 × Carrier, 4 LMG

Notes
1. Radios were in all AFV, Carrier PHQs and other PHQs.
2. Infantry had Hawkins No.75 anti-tank grenades.
3. Stuart 'Kangaroo' were turretless Stuart III seized and used as HQ APCs.
4. The Division formed battlegroups as required. Attachments were not permanent.
5. Artillery OPs can be in Crusader OP or Stuart III Kangaroo or Daimler Scout Car or Priest OP.

2.14 SOUTH AFRICAN 6TH ARMOURED DIVISION, ITALY, NOVEMBER 1944–JANUARY 1945

The Division's main combat elements were:
   11th Armoured Brigade (Pretoria, Special Service Battalion, Prince Alfred's Guard Armoured Regiments, Imperial Light Horse Motor Battalion)
   12th Motorised Brigade (Royal Natal Carabiniers, First City/Capetown Highlanders, Witwatersrand Rifles, 4th/13th Indian Frontier Force infantry battalions)
   British 24th Guards Infantry Brigade (5th Btn Grenadier Guards, 3rd Btn Coldstream Guards, 1st Btn Scots Guards)
   Divisional Armoured Recce Regiment (Natal Mounted Rifles)
Troops are rated good morale and average training, with ex-South African Air Force personnel acting as infantry rated as average morale and average training. In practice the Division formed mixed brigades by cross-attaching one armoured regiment to each Infantry Brigade Group, leaving the Armoured Brigade Group with one Armoured Regiment and the Motor Battalion.

SUPPORT UNITS

Divisional Support

Included:
7th/23rd Medium Artillery Regiment:
   Regiment HQ (6 rifle secs, 4AALMG, 1 PIAT, 8 lorries, 4 OP Teams)
     2 Batteries, each: (4 rifle secs, 2 AALMG, 4 lorries)
     2 Troops, each: 4 × 5.5" guns, 4 lorries, radio van, 2 AALMG
1st/11th Anti-Tank Regiment:
   1 Battery: Battery HQ (1 rifle sec, 1 truck)
     2 Troops, each: 4 × 17pdr A/T guns, 4 trucks, 2 LMG
1st/12th Light AA Regiment, South African Air Force:
   2 Batteries, each: Battery HQ (1 rifle sec,1 truck)
     3 Troops, each 6 × 40mmL60 Bofors, 6 trucks
17th Field Park Squadron: Sqdn HQ (3 (12 man) rifle secs, 4 lorries, 5 LMG, 4 PIAT)
   1 Bridge Troop: 1 × 40t 80' Bailey Bridges in 15 × 3-ton lorries, 51 men
   1 Stores Section: 12 assault boats, 3 bulldozers, 3 tractors, 29 men
   1 Workshop Section: 44 men, recovery lorries

Attached Corps Support

178th South African Medium Artillery Regiment:
   Regiment HQ (6 rifle secs, 4AALMG, 1 PIAT, 8 lorries, 4 OP Teams)

2 Batteries, each: (4 rifle secs, 2 AALMG, 4 lorries)
    2 Troops, each: 4 × 5.5" guns, 4 lorries, radio van, 2 AALMG
76th South African Heavy AA Regiment:
    3 Batteries, each: Battery HQ (2 rifle secs, 4 trucks)
    2 Troops, each: 4 × 3.7" AA guns, 6 lorries

Brigade Support

11th Armoured Brigade Group HQ (7 × Sherman V-HQ, 6 × Crusader OP, 7 × Daimler S/C) with:
    1 Defence Troop: 4 × Sherman V
    1 Mortar Platoon, Royal Durban Light Infantry: 4 × 4.2" mortars, 8 × Universal Carrier, 4 LMG
    1 A/T Battery, 1st/11th A/T Regiment: Battery HQ (1 rifle sec, 2 × M3 halftrack)
        3 Troops, each: 4 × M10 Wolverine, 1 × Universal Carrier Pl HQ
    12th Field Engineer Squadron: Sqdn HQ (4 (11 man) rifle secs, 4 LMG, 2 PIAT, 3 lorries)
        3 Troops, each: 1 (21 man) rifle/engineer Pl HQ sec, 1 LMG, 2 PIAT, 6 × Humber Scout Car, 4 (12
            man) rifle/engineer secs, 4 LMG, 4 lorries
    4/22nd Field SP Artillery Regiment:
        3 Batteries, each: Battery HQ (4 rifle secs, 2 AALMG, 4 lorries, 1 PIAT)
            1 Troop: 4 × 105mm M7 Priest, radio truck, 2 AALMG, 1 PIAT
            1 Troop: 3 × 105mm M7 Priest, radio truck, 2 AALMG, 1 PIAT
12th Motorised Brigade Group HQ (6 rifle secs, 6 trucks, 2 LMG) with:
    1 A/T Battery, 1st/11th A/T Regiment: Battery HQ (1 rifle sec, 2 × M3 halftrack)
        3 Troops, each: 4 × M10 Wolverine, 1 × Universal Carrier Pl HQ
    Group A, Royal Durban Light Infantry
        Btn HQ (2 rifle secs, 2 lorries)
        1 MG Company: Coy HQ (1 rifle sec, 1 truck)
            3 Platoons, each: 4 × Vickers MMG, 5 × Universal Carrier
        1 Mortar Platoon: 4 × 4.2" mortars, 8 × Universal Carrier
    8th Field Engineer Squadron: Sqdn HQ (4 (11 man) rifle secs, 4 LMG, 2 PIAT, 3 lorries)
        3 Troops, each: 1 (21 man) rifle/engineer Pl HQ sec, 1 LMG, 2 PIAT, 6 × Humber Scout Car, 4 (12
            man) rifle/engineer secs, 4 LMG, 4 lorries
    1st/6th Field Artillery Regiment:
        3 Batteries, each: Battery HQ (4 rifle secs, 2 AALMG, 4 lorries)
            2 Troops, each: 4 × 25pdr field guns, 6 trucks, 2 AALMG, OP Team
24th British Guards Brigade Group HQ (6 rifle secs, 4 lorries, Air Liaison Team, 2 LMG) with:
    1 A/T Battery, 1st/11th A/T Regiment: Battery HQ (1 rifle sec, 1 truck)
        3 Troops, each: 4 × 17pdr A/T guns, 4 trucks, 2 LMG
    Group B, Royal Durban Light Infantry
        Btn HQ (2 rifle secs, 2 lorries)
        1 MG Company: Coy HQ (1 rifle sec, 1 truck)
            3 Platoons, each: 4 × Vickers MMG, 5 × Universal Carrier
        1 Mortar Platoon: 4 × 4.2" mortars, 8 × Universal Carrier
    166th Newfoundland Field Artillery Regiment
        3 Batteries, each: Battery HQ (4 rifle secs, 2 AALMG, 4 lorries)
            2 Troops, each: 4 × 25pdr field guns, 6 trucks, 2 AALMG, OP Team
8th British Field Engineer Squadron:
    Sqdn HQ (4 (11 man) rifle secs, 4 LMG, 2 PIAT, 3 lorries)
    3 Troops, each: 1 (21 man) rifle/engineer Pl HQ sec, 1 LMG, 2 PIAT, 6 × Humber Scout Car, 4 (12
        man) rifle/engineer secs, 4 LMG, 4 lorries

MAIN COMBAT ELEMENTS

Prince Alfred's Guard, Pretoria Regiment, Special Service Battalion Armoured Regiments, each:

RHQ (4 × Sherman II or V, 3 × Crusader OP, 1 × Sherman ARV Mk.1)
2 Squadrons, each: Sqdn HQ (4 × Sherman II or V)
    4 Troops, each: 1 × Sherman II or V, 1 × Sherman IIA (76mm)
1 Squadron (dismounted): Sqdn HQ (4 × Sherman V, 4 (5 man) SMG crew secs)
    4 Troops, each: 3 (5 man) SMG crew secs as infantry, muleteers and stretcher bearers
D Reserve Squadron: spare tanks and spare crews
1 Assault Troop: 6 × Sherman 1B(105mm)
1 Scout Troop: Troop HQ (2 × Stuart IV)
    3 Sections, each: 3 × Stuart IV, 3 × Daimler Scout Car

Royal Natal Carabiniers, First City/Capetown Highlanders, Witwatersrand Rifles Infantry Battalions, each:

Btn HQ (3 rifle secs, 1 LMG, 2 lorries)
3 Companies, each: Coy HQ (1 rifle sec, 1 truck)
    3 Platoons, each: 1 (5 man) rifle Pl HQ sec, 1 × 2" mortar, 1 PIAT
        3 (6–8 man) rifle secs, 3 LMG, 2 lorries
1 Reserve Company, ex-SAAF personnel: Coy HQ (1 rifle sec, 1 truck)
    3 Platoons, each: 4 (7 man) rifle secs, 4 LMG, 1 × 2" mortar, 1 PIAT, 2 lorries
1 Support Company: Coy HQ (1 rifle sec, 1 truck)

1 battery: 6 × 3" mortars, 7 × Universal Carriers
1 Platoon: 6 × 6pdr A/T guns, 6 × Carriers, 3 LMG
1 Platoon: 3 (5 man) rifle/engineer secs, 3 LMG, 3 trucks
1 Platoon: Pl HQ: 1 × Universal Carrier, 1 LMG, 1 × Daimler Scout Car
    4 Sections, each: 3 × Carrier, 3 LMG, 1 × 2", 1 Boys, 1 (4 man) rifle sec

5th Btn Grenadier Guards, 3rd Btn Coldstream Guards, 1st Btn Scots Guards Infantry Battalions, each:

Btn HQ (4 rifle secs, 1 (8 man) sniper sec, 1 LMG, 2 lorries)
3 Companies, each: Coy HQ (1 (13 man) rifle sec, 1 truck)
    3 Platoons, each: 1 (7 man) rifle Pl HQ sec, 1 × 2" mortar, 1 PIAT
        3 (10 man) rifle secs, 3 LMG, 2 lorries
1 Support Company: Coy HQ (1 rifle sec, 1 truck)
    1 battery: 6 × 3" mortars, 7 × Universal Carriers, 3 PIAT
    1 Platoon: 3 (10 man) rifle secs, 1 (6 man) Pl HQ sec, 3–4 LMG, 1 PIAT, 1 × 2" mortar
    1 Platoon: 2 (8 man) rifle/engineer secs, 1 (5 man) Pl HQ Sec, 3 LMG, 3 trucks
    1 Platoon: 4 × Vickers MMG, 5 × Universal Carriers, 5 LMG, 1 × 2" mortar, 1 PIAT
    1 Platoon: Pl HQ: 1 × Universal Carrier, 1 LMG, 1 × Daimler Scout Car
        3 Sections, each: 3 × Carrier, 3 LMG, 1 × 2", 1 PIAT, 1 (6 man) rifle sec

Imperial Light Horse/Kimberley Motor Battalion (of Armoured Brigade)

Btn HQ (2 rifle secs, 4 trucks, 2 LMG)
3 Companies, each: Coy HQ (1 × Stuart III Kangaroo, 1 (6 man) rifle sec, 1 LMG, 1 PIAT)
    1 Section: 2 × 3" mortars, 2 × Universal Carriers
    2 Platoons, each: 1 × Stuart III Kangaroo Pl HQ, 3 trucks, 4 (6 man) rifle secs, 4 LMG, 1 × 2" mortar, 1 PIAT
    1 Platoon: Pl HQ: 1 × Stuart III Kangaroo, 1 LMG
    3 Sections, each: 3 × Carrier, 3 LMG, 1 PIAT, 1 × 2" mortar, 1 (5 man) rifle sec
    1 Platoon: 3 (8 man) rifle secs, 3 LMG, 1 PIAT, 1 × 2" mortar, 3 trucks (ex-SAAF personnel)
1 Support Company: Coy HQ (1 rifle sec, 1 truck, 1 × Universal Carrier)
    3 Platoons, each: 2 × 6pdr A/T guns, 2 trucks or Carriers, 1 LMG
    2 MG Platoons, each: 2 MMG, 2 × Universal Carriers

4th/13th Indian Frontier Force Infantry Battalion

Btn HQ (4 rifle secs, 1 LMG, 2 lorries)
4 Companies, each: Coy HQ (1 (13 man) rifle sec, 1 truck)
    3 Platoons, each: 1 (7 man) rifle Pl HQ sec, 1 × 2" mortar, 1 PIAT
        3 (10 man) rifle secs, 3 LMG, 2 lorries
1 Support Company: Coy HQ (1 rifle sec, 1 truck)
    1 battery: 6 × 3" mortars, 7 × Universal Carriers, 3 PIAT
    1 Platoon: 3 (10 man) rifle secs, 1 (6 man) Pl HQ sec, 3–4 LMG, 1 PIAT, 1 × 2" mortar
    1 Platoon: 2 (8 man) rifle/engineer secs, 1 (5 man) Pl HQ Sec, 3 LMG, 3 trucks
    1 Platoon: 4 × Vickers MMG, 5 × Universal Carriers, 5 LMG, 1 × 2" mortar, 1 PIAT
    1 Platoon: Pl HQ: 1 × Universal Carrier, 1 LMG, 1 × Daimler Scout Car
        3 Sections, each: 3 × Carrier, 3 LMG, 1 × 2" mortar, 1 PIAT,1 (6 man) rifle sec

Natal Mounted Rifles Divisional Armoured Recce Regiment

RHQ (4 × Sherman II, 1 × Sherman ARV)
3 Squadrons, each: Sqdn HQ (4 × Sherman II)
    1 Troop: 2 × Sherman II, 2 × Stuart III
    3 Troops, each: 4 (4 man) SMG crew secs as muleteers and stretcher bearers
    1 Platoon: 4 (8 man) rifle secs, 2 lorries, 4 LMG, 1 × 2" mortar, 1 PIAT
1 Scout/Liaison Troop: Troop HQ (3 × Daimler Scout Cars)
    3 Sections, each: 3 × Daimler Scout Cars
1 Assault Troop: 6 × Sherman 1B(105mm)
1 attached Mortar Platoon, Royal Durban Light Infantry: 4 × 4.2" mortars, 8 × Carrier, 4 LMG

Notes
1. Radios were in all AFV, Carrier PHQs and other PHQs.
2. Infantry had Hawkins No.75 anti-tank grenades.
3. Stuart 'Kangaroo' were turretless Stuart III seized and used as HQ APCs.
4. The Division formed battlegroups as required, attachments were not permanent.
5. Artillery OPs could be in Crusader OP or Stuart III Kangaroo or Daimler Scout Car or Priest OP.
6. The Division fought in the Apennine mountains, usually one brigade at a time in action with all the division's artillery available. Due to the terrain the armoured regiments dismounted many tank crews as infantry, muleteers and stretcher-bearers.
7. In January 1945 each armoured squadron can add one Firefly Vc

2.15 SOUTH AFRICAN 6TH ARMOURED DIVISION, ITALY, FEBRUARY–MAY 1945

The Division's main combat elements were:
    11th Armoured Brigade (Pretoria, Special Service Battalion, Prince Alfred's Guard Armoured Regiments, 1st Btn, US 135th Regimental Combat Team)
    12th Motorised Brigade (Royal Durban Light Infantry, First City/Capetown Highlanders, Witwatersrand Rifles, 4th/13th Indian Frontier Force infantry battalions)

13th Motorised Brigade (Royal Natal Carabiniers, Natal Mounted Rifles, Imperial Light Horse infantry battalions) Troops are rated good morale and average training, with Americans as average morale and average training. In practice the Division formed mixed brigades by cross-attaching one armoured Squadron and an Assault Troop to each Motorised Brigade Group, attaching one infantry company of the Imperial Light Horse to each Armoured Regiment, and the Pretoria Armoured Regiment carrying out recce duties previously done by the Natal Mounted Rifles.

SUPPORT UNITS

Divisional Support

Included:
7th/23rd Medium Artillery Regiment:
    Regiment HQ (6 rifle secs, 4AALMG, 1 PIAT, 8 lorries, 4 OP Teams)
    2 Batteries, each: (4 rifle secs, 2 AALMG, 4 lorries)
        2 Troops, each: 4 × 5.5" guns, 4 lorries, radio van, 2 AALMG
17th Field Park Squadron: Sqdn HQ (3 (12 man) rifle secs, 4 lorries, 5 LMG, 4 PIAT)
    1 Bridge Troop: 3 × 40t 80' Bailey Bridges in 15 × 3-ton lorries, 51 men
    1 Stores Section: 12 assault boats, 3 bulldozers, 3 tractors, 29 men
    1 Workshop Section: 44 men, recovery lorries
3rd/56th South African Heavy AA Battery: Battery HQ (2 rifle secs, 4 trucks)
    2 Troops, each: 4 × 3.7" AA guns, 6 lorries (trained for ground fire and indirect fire)

Attached Corps Support

American 178th Field Artillery Group
    3 battalions, each: 3 batteries, each; 4 × 105mm M2A1 howitzers, 2 OP Teams in Jeeps
    1 battalion: 3 batteries, each 4 × 155mm M1 howitzers, OP Team in Jeep
British 12th Battery, 54th Super Heavy Artillery Regiment: 4 × 8" M1 or 240mm M1 guns, static

Brigade Support

11th Armoured Brigade Group HQ (7 × Sherman V-HQ, 6 × Sherman V-OP, 7 × Daimler S/C) with:
    1 Defence Troop: 3 × Sherman V
    1 Bridge Troop: 3 × Valentine AVLB?
    3rd/24th A/T Battery, 1st/11th A/T Regiment: Battery HQ (1 rifle sec, 2 × M3 halftrack)
        3 Troops, each: 4 × M10 Wolverine, 1 × Universal Carrier Pl HQ
    8th Field Engineer Squadron: Sqdn HQ (4 (11 man) rifle secs, 4 LMG, 2 PIAT, 3 lorries)
        3 Troops, each: 1 (21 man) rifle/engineer Pl HQ sec, 1 LMG, 2 PIAT, 6 × Humber Scout Car, 4 (12 man) rifle/engineer secs, 4 LMG, 4 lorries
    4/22nd Field SP Artillery Regiment:
        3 Batteries, each: Battery HQ (4 rifle secs, 2 AALMG, 4 lorries, 1 PIAT)
        2 Troops, each: 4 × 25pdr Sexton, 1 × M3 halftrack, 2 AALMG, 1 PIAT
12th Motorised Brigade Group HQ (6 rifle secs, 6 trucks, 2 LMG) with:
    2nd/23rd A/T Battery, 1st/11th A/T Regiment: Battery HQ (1 rifle sec, 2 × M3 halftrack)
        3 Troops, each: 4 × M10 Wolverine, 1 × M3 halftrack Pl HQ
    12th Field Engineer Squadron: Sqdn HQ (4 (11 man) rifle secs, 4 LMG, 2 PIAT, 3 lorries)
        3 Troops, each: 1 (21 man) rifle/engineer Pl HQ sec, 1 LMG, 2 PIAT, 6 × Humber Scout Car, 4 (12 man) rifle/engineer secs, 4 LMG, 4 lorries
    1st/6th Field Artillery Regiment:
        3 Batteries, each: Battery HQ (4 rifle secs, 2 AALMG, 4 lorries)
        2 Troops, each: 4 × 25pdr field guns, 6 trucks, 2 AALMG, OP Team
13th Motorised Brigade Group HQ (6 rifle secs, 6 trucks, 2 LMG) with:
    15th Field Artillery Regiment:
        3 Batteries, each: Battery HQ (4 rifle secs, 2 AALMG, 4 lorries)
        2 Troops, each: 4 × 25pdr field guns, 6 trucks, 2 AALMG, OP Team
    5th Field Engineer Squadron: Sqdn HQ (4 (11 man) rifle secs, 4 LMG, 2 PIAT, 3 lorries)
        3 Troops, each: 1 (21 man) rifle/engineer Pl HQ sec, 1 LMG, 2 PIAT, 6 × Humber Scout Car, 4 (12 man) rifle/engineer secs, 4 LMG, 4 lorries
    1st/22nd A/T Battery, 1st/11th A/T Regiment: Battery HQ (1 rifle sec, 1 × M3 Halftrack)
        3 Troops, each: 4 × 17pdr A/T guns, 5 × M3 halftracks, 2 LMG

MAIN COMBAT ELEMENTS

Prince Alfred's Guard, Special Service Battalion Armoured Regiments, each:

RHQ (4 × Sherman II or V, 3 × Crusader or Sherman OP, 1 × Sherman ARV Mk.1)
3 Squadrons, each: Sqdn HQ (4 × Sherman IIA)
    4 Troops, each: 3 × Sherman IIA (76mm)
    1 Troop: 3 × Sherman Firefly Vc
D Reserve Squadron: spare tanks and spare crews
1 Assault Troop: 6 × Sherman 1B(105mm)
1 Scout Troop: Troop HQ (2 × Stuart III Recce)
    3 Sections, each: 3 × Stuart III Recce, 3 × Daimler Scout Car

Pretoria Regiment Armoured & Recce Regiment

RHQ (4 × Sherman II or V, 3 × Crusader or Sherman OP, 3 × Sherman ARV)

3 Squadrons, each: Sqdn HQ (2 × Sherman IIA)
    4 Troops, each: 3 × Sherman IIA(76mm)
    1 Troop: 3 × Sherman Firefly Vc
    1 Recce Platoon: 3 (8 man) rifle secs, 6 LMG, 3 PIAT, 3 × M3 halftracks
D Squadron: Sqdn HQ (2 × Sherman IIA)
    4 Troops, each: 3 × Sherman IIA (76mm)
    1 Troop: 3 × Sherman Firefly Vc
1 Recce Squadron: Sqdn HQ (3 × Stuart III or V)
    3 Troops, each: 3 × Stuart III or V
1 Assault Troop: 6 × Sherman 1B(105mm)
1 Scout/Liaison Troop: Troop HQ (2 × Daimler Scout Car)
    3 Sections, each: 3 × Daimler Scout Car

Natal Mounted Rifles, Royal Durban Light Infantry, Royal Natal Carabiniers, First City/Capetown Highlanders, Witwatersrand Rifles, Imperial Light Horse Infantry Battalions, each:

Btn HQ (2 rifle secs, 1 LMG, 1 (8 man) sniper sec, 4 lorries)
3 Companies, each: Coy HQ (1 rifle sec, 1 truck)
    3 Platoons, each: 1 (5 man) rifle Pl HQ sec, 1 × 2" mortar, 1 PIAT
        3 (8 man) rifle secs, 3 LMG, 2 lorries
1 Support Company: Coy HQ (1 rifle sec, 1 truck)
    1 battery: 6 × 3" mortars, 7 × Universal Carriers, 3 PIAT
    1 battery: 4 × 4.2" mortars, 9 × Universal Carriers, 4 LMG
    1 Platoon: 6 × 6pdr A/T guns, 6 × Carriers, 3 LMG
    1 Platoon: 4 × Vickers MMG, 5 × Universal Carrier
    1 Platoon: 3 (5 man) rifle/engineer secs, 3 LMG, 3 trucks or Universal Carriers
    1 Platoon: Pl HQ:1 × Universal Carrier, 1 LMG, 1 × Daimler Scout Car
        2–4 Sections, each: 3 × Carrier, 3 LMG, 1 × 2", 1 PIAT, 1 (6 man) rifle sec

4th/13th Indian Frontier Force Infantry Battalion

Btn HQ (4 rifle secs, 1 LMG, 1 (8 man) sniper sec, 4 lorries)
4 Companies, each: Coy HQ (1 (13 man) rifle sec, 1 truck)
    3 Platoons, each: 1 (7 man) rifle Pl HQ sec, 1 × 2" mortar, 1 PIAT, 3 (10 man) rifle secs, 3 LMG, 2 lorries
1 Support Company: Coy HQ (1 rifle sec, 1 truck)
    1 battery: 6 × 3" mortars, 7 × Universal Carriers, 3 PIAT
    1 Platoon: 3 (10 man) rifle secs, 1 (6 man) Pl HQ sec, 3–4 LMG, 1 PIAT, 1 × 2" mortar
    1 Platoon: 2 (8 man) rifle/engineer secs, 1 (5 man) Pl HQ Sec, 3 LMG, 3 trucks
    1 Platoon: 4 × Vickers MMG, 5 × Universal Carriers, 5 LMG, 1 × 2" mortar, 1 PIAT
    1 Platoon: Pl HQ: 1 × Universal Carrier, 1 LMG, 1 × Daimler Scout Car
        3 Sections, each: 3 × Carrier, 3 LMG, 1 × 2", 1 PIAT, 1 (6 man) rifle sec

American 1st Battalion, 135th Regimental Combat Team

Btn HQ (3 rifle secs, 3 Jeeps, 4 trucks)
3 Companies, each: Coy HQ (2 (8 man) rifle secs, 3 × 2.36" bazookas)
    3 platoons, each: 3 (12 man) rifle secs, 3 BAR, 1 (4 man) Pl HQ SMG sec
    1 platoon: 2 MMG teams, 1 × .50" HMG team, 3 × 60mm mortar teams, 1 (4 man) Pl HQ sec
1 Support Company: Coy HQ: 2 (8 man) rifle/carbine secs
    1 battery: 6 × 81mm M1 mortars, 3 × 2.36" bazookas
    1 platoon: 6 MMG teams, 3 × .50" HMG teams
1 Anti-Tank Platoon: 3 × 57mm M1 A/T guns, 3 trucks
1 Mine Platoon: 2 (12 man) carbine secs, mines
1 Intelligence & Recce Platoon: 2 (12 man) rifle secs, 2 BAR
1 Attached Tank Company: Coy HQ (2 × M4A3 Sherman, 2 × M4A3 (105mm)
    3 platoons, each: 3 × M4A3 Sherman, 2 × M4A3 (76mm) Sherman
Notes
1.   Radios were in all AFV, Carrier PHQs and other PHQs.
2.   Infantry had Hawkins No.75 anti-tank grenades.
3.   Artillery OPs could be in Crusader OP or Stuart III Kangaroo or Daimler Scout Car or Priest OP or Sherman OP.
4.   Organisation of the attached American forces is not confirmed.

2.16 BRITISH 8TH ARMOURED BRIGADE, TUNISIA, MARCH–JULY 1943

The Brigade's main combat elements were:
    3rd Royal Tank Regiment
    Nottinghamshire Yeomanry Armoured Regiment
    Staffordshire Yeomanry Armoured Regiment
    1st Battalion, Buffs Motor Battalion (up to June 16th 1943)
    7th Battalion, Rifle Brigade Motor Battalion (June 17th 1943+)

SUPPORT UNITS

Brigade Support

8th Armoured Brigade HQ (2 × Stuart-HQ, 3 × Sherman II, 1 × ACV, 3 × Daimler Scout Car) with:

111th Field Artillery Regiment
    3 Batteries, each: Battery HQ (2 rifle secs, 2 trucks radio van, 4 AALMG, 3 OP Teams)
        2 Troops, each: 4 × 25pdr field guns, 4 trucks, radio truck, 2 AALMG

MAIN COMBAT ELEMENTS

3rd Royal Tank Regiment

RHQ (1 × Crusader II, 3 × Sherman II)
A Squadron: Sqdn HQ (2 × Crusader II, 2 × Crusader IICS)
    4 Troops, each: 3 × Crusader III
B Squadron: Sqdn HQ (1 × M3 Lee)
    4 Troops, each: 3 × Sherman II
C Squadron: Sqdn HQ (1 × Sherman III)
    3 Troops, each: 3 × Sherman II
    1 Troop: 3 × Sherman III
Recce Troop: Troop HQ (1 × Marmon-Herrington II)
    3 Sections, each: 3 × Marmon-Herrington II

3rd Royal Tank Regiment (July 1943+)

RHQ (4 × Sherman II/III)
3 Squadrons, each: Sqdn HQ (4 × Sherman II/III)
    4 Troops, each: 3 × Sherman II/III
1 Recce Troop: Troop HQ (1 × Universal Carrier)
    3 Sections, each: 3 × Universal Carriers
    2 Sections, each: 3 × Daimler Scout Cars

Nottinghamshire Yeomanry, Staffordshire Yeomanry Armoured Regiments, each:

RHQ (3 × Crusader II, 1 × Sherman II)
1 Recce Troop: Troop HQ (1 × Daimler Scout Car)
    3 Sections, each: 3 × Daimler Scout Car
1 Squadron: Sqdn HQ (2 × Crusader II, 2 × Crusader IICS)
    4 Troops, each: 3 × Crusader III
    1 Troop: 3 × Crusader II
1 Squadron: Sqdn HQ (3 × Sherman II)
    4 Troops, each: 3 × Sherman II
1 Squadron: Sqdn HQ (3 × Sherman II or 1 × Grant I, 1 × Crusader II)
    4 Troops, each: 3 × Sherman II or 3 × Grant I

1st Battalion, Buffs Motor Battalion

Btn HQ (2 rifle secs, 2 trucks)
3 Companies, each: Coy HQ (1 rifle sec, 1 × 2" mortar, 2 trucks)
    1 section: 2 × 3" mortars, 2 × Universal Carrier
    2 platoons, each: 4 (8 man) rifle secs, 3 LMG, 1 × 2" mortar, 4 trucks
    1 platoon: 4 × Vickers MMG, 4 × Universal Carrier or trucks
    1 platoon: Pl HQ: 1 × Universal Carrier, 1 LMG, 1 × Daimler Scout Car)
        3 Sections, each: 3 × Carrier, 3 LMG, 1 Boys, 1 × 2" mortar, 1 rifle sec
1 Anti-tank Company: Coy HQ (1 rifle sec, 1 truck)
    4 platoons, each: 4 × 6pdr portees, 2 LMG

Notes
1. Radios were in all tanks and armoured cars, and all other Pl HQs.
2. Infantry sections had Hawkins 75 anti-tank grenades.
3. The Brigade saw action in Tunisia under the New Zealand Corps HQ.
4. The Stuart-HQ is a turretless command tank variant.
5. The Brigade stayed in North Africa until November 1943, being in Egypt from September 1943.
6. Artillery OP was in Universal Carrier-OP, turretless Marmon-Herrington or Stuart III tank.
7. Marmon-Herringtons were in poor condition, with only 1 MG as armament.

2.17 EGYPTIAN HOME DEFENCE FORCES, EGYPT, 1939–1942

In 1939 the Egyptian Army's main combat elements were:
    1st Egyptian Infantry Brigade (3 Infantry Battalions)
    2nd Egyptian Infantry Brigade (3 Infantry Battalions)
    3rd Egyptian Infantry Brigade (3 Infantry Battalions)
    Frontier Force
    1 Cavalry Armoured Regiment
    1 Cavalry Mechanised Regiment (later called Light Car Regiment)
    2 Machine Gun Battalions
    1 Royal Guard Regiment
Troops are rated bad morale and poor training, unless fighting the British, when they raise to average morale! The Frontier Force and AA Batteries are rated average morale and training.

By 1940 the Egyptian Army's main combat elements were:
    1st Egyptian Infantry Brigade, Cairo (2 Rifle Battalions, 1 Machine Gun Battalion)

2nd Egyptian Infantry Brigade, Alexandria (2 Infantry Battalions)
3rd Egyptian Infantry Brigade, Port Sudan (2? Infantry Battalions)
Frontier Force
1 Royal Guard Regiment
1 Cavalry Armoured Regiment
2 Independent Infantry Battalions
1st Egyptian MG Brigade, Mersa Matruh (2 Machine Gun Battalions)
Egyptian Mobile Force, Mersa Matruh (Light Car Regiment)

Troops are rated bad morale and poor training, unless fighting the British, when they raise to average morale! The Frontier Force and AA Batteries are rated average morale and training.

SUPPORT UNITS 1939
Included:
2 Cavalry Squadrons (1937–1938): Sqdn HQ (2 rifle secs, horses, sabres)
  3 Troops, each: 1 (9 man) rifle Pl HQ sec, 2 Lewis LMG, 1 Boys, horses
     4 (8 man) rifle secs, horses, sabres
4 Mule Batteries, each: Battery HQ (2 rifle secs, 1 truck, 1 car, horses, Obsolete FC)
  2 Troops, each: 4 × 3.7" pack howitzers, pack mules
1 Motor Machine Gun Battery: Battery HQ (2 rifle secs, 2 trucks, 1car)
  3 Troops, each: 4 × Vickers MMG, 4 trucks, 2 LMG
1 Howitzer Battery: Battery HQ (2 rifle secs, 4 trucks, Assigned FC)
  2 Troops, each: 4 × 3.7" pack howitzers on lorries, 1 radio van, 2 LMG
1 Field Artillery Battery: Battery HQ (2 rifle secs, 2 Lewis AAMG, 2 Boys, 4 trucks)
  2 Troops, each: 4 × 25pdr Mk.1 field guns, 6 trucks, 2 AAMG, 1 Boys
1 Medium Artillery Battery: Battery HQ (4 rifle secs, 4 lorries, 2 AAMG, 2 Boys)
  2 Troops, each: 4 × 6" 26cwt howitzers, 6 lorries, 2 LMG
1 Anti-tank Regiment:
  1 A/T Battery: Battery HQ (1 rifle sec, 1 truck)
    3 Troops, each: 4 × 2pdr A/T guns, 4 trucks, 2 LMG
  1 A/T Battery: Battery HQ (1 rifle sec, 1 truck)
    3 Troops, each: 4 × 2pdr portees, 2 LMG
1 Engineer Company: Coy HQ (2 rifle secs, 2 LMG, 2 Boys, 2 lorries)
  3 Sections, each: 4 (12 man) rifle/engineer secs
1 Garrison Artillery Company (unknown equipment)

SUPPORT UNITS 1940

Corps Support
Included:
1 Engineer Company: Coy HQ (2 rifle secs, 2 LMG, 2 Boys, 2 lorries)
  3 Sections, each: 4 (12 man) rifle/engineer secs
2 Field Artillery Batteries, each: Battery HQ (4 rifle secs, 3 lorries, 1 radio van, Assigned FC) 2 Troops, each: 4 ×
  18pdr Mk.IV or 25pdr Mk.I field guns, 4 trucks, radio truck
  1 Medium Artillery Battery: Battery HQ (4 rifle secs, 4 lorries, Assigned FC)
    2 Troops, each: 4 × 60pdr or 6" 26cwt howitzers, 4 lorries, radio van, 1 MG
1 Anti-tank Regiment:
  1 Anti-tank Battery: Battery HQ (1 rifle sec, 1 truck)
    3 Troops, each: 4 × 37mm Bofors A/T guns, 4 trucks, 1 LMG
  1 Anti-tank Battery: Battery HQ (1 rifle sec, 1 truck)
    3 Troops, each: 4 × 2pdr A/T guns, 4 trucks, 2 LMG
Alexandria Coastal Artillery Detachment: 4 × 6" guns, 4 × 4" coastal guns
Suez AA Troop: 1 Section: 2 × 40mmL60 Bofors 2 trucks
  1 Section: 1 × 3.7" AA gun
  1 Section: 6 × searchlights
1 AA Battery: Battery HQ (1 rifle sec, 1 lorry)
  2 Troops, each: 4 × 40mmL60 Bofors, 4 trucks
3 Fighter Flights, each: 4 × Gladiator Mk.1
3 Fighter Flights, each: 4 × Hawker Hart
6 Army Co-Operation Flights, each: 4 × Lysander or Percival Q-6
3 Army Co-Operation Flights, each: 3 × Blenheim I or Avro-Anson
6 Fighter Flights, each: 4 × Hurricane (1942+)
3 Fighter Flights, each: 4 × Tomahawk IIB (1942+)

Brigade Support 1940
1st Egyptian Infantry Brigade HQ (2 rifle secs, 1 car, 2 lorries) with:
  1st Egyptian Light Artillery Regiment:
    3 Batteries, each: 1 Troop: 4 × 3.7" pack howitzers, trucks or pack camels
  2nd Egyptian AA Regiment:
    1 Battery: Battery HQ (2 rifle secs, 1 lorry)
      2 Troops, each: 4 × 3.7" AA guns, 4 lorries

2 Batteries, each: Battery HQ (2 rifle secs, 1 lorry)
2 Troops, each: 4 × 3" 20cwt AA, 4 lorries
1 Searchlight Detachment: 16 × searchlights
2nd Egyptian Infantry Brigade HQ (2 rifle secs, 1 car, 2 lorries) with:
1st Egyptian AA "Brigade":
2 Batteries, each: Battery HQ (2 rifle secs, 1 lorry)
2 Troops, each: 4 × 3" 20cwt AA, 4 lorries
1st Egyptian Searchlight Regiment: 24 × searchlights
3rd Egyptian Infantry Brigade HQ (2 rifle secs, 1 car, 2 lorries) with:
1 Coastal Artillery Battery (Port Sudan)
1st Egyptian Machine Gun Brigade (2 rifle secs, 1 car, 2 trucks)

MAIN COMBAT ELEMENTS

Royal Guard Regiment

RHQ (4 rifle secs, 4 trucks, 3 cars)
1 Guard Cavalry Squadron: Sqdn HQ (2 rifle secs, horses, sabres)
3 Troops, each: 1 (9 man) rifle Pl HQ sec, 2 Lewis LMG, 1 Boys, horses
4 (8 man) rifle secs, horses, sabres
1 Guard Infantry Battalion (as Infantry Battalion, below)
1 Motorcycle Squadron: Sqdn HQ (3 rifle secs, 2 Boys, 2 trucks, 10 motorcycles)
3 Troops, each: 3 rifle secs, 3 LMG, 1 Boys, 1 × 2" mortar, 11 × M/C Combinations

Frontier Force

Force HQ (2 rifle secs, 3 trucks, 1 car)
5 Border Recce Squadrons, each: Sqdn HQ (1 rifle sec, horses)
3 platoons, each: 1 (6 man) rifle Pl HQ sec
3 (8 man) rifle secs, 4 × Ford pickup trucks
1 platoon: 1 (6 man) rifle Pl HQ sec, 1 Lewis MG
3 (8 man) rifle secs, 3 Lewis MG, 4 Ford pickup trucks

Egyptian Mobile Force

Group HQ (4 rifle secs, 5 trucks, 1 car, 2 AALMG?)
1 Light Tank Squadron: Sqdn HQ (3 × Vickers VIB)
1 Troop: 3 × Vickers VIB
1 Troop: 4 × Vickers Medium Mk.IIA
1 Light Howitzer Battery: Battery HQ (4 rifle secs, 3 lorries, 1 radio van)
2 Troops, each: 4 × 3.7" pack howitzers, trucks or pack camels
1 Anti-tank Battery: Battery HQ (1 rifle sec, 1 truck)
3 Troops, each: 4 × 2pdr portees 1 LMG
1 Machine Gun Company: Coy HQ (2 rifle secs, 2 trucks)
3 platoons, each: 4 × Vickers MMG, 4 trucks

1 Light Car Regiment

RHQ (4 rifle secs, 4 trucks, 2 cars)
3 Squadrons, each: Sqdn HQ (2 rifle secs, 2 trucks)
3 Troops, each: 1 (9 man) rifle Pl HQ sec, 2 Lewis LMG, 1 Boys, 2 cars, 4 (8 man) rifle secs, 4 Ford pickup
trucks

Cavalry Armoured Regiment

RHQ (4 × Vickers VIB)
1 Tank Squadron: Sqdn HQ (2 × Vickers Medium II)
2 Troops, each: 4 × Vickers Medium II
1 Tank Squadron: Sqdn HQ (3 × Vickers VIB)
2 Troops, each: 3 × Vickers VIB
2 Tank Training Units, each: Sqdn HQ (1 × Vickers Light Mk.II or III)
3 Troops, each: 3 × Vickers Light Mk.II or III

Egyptian Infantry Battalion, Rifle Battalion

Btn HQ (4 rifle secs)
4 Companies, each: Coy HQ (2 rifle secs)
3 platoons, each: 1 (6 man) rifle Pl HQ sec,
1 (10 man) rifle sec, 2 Lewis MG
3 (10 man) rifle secs
0–1 Mortar Section: 2 × 3" mortars, 2 trucks (1942+)

Machine Gun Battalion

Btn HQ (4 rifle secs, 2 lorries, 1 car)
3 Companies, each: Coy HQ (2 rifle secs, 2 trucks)
3 platoons, each: 4 × Vickers MMG, 2 trucks or pack camels

Notes
1. Radios were in Btn HQs and above.
2. Infantry had no A/T grenades.

3.   Brigade HQs were administrative only, and had no cohesive command function. The British planned to take over brigade command and control, if it was needed.

4.   Egyptian forces can only be used in defence of Cairo and the Suez canal, where they come under British command. The Frontier Force and Mobile Force were deployed outside this area, towards the Libyan border, but withdrew from the border before being engaged by the Italian advance in 1940.

5.   This list can be classed as Army level support for Commonwealth forces operating in the desert during 1940–42 if defending Cairo or the Suez.

6.   In late 1942 the Light Car Regiment was re-equipped with 38 × Scout Cars of some sort, and infantry received 298 Bren LMG, enough for 2 per platoon.

2.18 BRITISH GARRISON, ADEN, 1939–1945

MAIN COMBAT ELEMENTS 1939

2nd/th Mahratta Light Infantry Indian Infantry Battalion
    Btn HQ (4 rifle secs)
    3 Companies, each: Coy HQ (2 rifle secs)
        4 platoons, each: 1 (6 man) rifle Pl HQ secretary, 1 (10 man) rifle sec, 1 LMG, 3 (10 man) rifle secs
    1 MG Company: Coy HQ (1 rifle sec)
        2 platoons, each: 4 × Vickers MMG, pack mules
8th AA Battery: 1 Detachment: 2 × 3.7" AA guns, 2 lorries
9th Heavy Coastal Artillery Battery: 2 Troops, each: 2 × 6" guns
20th Fortress Engineer Company: 3 Sections
1 RAF Independent Armoured Car Flight: 12x Rolls-Royce/Fords on armoured cars, 30cwt trucks
Aden Protectorate Levies: Coy HQ: 2 British officers, 8 mules,
    2 Camel Sections, each: 2 (12 man) rifle sections, camels
    5 Platoons, each: one Company of Arab Infantry (approx 150 men)
    1 MG Troop: 4 × Vickers MMG, 4 trucks
    1 AA Troop: 2?x 40mmL60 Bofors, October 1939+

Troops rated average training and morale.

8th Squadron RAF: Vincent anti-submarine bombers
11th, 39th Squadrons, RAF: Blenheim bombers
94th Squadron, RAF: Gladiator fighters
203rd Ground Recce Squadron: later Wellingtons
Government Guards Unit: 100 experienced Arabs in local patrols and border posts, rifles, camel patrols, car patrol, in seven man secs.
Troops rated good morale, poor training.

Tribal Guards
Lahej Trained Force
Kathiri Armed Constabulary (1939–1945): 200 Arabs, 6.5mm Italian rifles, Austrian 8mm carbines
Mukalla Regular Army (1937+):
    400 regular infantry with Lee-Enfields in 1 Infantry Battalion
    1000 irregulars with .45" Martini-Henry single shot black powder breech loading rifles
    1 gun section: 2 × 2.75" mountain guns, pack camels
    1 Band
    1 Bodyguard Lancer Troop: camels, lances
Hadhrami Bedouin Legion (1940–1945): 50+ local Arabs in 4 forts, rifles

MAIN COMBAT ELEMENTS 1940+

As 1939, but add:
1401st Pioneer Company (December 1940–May 1941): 570 Arab labourers, unarmed
1402nd Pioneer Company (February–April 1941): 185 unarmed Arab labourers, 4 British officers/NCOs
2nd/5th Mahratta Light Infantry left August 1940
1st/2nd Punjab Regiment Infantry Battalion (May 1940+)
3rd/15th Punjab Regiment Infantry Battalion (July 1940+)
2nd Btn, Black Watch Infantry Battalion (July–August 1940)
1st Btn, North Rhodesia Regiment (August–September 1940)
3rd/7th Rajput Regiment Infantry Battalion (August–September 1940) (December 1942–May 1944)
2nd/10th Ghurka Rifles Battalion (May–December 1942)
3rd/1st Punjab Regiment Infantry Battalion (November 1942+)
Mewar Bhopal Infantry (ISF) Battalion (December 1942–May 1944)
1st Rampur Infantry (ISF) Battalion (May–November 1944), each:
    Btn HQ (4 rifle secs, 1 LMG)
    4 Companies, each: Coy HQ (1 (13 man) rifle sec)
        3 platoons, each: 1 (6 man) rifle Pl HQ sec, 1 Boys, 1 × 2" mortar, 3 (10 man) rifle secs, 3 Bren LMG
    1 Support Company: Coy HQ (1 rifle sec)
        1 platoon: 4 × Bren AALMG, 4 trucks, 4 Boys A/T Rifles
        1 platoon: 2 × 3" mortars, 2 trucks or 40 pack mules
        1 platoon: 3 (6 man) rifle/engineer secs, 1 stores truck
        1 platoon: Pl HQ (1 × Universal Carrier, 1 LMG)

3 Sections, each: 3 × Carriers, 3 LMG, 1 Boys, 1 × 2" mortar, 1 rifle sec
1st Hyderabad Lancers (ISF) Armoured Car Regiment (November 1944–December 1945)
RHQ (4 × Humber III armoured cars)
3 Squadrons, each: Sqdn HQ (2 × Humber III, 1 × Daimler II)
5 Troops, each: 2 × Humber III, 1 × Daimler II
1 Liaison Troop: Troop HQ (2 × HUmber Scout Cars)
3 Sections, each: 3 × Humber Scout Cars
Somaliland Camel Corps (August–September 1940) (see Vol.1 pg.52)
Bikanir Ganga Risala (ISF) Camel Unit (September 1940–1942)
5th Heavy Artillery Regiment (October 1939–March 1944)
15th AA Battery, Hong Kong Singapore Royal Artillery (October 1939+)
2 Troops, each: 2 guns
23rd AA Battery, Hong Kong Singapore Royal Artillery (March 1940+): 2 Troops, each: 4 guns
24th Searchlight Battery, Hong Kong Singapore Royal Artillery (April 1940+)
1st Hong Kong Singapore Heavy AA Regiment (March 1944–1945):
15th, 23rd, 24th Heavy AA Batteries
18th Indian Mountain Artillery Battery (October 1940+): 4 × 3.7" pack howitzers portee on trucks
27th Indian Mountain Artillery Battery (December 1939–August 1940): 4 × 3.7" pack howitzers, 5 trucks
Aden Protectorate Levies: RHQ:by 1942
10 Rifle Companies, each: 140 men approx
1 Heavy AA Battery: 2 Troops, each: 4?x 40mmL60 Bofors
1 Signals Company
1 Training Company
2 more Rifle Companies in 1943 (Socotra island)
1 anti-submarine battery: 2 × 75mm field guns(Socotra island, 1943)
1 Camel Company
Government Guards: in 1940 add 1 flotilla: 4 × powered Dhows, each: 1 × 2pdr gun
Hadhrami Bedouin Legion (1940–1945): 50+ local Arabs in 4 forts, rifles, Schwarzlose MMGs
RAF Independent Aden Armoured Car Flight: 12 × Alvis-Straussler armoured cars
Notes
1. Radios were in CHQs and most forts. Artillery was rated Assigned FC.
2. Infantry had no anti-tank weapons.
3. Local forces include regional tribes and local Sultans' levies, armed with black-powder rifles or loaned Lee-Enfields.
4. ISF is Indian State Forces, most rated average morale and average or poor training.
5. Other battalions were rated good morale and average training.

2.19 MALTA GARRISON 1939

The Garrison's main combat elements were:
1st Maltese Infantry Battalion (1st Battalion, King's Own Malta Regiment)
1st Malta Infantry Brigade (2nd Devonshire Regiment, 1st Dorsetshire Regiment 2nd Queen's Own Royal West
Kent Regiment 2nd Royal Irish Fusiliers Infantry Battalions)
Troops are rated average morale and average training.

SUPPORT UNITS

Included:
Royal Malta Artillery Regiment
Harbour Fire Command: (became 1st Malta Heavy Coastal Regiment late 1939)
1st, 2nd, 3rd, 4th Heavy Coastal Batteries sharing 10 × 6", 6 × 12pdr, 9 × twin 6pdr
5th Malta Heavy AA Battery (March 1939+): 2 Troops, each: 4 × 3" 20cwt AA or 3.7" AA
6th Malta Heavy AA Battery (August 1939+): 2 Troops, each: 4 × 3" 20cwt AA or 3.7" AA
7th Malta Searchlight Battery (September 1939+)
4th Coastal Artillery Regiment: 7 × 9.2" coastal guns
7th Anti-Aircraft Regiment:
3 Batteries, each: 2 Troops, each: 4 × 3" 20cwt or 3.7" AA guns
16th, 24th Royal Engineer Fortress Companies
Malta Auxiliary Corps
1st, 2nd Malta Artisan Works Companies
No.1, No.2 Royal Engineer Bomb Disposal Companies

Brigade Support

Infantry Brigade HQ (5 rifle secs, 4 lorries, 1 car)

MAIN COMBAT ELEMENTS

1st Battalion, King's Own Malta Regiment

Btn HQ (3 rifle secs)
4 Companies, each: Coy HQ (1 (6 man) rifle sec)
4 platoons, each: 3 rifle secs, 3 LMG
1 MG platoon: 4 × Vickers MMG, 4 (6 man) crews

British Infantry Battalion
Btn HQ (2 rifle secs, 1 car, 2 trucks)
4 Companies, each: Coy HQ (1 (13 man) rifle sec)
        3 platoons, each: 1 (7 man) rifle Pl HQ sec, 1 × 2" mortar, 1 Boys
                3 (10 man) rifle secs, 3 LMG
1 Support Company: Coy HQ (1 rifle sec)
        1 platoon: 2 × 3" mortars, 2 trucks
        1 platoon: 4 × twin Bren AALMG on trucks, 4 Boys A/T rifles
        1 platoon: 2 rifle/engineer secs, 1 stores truck
        1 platoon: Pl HQ (1 × Bren Carrier, 1 LMG)
                3 Sections, each: 3 × Bren Carrier, 3 LMG, 1 (6 man) rifle sec

Notes
1. Radios were in all Coy HQ and above.
2. Infantry had no anti-tank grenades.
3. Artillery was rated Assigned FC.

2.20 MALTA GARRISON 1940
The Garrison's main combat elements were:
    1st Malta Infantry Brigade (January–July 1940) (2nd Btn Devonshire Regiment, 1st Btn Dorsetshire Regiment, 2nd Btn Queen's Own Royal West Kent Regiment, 2nd Btn Royal Irish Fusiliers, 1st & 2nd Btns King's Own Malta Regiment, 8th Btn Manchester Regiment in May 1940, 3rd Btn King's Own Malta Regiment in July 1940)

    North Malta Infantry Brigade (August 1940+) (2nd Royal Irish Fusiliers, 8th Btn Manchester Regiment, 1st Btn and 2nd Btn King's Own Malta Regiment)

    South Malta Infantry Brigade (August 1940+) (2nd Btn Devonshire Regiment, 1st Btn Dorsetshire Regiment, 3rd Btn King's Own Malta Regiment, 2nd Btn Queen's Own Royal West Kent Regiment)

Troops are rated average morale and average training.

SUPPORT UNITS
Included:
Royal Malta Artillery:
    1st Malta Heavy Coastal Regiment:
        1st, 2nd, 3rd, 4th Heavy Coastal Batteries sharing 11 × 6", 6 × 12pdr, 9 × twin 6pdr
    2nd Malta Heavy AA Regiment:
        5th, 6th Malta Heavy AA Batteries, each: 2 Troops, each: 4 × 3" 20cwt AA or 3.7" AA
        9th Malta Heavy AA Battery (November 1940+): 2 Troops, each: 4 × 3.7" AA
        7th, 8th Malta Searchlight Batteries
        10th Light AA Battery (November 1940+): 3 Troops, each: 4 × 40mmL60 Bofors
    11th Malta Territorial Heavy AA Regiment:
        20th, 21st Heavy AA Batteries, each: 2 Troops, each: 4 × 3.7" AA guns
        22nd Heavy AA Battery (September 1940+): 2 Troops, each: 4 × 3.7" AA guns
Royal Artillery:
    4th Coastal Artillery Regiment: 7 × 9.2" coastal guns
        59th Light AA Battery: 3 Troops, each: 4 × 40mmL60 Bofors
    7th, 10th Anti-Aircraft Regiments, each:
        3 Batteries, each: 2 Troops, each: 4 × 3" 20cwt or 3.7" AA guns
    4th Searchlight Regiment: 1 Battery Royal Artillery, 1 Battery Royal Malta Artillery
    26th Anti-tank Regiment:
        1 Battery: 2 Troops, each: 4 × 3.7" howitzers, 6 trucks, 2 LMG
        1 Battery: 2 Troops, each: 4 × 6" howitzers, 6 lorries, 2 AALMG
Malta Auxiliary Corps
Malta Volunteer Defence Force (June 1940+) (Home Guard)
16th, 24th Royal Engineer Fortress Companies
1st, 2nd Malta Artisan Works Companies
No.1, No.2 Royal Engineer Bomb Disposal Companies
St Angelo Royal Marine Light AA Battery: Lewis AAMG, clerks etc as crews

Brigade Support
Infantry Brigade HQ (5 rifle secs, 4 lorries, 1 car)

MAIN COMBAT ELEMENTS

Infantry Battalion, King's Own Malta Regiment
Btn HQ (3 rifle secs)
4 Companies, each: Coy HQ (1 (6 man) rifle sec)
        4 platoons, each: 3 rifle secs, 3 LMG
        1 MG platoon: 4 × Vickers MMG, 4 (6 man) crews

British Infantry Battalion
Btn HQ (2 rifle secs, 1 car, 2 trucks)
4 Companies, each: Coy HQ (1 (13 man) rifle sec)
        3 platoons, each: 1 (7 man) rifle Pl HQ sec, 1 × 2" mortar, 1 Boys,
           3 (10 man) rifle secs, 3 LMG
1 Support Company: Coy HQ (1 rifle sec)
        1 platoon: 2 × 3" mortars, 2 trucks
        1 platoon: 4 × twin Bren AALMG on trucks, 4 Boys A/T rifles
        1 platoon: 2 rifle/engineer secs, 1 stores truck
        1 platoon: Pl HQ (1 × Bren Carrier, 1 LMG)
           3 Sections, each: 3 × Bren Carrier, 3 LMG, 1 (6 man) rifle sec

Notes
1. Radios were in all Coy HQ and above.
2. Infantry had no anti-tank grenades.
3. Artillery is rated Assigned FC.

2.21 MALTA GARRISON 1941

The Garrison's main combat elements were:
    North Malta Infantry Brigade (4th Btn Buffs, 2nd Royal Irish Fusiliers, 8th Btn Manchester Regiment, 1st Btn and 2nd Btn King's Own Malta Regiment)

    South Malta Infantry Brigade (2nd Btn Devonshire Regiment, 1st Btn Dorsetshire Regiment, 1st Btn Hampshire Regiment, 3rd Btn King's Own Malta Regiment, 2nd Btn Queen's Own West Kent Regiment up to June 1941, 8th Btn King's Own Regiment from July 1941)

    Central Malta Infantry Brigade (July 1941+) (11th Btn Lancashire Fusiliers, 1st Btn Cheshire Regiment MG Battalion, 2nd Btn Queen's Own West Kent Regiment)

Troops are rated average morale and average training.

SUPPORT UNITS

Included:
Royal Malta Artillery:
    1st Malta Heavy Coastal Regiment:
        1st, 2nd, 3rd, 4th Heavy Coastal Batteries sharing 12 × 6", 2 × 4.7", 5 × 4", 4 × 12pdr, 10 × twin 6pdr guns
    10th Heavy AA Brigade:
2nd Malta Heavy AA Regiment:
    5th, 6th Malta Heavy AA Batteries, each: 2 Troops, each: 4 × 3.7" AA
    9th Malta Heavy AA Battery: 2 Troops, each: 4 × 3.7" AA
11th Malta Territorial Heavy AA Regiment:
    20th, 21st Heavy AA Batteries, each: 2 Troops, each: 4 × 3.7" AA guns
    22nd Heavy AA Battery: 2 Troops, each: 3 × 4.5" AA guns
    23rd Heavy AA Battery (March 1941+): 1 Troop: 4 × 3" 20cwt AA guns
        1 Troop: 3 × 3" 20cwt AA guns
4th Heavy AA Regiment:
    2 Batteries, each: 2 Troops, each: 4 × 3.7" AA guns
7th Heavy AA Regiment:
    2 Batteries, each: 2 Troops, each: 4 × 3.7" AA guns
    1 Battery: 1 Troop: 4 × 3" 20cwt AA guns
        1 Troop: 4 × 3.7" AA guns
10th Heavy AA Regiment:
    2 Batteries, each: 2 Troops, each: 4 × 3.7" AA guns
    1 Battery: 1 Troop: 4 × 4.5" AA guns
        1 Troop: 4 × 3" AA guns
    7th Light AA Brigade:
32nd, 65th, 74th Light AA Regiments, each:
    3 Batteries, each: 3 Troops, each: 4 × 40mmL60 Bofors
3rd Malta Light AA Regiment:
    3 Batteries, each: 3 Troops, each: 4 × 40mmL60 Bofors
4th Searchlight Regiment:
    7th, 8th Malta Batteries, 2 Royal Artillery Batteries, each: 18 × searchlights
4th Coastal Artillery Regiment: 7 × 9.2" coastal guns
26th Royal Artillery Defence Regiment:
    15th/40th, 48th/71st RA Batteries, each: 3 Troops, each: 4 × 3.7" howitzers, 6 trucks, 2 LMG
    13th Malta Battery: 2 Troops, each: 4 × 6" howitzers, 6 lorries, 2 AALMG
12th Field Artillery Regiment:
    3 Batteries, each: 2 Troops, each: 4 × 25pdr field guns, 6 trucks, 2 AALMG
1st Independent Tank Troop, RTR: 2 × Vickers VIC, 4 × Matilda II
Malta Auxiliary Corps
Malta Volunteer Defence Force (Home Guard)

16th, 24th Royal Engineer Fortress Companies
173rd Royal Engineers Tunnelling Company (August 1941+)
1st, 2nd Malta Artisan Works Companies
No.1, No.2 Royal Engineer Bomb Disposal Companies
St Angelo Royal Marine Light AA Battery: 2 × 40mm Bofors, clerks etc as crews

Brigade Support
Infantry Brigade HQ (5 rifle secs, 4 lorries, 1 car)

MAIN COMBAT ELEMENTS

Infantry Battalion, King's Own Malta Regiment
Btn HQ (3 rifle secs)
4 Companies, each: Coy HQ (1 (6 man) rifle sec)
    4 platoons, each: 3 rifle secs, 3 LMG
    1 MG platoon: 4 × Vickers MMG, 4 (6 man) crews

British Infantry Battalion
Btn HQ (2 rifle secs, 1 car, 2 trucks)
4 Companies, each: Coy HQ (1 (13 man) rifle sec)
    3 platoons, each: 1 (7 man) rifle Pl HQ sec, 1 × 2" mortar, 1 Boys,
        3 (10 man) rifle secs, 3 LMG
1 Support Company: Coy HQ (1 rifle sec)
    1 platoon: 2 or 4 × 3" mortars, 3 trucks
    1 platoon: 4 × twin Bren AALMG on trucks, 4 Boys A/T rifles
    1 platoon: 2 rifle/engineer secs, 1 stores truck
    1 platoon: Pl HQ (1 × Universal Carrier, 1 Daimler Scout Car, 1 LMG)
        4 Sections, each: 3 × Carrier, 3 LMG, 1 (9 man) rifle sec, 1 Boys, 1 × 2" mortar

Cheshire Regiment Machine Gun Battalion
Btn HQ (2 rifle secs, 2 trucks, 1 car)
4 Companies, each: Coy HQ (2 rifle secs, 4 LMG, 1 lorry)
    3 platoons, each: 4 × Vickers MMG, 4 trucks, 1 Boys A/T rifle
Notes
1.   Radios were in all Coy HQ and above, and in all tanks.
2.   Infantry had no anti-tank grenades.
3.   Artillery was rated Assigned FC.

2.22 MALTA GARRISON, 1942
The Garrison's main combat elements were:
    North Malta Infantry Brigade (January–June 1942) (4th Btn Buffs, 2nd Btn Royal Irish Fusiliers, 8th Btn Manchester Regiment, 1st Btn and 2nd Btn King's Own Malta Regiment)

    South Malta Infantry Brigade (January–June 1942) (8th Btn King's Own Regiment, 1st Btn Dorsetshire Regiment, 1st Btn Hampshire Reg, 3rd Btn King's Own Malta Reg, 2nd Btn Devonshire Regiment)

    Central Malta Infantry Brigade (January–June 1942) (11th Btn Lancashire Fusiliers, 1st Btn Cheshire Regiment MG Battalion, 2nd Btn Queen's Own West Kent Regiment, 1st Btn Durham Light Infantry)

    1st Malta Infantry Brigade (July 1942+) (1st Btn Dorsetshire Regiment, 1st Btn Hampshire Regiment, 2nd Devonshire Regiment, 3rd Btn King's Own Malta Regiment)

    2nd Malta Infantry Brigade (July 1942+) (2nd Btn Royal Irish Fusiliers, 8th Btn Manchester Regiment, 1st Btn and 2nd Btn King's Own Malta Regiment)

    3rd Malta Infantry Brigade (July 1942+) (11th Btn Lancashire Fusiliers, 1st Btn Cheshire Regiment MG Battalion, 2nd Btn Queen's Own West Kent Regiment, 10th Btn King's Own Malta Regiment)

    Western or 4th Malta Infantry Brigade (July 1942+) (4th Btn Buffs Regiment, 8th Btn King's Own Regiment, 1st Btn Durham Light Infantry)

Troops are rated average morale and average training.

SUPPORT UNITS
Included:
Royal Malta Artillery:
    1st Malta Heavy Coastal Regiment:
        1st, 2nd, 3rd, 16th Heavy Coastal Batteries sharing 12 × 6", 2 × 4.7", 5 × 4", 4 × 12pdr, 10 × twin 6pdr
            guns
    5th Malta Heavy Coastal Regiment (June 1942+):
        4th, 17th Heavy Coastal Batteries sharing 7 × 9.2" guns

13th Defence Battery: 2 Troops, each: 4 × 6" howitzers, 6 lorries, 2 AALMG, OP Team
10th Heavy AA Brigade:
    2nd Malta Heavy AA Regiment:
        5th, 6th, 9th, 14th Malta Heavy AA Batteries, each: 2 Troops, each: 4 × 3.7" AA
    11th Malta Territorial Heavy AA Regiment:
        20th, 21st Heavy AA Batteries, each: 2 Troops, each: 4 × 3.7" AA guns
        22nd Heavy AA Battery: 2 Troops, each: 3 × 4.5" AA guns
        23rd Heavy AA Battery: 2 Troops, each: 4 × 3" 20cwt AA guns
    4th Heavy AA Regiment:
        2 Batteries, each: 2 Troops, each: 4 × 3.7" AA guns
    7th Heavy AA Regiment:
        2 Batteries, each: 2 Troops, each: 4 × 3.7" AA guns
        1 Battery: 1 Troop: 4 × 4.5" AA guns
            1 Troop: 4 × 3.7" AA guns
7th Light AA Brigade:
    32nd, 65th, 74th Light AA Regiments, each:
        3 Batteries, each: 3 Troops, each: 4 × 40mmL60 Bofors
    3rd Malta Light AA Regiment:
        3 Batteries, each: 3 Troops, each: 4 × 40mmL60 Bofors
    4th Searchlight Regiment:
        7th, 8th Malta Batteries, 2 Royal Artillery Batteries, each: 18 × searchlights
    26th Royal Artillery Defence Regiment:
        15th/40th, 48th/71st RA Batteries, each: 3 Troops, each: 4 × 3.7" howitzers, 6 trucks, 2 LMG
        13th Malta Battery (January–May 1942) 2 Troops, each: 4 × 6" howitzers, 6 lorries, 2 AALMG
    Possibly 3 other Royal Artillery Field Regiments, each:
        3 Batteries, each: 2 Troops, each: 4 × 25pdr field guns, 6 trucks, 2 AALMG, 1 Boys
1st Independent Tank Troop, RTR: 2 × Vickers VIC, 4 × Matilda II
Malta Auxiliary Corps
Malta Volunteer Defence Force (Home Guard)
16th, 24th Royal Engineer Fortress Companies
173rd Royal Engineers Tunnelling Company
1st, 2nd Malta Artisan Works Companies
No.1, No.2 Royal Engineer Bomb Disposal Companies
St Angelo Royal Marine Light AA Battery: 2 × 40mm Bofors, clerks etc as crews

Brigade Support

Infantry Brigade HQ (5 rifle secs, 4 lorries, 1 car) with:
        HQ Defence Platoon: 1 (7 man) rifle Pl HQ sec, 1 × 2" mortar, 1 Boys, 3 (10 man) rifle secs, 3 Bren LMG
        1 MP Company (3rd Brigade only)

MAIN COMBAT ELEMENTS

Infantry Battalion, King's Own Malta Regiment

Btn HQ (3 rifle secs)
4 Companies, each: Coy HQ (1 (6 man) rifle sec)
        4 platoons, each: 3 rifle secs, 3 LMG
        1 MG platoon: 4 × Vickers MMG, 4 (6 man) crews

British Infantry Battalion

Btn HQ (2 rifle secs, 1 car, 2 trucks)
4 Companies, each: Coy HQ (1 (13 man) rifle sec)
        3 platoons, each: 1 (7 man) rifle Pl HQ sec, 1 × 2" mortar, 1 Boys,
            3 (10 man) rifle secs, 3 LMG
1 Support Company: Coy HQ (1 rifle sec)
        1 platoon: 4 or 6 × 3" mortars, 7 × Universal Carriers
        1 platoon: 4 × twin Bren AALMG on trucks, 4 Boys A/T rifles
        1 platoon: 2 rifle/engineer secs, 1 stores truck
        0–1 platoon: 4 × 2pdr A/T guns, 4 trucks, 2 LMG (June 1942+)
        1 platoon: Pl HQ (1 × Universal Carrier, 1 Daimler Scout Car, 1 LMG)
            4 Sections, each: 3 × Carrier, 3 LMG, 1 (9 man) rifle sec, 1 Boys, 1 × 2" mortar

Cheshire Regiment Machine Gun Battalion

Btn HQ (2 rifle secs, 2 trucks, 1 car)
4 Companies, each: Coy HQ (2 rifle secs, 4 LMG, 1 lorry)
        3 platoons, each: 4 × Vickers MMG, 4 trucks, 1 Boys A/T rifle

Notes
1.   Radios were in all Coy HQ and above, and in all tanks.
2.   Infantry had no anti-tank grenades.
3.   Artillery was rated Assigned FC until late 1942 when it became Flexible FC, with 3 OP Teams per Battery.
4.   Infantry Battalions may have received the 2pdr A/T platoon by mid 1942.

2.23 MALTA GARRISON 1943

The Garrison's main combat elements were:

1st Malta Infantry Brigade (January–March 1943) (1st Btn Dorsetshire Regiment, 1st Btn Hampshire Regiment, 2nd Devonshire Regiment, 2nd and 3rd Btns King's Own Malta Regiment)

2nd Malta Infantry Brigade (January–March 1943) (2nd Btn Royal Irish Fusiliers, 8th Btn Manchester Regiment, 1st Btn King's Own Malta Regiment, 8th King's Own Royal Regiment)

3rd Malta Infantry Brigade (January–March 1943) (11th Btn Lancashire Fusiliers, 2nd Btn Queen's Own West Kent Regiment, 10th Btn King's Own Malta Regiment)

4th Malta Infantry Brigade (January–March 1943) (4th Btn Buffs Regiment, 8th Btn King's Own Regiment, 1st Btn Cheshire MG Regiment, 1st Btn Durham Light Infantry)

232nd Infantry Brigade (April–August 1943) (8th Btn Manchester Regiment, 8th King's Own Royal Regiment, 2nd Btn and 3rd Btn King's Own Malta Regiment)

233rd Infantry Brigade (April–August 1943) (11th Lancashire Fusiliers, 4th Buffs, 1st Btn, 10th Btn King's Own Malta Regiment)

233rd Infantry Brigade (September 1943–May 1944) (11th Lancashire Fusiliers, 1st Btn, 2nd Btn, 3rd Btn King's Own Malta Regiment)

Troops are rated average morale and average training.

SUPPORT UNITS

Included:
Royal Malta Artillery:
    1st Malta Heavy Coastal Regiment:
        1st, 2nd, 3rd, 16th Heavy Coastal Batteries sharing 12 × 6", 2 × 4.7", 5 × 4", 4 × 12pdr, 10 × twin 6pdr
            guns
    5th Malta Heavy Coastal Regiment:
        11th, 12th Heavy Coastal Batteries sharing 7 × 9.2" guns
        13th Defence Battery: 2 Troops, each: 4 × 6" howitzers, 6 lorries, 2 AALMG, OP Team
10th Heavy AA Brigade:
    2nd Malta Heavy AA Regiment:
        5th, 6th, 9th, 14th Malta Heavy AA Batteries, each: 2 Troops, each: 4 × 3.7" AA
    11th Malta Territorial Heavy AA Regiment:
        20th, 21st, 23rd Heavy AA Batteries, each: 2 Troops, each: 4 × 3.7" AA guns
        22nd Heavy AA Battery: 2 Troops, each: 3 × 4.5" AA guns
    4th Heavy AA Regiment:
        2 Batteries, each: 2 Troops, each: 4 × 3.7" AA guns
    7th Heavy AA Regiment:
        2 Batteries, each: 2 Troops, each: 4 × 3.7" AA guns
        1 Battery: 1 Troop: 4 × 4.5" AA guns
            1 Troop: 4 × 3.7" AA guns
7th Light AA Brigade:
    3rd Malta Light AA Regiment:
        10th, 15th, 19th Batteries, each: 3 Troops, each: 4 × 40mmL60 Bofors
    4th Searchlight Regiment:
        7th, 8th Malta Batteries, 2 Royal Artillery Batteries, each: 18 × searchlights
    26th Royal Artillery Defence Regiment (January–September 1943):
        15th/40th, 48th/71st RA Batteries, each: 3 Troops, each: 4 × 3.7" howitzers, 6 trucks, 2 LMG
16th, 24th Royal Engineer Fortress Companies
171st, 173rd Royal Engineers Tunnelling Companies
1st, 2nd Malta Artisan Works Companies
No.1, No.2 Royal Engineer Bomb Disposal Companies

Brigade Support

Infantry Brigade HQ (5 rifle secs, 4 lorries, 1 car) with:
    HQ Defence Platoon: 1 (7 man) rifle Pl HQ sec, 1 × 2" mortar, 1 Boys, 3 (10 man) rifle secs, 3 Bren LMG
    1 MP Company

MAIN COMBAT ELEMENTS

Infantry Battalion, King's Own Malta Regiment

Btn HQ (3 rifle secs)
4 Companies, each: Coy HQ (1 (6 man) rifle sec)
        4 platoons, each: 3 rifle secs, 3 LMG, 1 Boys
        1 MG platoon: 4 × Vickers MMG, 4 (6 man) crews

British Infantry Battalion

Btn HQ (2 rifle secs, 1 car, 2 trucks)
4 Companies, each: Coy HQ (1 (13 man) rifle sec)
        3 platoons, each: 1 (7 man) rifle Pl HQ sec, 1 × 2" mortar, 1 Boys,
            3 (10 man) rifle secs, 3 LMG
1 Support Company: Coy HQ (1 rifle sec)
        1 platoon: 6 × 3" mortars, 7 × Universal Carriers
        1 platoon: 2 rifle/engineer secs, 1 stores truck, 2 LMG
        1 platoon: 4 × 2pdr or 6pdr A/T guns, 4 trucks, 2 LMG
        1 platoon: Pl HQ (1 × Universal Carrier, 1 Daimler Scout Car, 1 LMG)
            4 Sections, each: 3 × Carrier, 3 LMG, 1 (9 man) rifle sec, 1 Boys, 1 × 2" mortar

Cheshire Regiment Machine Gun Battalion

Btn HQ (2 rifle secs, 2 trucks, 1 car)
4 Companies, each: Coy HQ (2 rifle secs, 4 LMG, 1 lorry)
        3 platoons, each: 4 × Vickers MMG, 4 trucks, 1 Boys A/T rifle

Notes
1.   Radios were in all Pl HQ and above, and in all tanks.
2.   Infantry had No.75 Hawkins anti-tank grenades.

2.24 BRITISH GARRISON IN CYPRUS 1939–APRIL 1941

The island's Garrison consisted of:
    C Company, 1st Btn Essex Regiment: 179 men (1938–May 1940)
    D Company, 1st Btn Sherwood Foresters (1939–May 1940)
    1st Battalion, Sherwood Foresters Infantry Battalion (June 1940+)
        Btn HQ (4 rifle secs)
    4 Companies, each: Coy HQ (1 rifle sec, 1 × 2" mortar, 1 Boys)
        3 platoons, each: 1 (6 man) rifle Pl HQ sec, 3 (10 man) rifle secs, 3 LMG
    1 Support Company: Coy HQ (1 rifle sec)
        1 battery: 2 × 3" mortars, 2 trucks
        1 AA platoon: 2 × Lewis AAMG
        1 platoon: 2 (6 man) rifle/engineer secs, 1 stores truck
        1 platoon: Pl HQ: 1 × Bren Carrier, 1 LMG
            3 Sections, each: 3 × Bren Carrier, 3 LMG
    Cyprus Regiment (April 1940+)
        1st Infantry Battalion
            Btn HQ (2 rifle secs)
            4 Infantry Companies, each: Coy HQ (1 rifle sec)
                3 platoons, each: 4 (6 man) rifle secs, 1 LMG
        Depot Infantry unit
        1 Transport Company: 30 trucks
        1 Pack Transport Mule Company: 90 mules 30 rifle armed crew
        1007th, 1008th Cypriot Pioneer Companies (November 1940+), each: Coy HQ (1 rifle sec)
            3 platoons, each: 4 (12 man) rifle/pioneer secs
    15th Coastal Artillery Regiment: (November 1940+)
        1 Squadron: 2 Batteries, each: 4 × 6" naval guns, 4 AAMG, 120 crew
    Cyprus Volunteer Defence Force (June 1940–July 1942) (Home Guard type force)
    Cyprus Coast Battery (September 1940+): 2 × 4" guns
    Cyprus Commando Troop (few months in 1941): Troop HQ (1 (4 man) SMG sec)
        2 Platoons, each: 2 (6 man) rifle/SMG secs, 2 LMG, 1 (3 man) SMG Pl HQ sec, 1 × 2" mortar

Notes
1.   Radios were in all Coy HQs and above.
2.   Infantry may have had molotovs if in defence.
3.   Troops were rated average morale and training, with the Cyprus Regiment being poor morale and poor training, and the Cyprus Commando Troop being good morale and average training.

2.25 BRITISH GARRISON IN CYPRUS, MAY–AUGUST 1941

The Garrison's main combat elements were:
    1st Btn Sherwood Foresters Infantry Battalion
    11th Scottish Commando (C Battalion, Layforce)
    Cyprus Regiment
    Cyprus Volunteer Defence Force (Home Guard)
    7th Australian Divisional Cavalry Regiment
Troops are rated average morale and training, with Commandos at good morale and training, the Australian Cavalry at good morale and average training, and the Cyprus Regiment at poor morale and training.

SUPPORT UNITS

Included:
15th Coastal Artillery Regiment:
    1 Squadron: 2 Batteries, each: 4 × 6" naval guns, 4 AAMG, 120 crew

Cyprus Volunteer Defence Force (June 1940–July 1942) (Home Guard type force)
Cyprus Coast Artillery: C, D Batteries, each: 2 × 4" naval guns
C Troop, 237th Battery, 60th Field Artillery Regiment: 4 × 18pdr field guns (May–July 1941)
1 Light AA Troop, 103rd Light AA Battery: 4 × 40mmL60 Bofors, 4 trucks or dugouts
296th Army Field Engineer Company: Coy HQ (2 rifle secs)
        4 Troops, each: 4 rifle/engineer secs, 1 LMG

MAIN COMBAT ELEMENTS

1st Btn Sherwood Foresters Infantry Battalion
Btn HQ (4 rifle secs)
4 Companies, each: Coy HQ (1 rifle sec, 1 × 2" mortar, 1 Boys)
        3 platoons, each: 1 (6 man) rifle Pl HQ sec, 3 (10 man) rifle secs, 3 LMG
1 Support Company: Coy HQ (1 rifle sec)
        1 battery: 2 × 3" mortars, Assigned FC
        1 AA platoon: 2 × Lewis AAMG
        1 platoon: 2 (6 man) rifle/engineer secs, 1 stores truck
        1 platoon: Pl HQ: 1 × Bren Carrier, 1 LMG
                3 Sections, each: 3 × Bren Carrier, 3 LMG

Cyprus Regiment
RHQ (4 rifle secs, 2 lorries, 1 car)
1st Infantry Battalion
        Btn HQ (2 rifle secs)
        4 Infantry Companies, each: Coy HQ (1 rifle sec)
                3 platoons, each: 4 (6 man) rifle secs, 1 LMG
Depot Infantry unit
1 Transport Company: 30? trucks
1 Pack Transport Mule Company: 90 mules? 30 rifle armed crew
1007th, 1008th Cypriot Pioneer Companies, each: Coy HQ (1 rifle sec)
        3 platoons, each: 4 (12 man) rifle/pioneer secs

11th Commando
5 Companies, each: 2 Troops, each: Troop HQ (1 (4 man) SMG sec)
        2 Platoons, each: 2 (10 man) rifle/SMG secs, 2 LMG
                1 (3 man) SMG Pl HQ sec, 1 × 2" mortar

Australian 7th Divisional Cavalry Regiment
RHQ (2 rifle secs, 2 trucks + LMG)
1 Tank Squadron: Sqdn HQ (3 × Vickers VIB)
        4 Troops, each: 3 × Vickers VIB light tanks
1 Machine Gun Squadron: Sqdn HQ (2 rifle secs, 2 trucks, 2 LMG)
        3 Troops, each: 4 × Vickers MMG, 4 trucks
1 Motor Squadron: Sqdn HQ (1 rifle sec, 1 × 2" mortar, 1 truck)
        3 Troops, each: 4 (8 man) rifle secs, 4 trucks, 4 LMG, 1 Boys, 1 × 2" mortar
        1 Troop: Troop HQ (2 × Bren Carrier, 2 LMG)
                3 Sections, each: 3 × Carrier, 1 Boys, 2 LMG, 1 (6 man) rifle sec
1 Anti-Tank Troop: Troop HQ (3 × Bren Carrier, 3 LMG)
        3 Sections, each: 4 × 2pdr portees
Notes
1.   Radios were in all tanks and other CHQs.
2.   Infantry secs have had molotovs if in home defence.
3.   In June the 11th Commando was briefly used in Syria in support of the invasion against Vichy held territory, but remained
        based in Cyprus for most of the time.

2.26 BRITISH GARRISON, CYPRUS, AUGUST–NOVEMBER 1941
The Garrison's main combat elements were:
British 50th Northumbrian Infantry Division:
        69th Brigade (5th Btn East Yorkshire Reg, 6th Btn and 7th Btns Green Howards)
        150th Brigade (4th Btn East Yorkshire Reg, 4th and 5th Btns Green Howards)
        151st Brigade (6th, 8th, 9th Btns Durham Light Infantry Battalions)
        Divisional MG Battalion (2nd Btn Cheshire MG Regiment)
        Divisional Recce Battalion (50th Btn Recce Corps)
        1st Battalion, Sherwood Foresters Infantry Battalion
        Cyprus Regiment
        Cyprus Volunteer Defence Force (Home Guard)
        3rd Hussars Armoured Regiment
        11th Commando (No.3 Troop, Middle East Commando)
        Yorkshire Dragoons Motor Battalion.
Troops are rated average morale and training, with Commandos at good morale and training, and the Cyprus Regiment at
poor morale and training.

SUPPORT UNITS

Garrison Support

Included:
15th Coastal Artillery Regiment:
      1 Squadron: 2 Batteries, each: 4 × 6" naval guns, 4 AAMG, 120 crew
Cyprus Volunteer Defence Force (June 1940–July 1942) (Home Guard type force)
Cyprus Coast Artillery: C, D Batteries, each: 2 × 4" naval guns
1 Light AA Troop, 103rd Light AA Battery: 4 × 40mmL60 Bofors, 4 trucks or dugouts
296th Army Field Engineer Company: Coy HQ (2 rifle secs)
      4 Troops, each: 4 rifle/engineer secs, 1 LMG

50th Infantry Divisional Support

Included:
235th Field Park Company: Workshp Section, Stores Section

Brigade Support

69th Infantry Brigade HQ (5 rifle secs, 3 lorries) with:
      124th Field Artillery Regiment:
            3 Batteries, each: Battery HQ (4 rifle secs, 4 lorries, 2 AALMG, 1 Boys)
                2 Troops, each: 4 × 25pdr field guns, 6 trucks, 2 LMG
      505th Field Engineer Company: Coy HQ (2 rifle secs)
            3 platoons, each: 4 (12 man) rifle/engineer secs, 1 LMG
150th Infantry Brigade HQ (5 rifle secs, 3 lorries) with:
      72nd Field Artillery Regiment (as 69th Brigade above)
      232nd Field Engineer Company
151st Infantry Brigade HQ (5 rifle secs, 3 lorries) with:
      74th Field Artillery Regiment (as above)
      233rd Field Engineer Company (as above)

MAIN COMBAT ELEMENTS

British Infantry Battalion

Btn HQ (4 rifle secs)
4 Companies, each: Coy HQ (1 (13 man) rifle sec)
      3 platoons, each: 1 (7 man) rifle Pl HQ sec, 1 × 2" mortar, 1 Boys, 3 (10 man) rifle secs, 3 LMG
1 Support Company: Coy HQ (1 rifle sec)
      1 battery: 2 × 3" mortars, 2 trucks, Assigned FC
      1 AA platoon: 4 × twin Bren AALMG, 4 Boys
      1 platoon: 2 rifle/engineer secs, 1 stores truck
      1 platoon: Pl HQ: 1 × Universal Carrier, 1 LMG
            4 Sections, each: 3 × Carrier, 3 LMG, 1 rifle sec, 1 × 2" mortar,1 Boys

Cyprus Regiment (local recruits)

RHQ (4 rifle secs, 2 lorries, 1 car)
1st Infantry Battalion
      Btn HQ (2 rifle secs)
      4 Infantry Companies, each: Coy HQ (1 rifle sec)
            3 platoons, each: 4 (6 man) rifle secs, 1 LMG
Depot Infantry unit
1 Transport Company: 30 trucks
1 Pack Transport Mule Company: 90 mules 30 rifle armed crew
1007th, 1008th Cypriot Pioneer Companies, each: Coy HQ (1 rifle sec)
      3 platoons, each: 4 (12 man) rifle/pioneer secs

Divisional 50th Recce Battalion, 50th Infantry Division

Btn HQ (4 rifle secs, 4 trucks, 3 LMG, 2 Boys)
3 Companies, each: Coy HQ (3 rifle secs, 1 LMG, 3 trucks)
      3 platoons, each: Pl HQ: 1 × Universal Carrier, 1 LMG, 1 × 2" mortar
            2 sections, each: 2 × Universal Carriers, 2 LMG, 1 Boys
            2 sections, each: 2 trucks + LMG
      1 platoon: 4 (8 man) rifle secs, 4 trucks, 1 Boys, 4 LMG
1 AA Platoon: 4 × twin AALMG, 4 trucks, 4 Boys
1 Battery: 2 × 3" mortars, 2 trucks, Assigned FC
1 Anti-tank platoon: 8 × Boys, 8 trucks

2nd Btn Cheshire Regiment Divisional Machine Gun Battalion, 50th Infantry Division

Btn HQ (2 rifle secs, 2 trucks)
4 Companies, each: Coy HQ (1 rifle sec, 1 truck)
      3 platoons, each: 4 × Vickers MMG, 1 LMG, 4 trucks

11th Commando

5 Companies, each: 2 Troops, each: Troop HQ (1 (4 man) SMG squad)

2 Platoons, each: 2 (10 man) rifle/SMG secs, 2 LMG
1 (3 man) SMG Pl HQ sec, 1 × 2" mortar

Yorkshire Dragoons Motor Battalion

Btn HQ (2 trucks, 1 lorry, 2 rifle secs)
3 Companies, each: Coy HQ (1 rifle sec, 1 × 2" mortar, 1 Boys, 2 trucks)
3 platoons, each: 4 (8 man) rifle secs, 3 LMG, 1 Boys, 4 trucks
1 platoon: 2 × 3" mortars, 2 MMG, 4 trucks
1 platoon: Pl HQ: 1 truck + LMG or Universal Carrier
3 Sections, each: 3 × truck + LMG or Carrier, 3 LMG, 1 Boys, 1 × 2" mortar, 1 rifle sec

3rd Hussars Armoured Regiment

RHQ (2 trucks + LMG, 3 × Scout Cars)
3 Squadrons, each: Sqdn HQ (1 × Stuart)
1 Troop: 3 × Vickers VIB
2–3 Troops, each: 3 trucks + LMG &/or Vickers VIB

Notes
1. Radios were in all tanks and other CHQs. Artillery is rated Assigned FC.
2. Infantry secs had Hawkins 75 anti-tank grenades.

2.27 ALLIED GARRISON, CYPRUS, NOVEMBER 1941–AUGUST 1942

The Garrison's main combat elements were:
Indian 5th Infantry Division (November 1941–March 1942)
9th Brigade (2nd West Yorkshire Reg, 3rd/5th Mahratta Light Infantry Reg, 3rd/12th Frontier Force Regiment Infantry Battalions)
10th Brigade (2nd Highland Light Infantry Btn, 4th/10th Baluch Regiment, 3rd/18th Royal Garwhal Rifles Infantry Battalions)
161st British Brigade (1st/4th Essex Regiment, 3rd/7th and 4th/7th Rajput Reg) Divisional Recce Regiment (Skinners Horse Recce Regiment)
7th Indian infantry Brigade (March–August 1942)(1st Royal Sussex Regiment, 4th/16th Punjab Regiment, 1st/2nd Gurkha Rifles Infantry Btns)
1st Battalion, Sherwood Foresters Infantry Battalion (November 1941–January 1942)
Mewar Bhopal Indian Garrison Infantry Battalion (November 1941+)
Bhopal Sultania Indian Garrison Infantry Battalion (April 1942+)
1st Btn Jaipur Indian Garrison Infantry Regiment (April 1942+)
1st Btn Rampur Indian Garrison Infantry Regiment (April 1942+)
Cyprus Regiment
Cyprus Volunteer Defence Force (Home Guard)
Crusader Force:
3rd Hussars Armoured Regiment (November 1941–March 1942)
Yorkshire Dragoons Motor Battalion (November 1941–August 1942)
1st Household Cavalry Regiment (March–August 1942)
Yorkshire Hussars Yeomanry Armoured Regiment (March 1942+)
Troops are rated average morale and training, with Gurkhas at good morale and good training, Indian Garrison Infantry Battalions at average morale and poor training, and the Cyprus Regiment at poor morale and training.

SUPPORT UNITS

Garrison Support

Included:
15th Coastal Artillery Regiment:
1 Squadron: 2 Batteries, each: 4 × 6" naval guns, 4 AAMG, 120 crew
Cyprus Volunteer Defence Force (June 1940–July 1942) (Home Guard type force)
Cyprus Coast Artillery: C, D Batteries, each: 2 × 4" naval guns
1 Light AA Battery: 3 Troops, each: 6 × 40mmL60 Bofors, 6 trucks or dugouts
295th, 296th Army Field Engineer Companies, each: Coy HQ (2 rifle secs)
3 Troops, each: 4 (12 man) rifle/engineer secs, 1 LMG
1 Detachment, 36th New Zealand Survey Battery
39th Royal Tank Regiment (50 x dummy tanks on lorries)
2nd Heavy AA Regiment:
2 Batteries, each: Battery HQ (2 rifle secs, 2 lorries)
2 Troops, each: 4 × 3.7" AA guns, 6 lorries
606th Palestinian Pioneer Company: Coy HQ (1 rifle sec)
3 platoons, each: 4 (12 man) rifle/pioneer secs

Indian 5th Infantry Divisional Support

21st Bombay Field Engineer Company: Coy HQ (2 rifle secs, 2 LMG, 2 trucks)
3 Sections, each: 4 (12 man) rifle/engineer secs, 4 lorries
44th Madras Field Park Company: Workshop Section, Supply Section

Brigade Support

9th Indian Infantry Brigade HQ (5 rifle secs, 6 lorries, 2 LMG) with:

9th Brigade Machine Gun Company: Coy HQ (2 rifle secs, 2 trucks)
                3 platoons, each: 4 × Vickers MMG, 4 trucks, 2 LMG
        4th Field Artillery Regiment:
                3 Batteries, each: Battery HQ (4 rifle secs, 4 lorries, 2 AALMG, Assigned FC)
                        2 Troops, each: 4 × 25pdr field guns, 6 trucks, 2 LMG
        20th Indian Field Engineer Company: Coy HQ (2 rifle secs, 2 LMG, 2 trucks)
                3 Sections, each: 4 (12 man) rifle/engineer secs, 4 lorries
10th Indian Infantry Brigade HQ (5 rifle secs, 6 lorries, 2 LMG) with:
        10th Brigade Machine Gun Company (as above)
        28th Field Artillery Regiment (as above)
        2nd Indian Field Engineer Company (as above)
161st Indian Infantry Brigade HQ (5 rifle secs, 6 lorries, 2 LMG) with:
        161st Brigade Machine Gun Company (as above)
7th Indian Infantry Brigade HQ (5 rifle secs, 6 lorries, 2 LMG) with:
        31st Field Artillery Regiment (as above)
        Indian Field Engineer Company (as above)

MAIN COMBAT ELEMENTS

Cyprus Regiment (local recruits)

RHQ (4 rifle secs, 2 lorries, 1 car)
1st Infantry Battalion
        Btn HQ (2 rifle secs)
        4 Infantry Companies, each: Coy HQ (1 rifle sec)
                3 platoons, each: 4 (6 man) rifle secs, 1 LMG
Depot Infantry unit
1 Transport Company: 30 trucks
1 Pack Transport Mule Company: 90 mules 30 rifle armed crew
1011th Cypriot Pioneer Company: Coy HQ (1 rifle sec)
        3 platoons, each: 4 (12 man) rifle/pioneer secs

British & Indian Infantry Battalions

Btn HQ (4 rifle secs)
4 Companies, each: Coy HQ (1 (13 man) rifle sec)
        3 platoons, each: 1 (8 man) rifle Pl HQ sec, 1 × 2" mortar, 1 Boys,
                3 (10 man) rifle secs, 3 LMG
1 Support Company: Coy HQ (1 rifle sec)
        1 battery: 2 or 4 × 3" mortars, 3 trucks, Assigned FC
        1 AA platoon: 4 × twin Bren AALMG, 4 Boys, 4 trucks
        1 platoon: 2 rifle/engineer secs, 1 stores truck
        1 platoon: Pl HQ: 1 × Universal Carrier, 1 LMG
                4 Sections, each: 3 × Universal Carriers, 3 LMG, 1 rifle sec, 1 × 2" mortar, 1 Boys

Skinners Horse Divisional Recce Regiment, 5th Indian Infantry Division (November 1941–January 1942)

RHQ (2 rifle secs, 4 trucks, 2 LMG, 1 Boys)
3 Companies, each: Coy HQ (3 rifle secs, 1 LMG, 3 trucks)
        3 platoons, each: Pl HQ: 1 × Universal Carrier, 1 LMG, 1 × 2" mortar
                2 sections, each: 2 × Universal Carrier, 2 LMG, 1 Boys
                2 sections, each: 2 trucks + LMG
        1 platoon: 4 (8 man) rifle secs, 4 trucks, 1 Boys, 4 LMG
1 AA Platoon: 4 × twin AALMG, 4 trucks, 4 Boys
1 Battery: 2 × 3" mortars, 2 trucks, Assigned FC
1 Anti-tank platoon: 8 × Boys, 8 trucks

Skinners Horse Divisional Recce Regiment, 5th Indian Infantry Division (January–March 1942)

RHQ (2 rifle secs, 4 trucks, 2 LMG, 1 Boys)
2 Squadrons, each: Sqdn HQ (1 × Vickers VIB)
        2–3 Troops, each: 3 × Vickers VIB
1 Squadron: Sqdn HQ (3 rifle secs, 1 LMG, 3 trucks)
        3 Troops, each: Troop HQ: 1 × Universal Carrier, 1 LMG, 1 × 2" mortar
                2 sections, each: 2 × Universal Carrier, 2 LMG, 1 Boys
                2 sections, each: 2 trucks + LMG
        1 platoon: 4 (8 man) rifle secs, 4 trucks, 1 Boys, 4 LMG
1 AA Platoon: 4 × twin AALMG, 4 trucks, 4 Boys
1 Battery: 2 × 3" mortars, 2 trucks, Assigned FC
1 Anti-tank platoon: 8 × Boys, 8 trucks

Yorkshire Dragoons Motor Battalion

Btn HQ (2 trucks, 1 lorry, 2 rifle secs)
3 Companies, each: Coy HQ (1 rifle sec, 1 × 2" mortar, 1 Boys, 2 trucks)

3 platoons, each: 4 (8 man) rifle secs, 3 LMG, 1 Boys, 4 trucks
1 platoon: 2 × 3" mortars, 2 MMG, 4 trucks
1 platoon: 2 × 2pdr A/T guns, 2 × Carriers
1 platoon: Pl HQ: 1 × Universal Carrier, 1 LMG
    3 Sections, each: 3 × Universal Carriers, 3 LMG, 1 Boys, 1 × 2" mortar, 1 rifle sec

3rd Hussars Armoured Regiment (November 1941–January 1942)

RHQ (2 trucks + LMG, 3 × Scout Cars, 1 × Stuart)
A, C Squadrons, each: Sqdn HQ (1 × Stuart)
    1 Troop: 3 × Vickers VIB
    3 Troops, each: 3 × A-13 Mk.II
(B Squadron in Java, February 1942)

3rd Hussars Armoured Regiment (January–March 1942)

RHQ (2 trucks + LMG, 3 × Scout Cars, 2 × Stuart I)
2 Squadrons, each: 1 × Stuart, several crews

1st Household Cavalry Regiment (March–mid April 1942)

RHQ (2 rifle secs, 4 trucks, 2 LMG, 1 Boys)
3 Squadrons, each: Sqdn HQ (3 rifle secs, 1 LMG, 3 trucks)
    3 platoons, each: Pl HQ: 1 × Universal Carrier, 1 LMG, 1 × 2" mortar
        2 sections, each: 2 × Universal Carrier, 2 LMG, 1 Boys
        2 sections, each: 2 trucks + LMG
    1 platoon: 4 (8 man) rifle secs, 4 trucks, 1 Boys, 4 LMG
1 AA Platoon: 4 × twin AALMG, 4 trucks, 4 Boys
1 Battery: 2 × 3" mortars, 2 trucks, Assigned FC
1 Anti-tank platoon: 8 × Boys, 8 trucks

1st Household Cavalry Regiment (mid April–May 1942)

RHQ (2 × Marmon-Herrington III, 2 cars, 2 trucks + LMG)
3 Squadrons, each: Sqdn HQ (1 × Marmon-Herrington III, 8 motorcycles)
    2 Troops, each: 3 × Marmon-Herrington III
    1 Troop: Troop HQ: 1 × Universal Carrier, 1 LMG, 1 × 2" mortar
        2 sections, each: 2 × Universal Carrier, 2 LMG, 1 Boys
        2 sections, each: 2 trucks + LMG
    1 Assault Troop: 4 (8 man) rifle secs, 4 trucks, 1 Boys, 4 LMG
1 AA Platoon: 4 × twin AALMG, 4 trucks, 4 Boys
1 Battery: 2 × 3" mortars, 2 trucks, Assigned FC
1 Anti-tank platoon: 8 × Boys, 8 trucks

1st Household Cavalry Regiment (May–August 1942)

RHQ (4 × Marmon-Herrington III)
3 Squadrons, each: Sqdn HQ (3 × Marmon-Herrington III)
    3 Troops, each: 3 × Marmon-Herrington III
1 AA Platoon: 4 × twin AALMG, 4 trucks, 4 Boys
1 Battery: 2 × 3" mortars, 2 trucks, Assigned FC
1 Anti-tank Platoon: 2 Troops, each: 4 × 2pdr A/T guns, 4 trucks, 2 LMG

Indian Garrison Infantry Battalion

Btn HQ (3 rifle secs, 1 LMG)
4 Companies, each: Coy HQ (1 rifle squad, 1 × 2" mortar, 1 Boys)
    3 platoons, each: 1 (6 man) rifle Pl HQ sec, 3 (10 man) rifle secs, 3 LMG
1 Support Company: Coy HQ (1 rifle sec)
    1 AA platoon: 2 × Lewis or Bren AALMG
    1 platoon: 2 (6 man) rifle/engineer secs, 1 stores truck
    1 Scout platoon: Pl HQ: 1 truck, 1 (4 man) rifle squad
        3 Sections, each: 3 trucks, 3 LMG, 3 (4 man) rifle secs

Yorkshire Hussars Armoured Regiment (March–August 1942)

RHQ (2 trucks + LMG, 4 (6 man) SMG secs
3 Squadrons, each: Sqdn HQ (2 trucks or cars, 3 (5 man) SMG secs)
    4 Troops, each: 3 (5 man) rifle/SMG crew secs, 4 trucks

Notes
1.   Radios were in all tanks and armoured cars, Carrier Pl HQ and other CHQs. Artillery is rated Assigned FC.
2.   Infantry secs had Hawkins 75 anti-tank grenades.
3.   The 5th Indian Division left on March 1942 and was replaced by the 7th Indian infantry Brigade.
4.   The mobile Armoured forces were formed into "Crusader Force", the garrison's mobile reserve.
5.   The 39th RTR was a deception unit equipped with dummy tanks on lorries.
6.   The Yorkshire Hussars Yeomanry Armoured Regiment came from 9th Armoured Brigade, apparently without any tanks. It may have taken over the A-13 Mk.IIs left by the 3rd Hussars, at 6 per squadron.

2.28 ALLIED GARRISON, CYPRUS, AUGUST 1942–1944

The Garrison's main combat elements were:

Mewar Bhopal Indian Garrison Infantry Battalion (August–November 1942) (June–September 1944)
Bhopal Sultania Indian Garrison Infantry Battalion (August 1942–May 1944)
1st Rampur Indian Garrison Infantry Battalion (April–December 1942)
Nabha Akal Indian Garrison Infantry Battalion (December 1942–August 1944)
3rd/7th Rajput Regiment Indian Infantry Battalion (April–July 1944)
4th Gwalior Indian Infantry Regiment (May–August 1944)
9th/8th Punjab Infantry Regiment (August 1944–May 1945)
8th Irish Hussars Armoured Regiment (December 1942–June 1943)
Yorkshire Hussars Yeomanry Armoured Regiment (August 1942–December 1943)
Cyprus Regiment
10th Indian Division (August 1942–May 1943)
10th Brigade (August 1942–January 1944) (3rd/18th Royal Garhwal Rifles, 4th/10th Baluch Regiment, 2nd/4th Gurkha Rifles, +4th/13th Frontier Force Rifles (May 1943+))
20th Brigade (2nd/3rd Gurkha Rifles Infantry Battalion, 39th RTR, +4th Hussars Armoured Regiment (January–June 1943))
25th Indian Infantry Brigade (1st King's Own Regiment, 2nd/11th Sikh Regiment, 3rd/5th Mahrata Light Infantry Battalions)
The Poona Horse Indian Cavalry Regiment (September 1944–May 1945)
Troops were rated average morale and training, with Gurkhas at good morale and good training, Indian Garrison Infantry Battalions at average morale and poor training, and the Cyprus Regiment at poor morale and training.

SUPPORT UNITS

Garrison Support
Included:
15th Coastal Artillery Regiment:
　　1 Squadron: 2 Batteries, each: 4 × 6" naval guns, 4 AAMG, 120 crew
Cyprus Coast Artillery: C, D Batteries, each: 2 × 4" naval guns
295th, 296th Army Field Engineer Companies, each: Coy HQ (2 rifle secs)
　　3 Troops, each: 4 (12 man) rifle/engineer secs, 1 LMG
1 Light AA Battery: Coy HQ (1 rifle sec, 1 truck)
　　3 Troops, each: 6 × 40mmL60 Bofors, 6 trucks

10th Indian Infantry Divisional Support
97th Field Artillery Regiment: (January–May 1943 only)
　　3 Batteries, each: BHQ (3 rifle secs, 4 lorries, 1 AALMG)
　　　　2 Troops, each: 2 × 25pdr field guns, 3 trucks
10th, 61st Madras Field Engineer Companies, each: Coy HQ (1 rifle sec)
　　3 platoons, each: 2 rifle/engineer secs, 1 LMG, 1 lorry

Brigade Support
Indian Infantry Brigade HQ (4 rifle secs, 4 lorries, 1 LMG)

MAIN COMBAT ELEMENTS

British & Indian Infantry Battalions, 10th Indian Division
Btn HQ (2 rifle secs)
4 Companies, each: Coy HQ (1 (7 man) rifle squad)
　　3 platoons, each: 1 (3 man) rifle Pl HQ sec, 1 × 2" mortar
　　　　3 (6 man) rifle secs, 2 LMG
1 Support Company: Coy HQ (1 rifle sec)
　　1 battery: 2 × 3" mortars
　　1 platoon: 1 rifle/engineer sec, 1 LMG
　　1 platoon: 4 × 2pdr portees
　　1 platoon: 2 Bren AALMG,1 truck
　　1 platoon: Pl HQ: 1 × Universal Carrier, 1 LMG
　　　　2 Sections, each: 2–3 × Universal Carriers, 2 LMG, 1 (6 man) rifle sec

8th Irish Hussars Armoured Regiment (December 1942–June 1943)
RHQ (3 × Marmon-Herrington III, 2 trucks)
3 Squadrons, each: Sqdn HQ (2 × Marmon-Herrington III, 2 × Universal Carriers)
　　4 Troops, each: 3 × Marmon-Herrington III
　　1 Troop: 3 × Universal Carrier, 3 LMG, 1 rifle sec

Indian Garrison Infantry Battalion
Btn HQ (4 rifle secs, 1 LMG)
4 Companies, each: Coy HQ (1 rifle squad, 1 × 2" mortar)
　　3 platoons, each: 1 (8 man) rifle Pl HQ sec, 1 Boys
　　　　3 (10 man) rifle secs, 3 LMG
1 Support Company: Coy HQ (1 rifle sec)
　　1 platoon: 2 or 6 × 3" mortars
　　1 platoon: 2 (8 man) rifle/engineer secs, 1 stores truck
　　1 platoon: 2–6 × 2pdr anti-tank guns, trucks

1 Scout platoon: Pl HQ: 1 × Universal Carrier, 1 LMG
4 Sections, each: 3 × Universal Carriers, 3 LMG, 1 rifle sec, 1 × 2" mortar

4th Hussars Armoured Regiment (August 1942–January 1944)

RHQ (2 × Crusader II, 2 × Daimler Scout Car)
1 Squadron: Sqdn HQ (1 × Crusader III, 1 × Crusader CS)
2 Troops, each: 3 × Crusader II
1 Squadron: Sqdn HQ (2 × Valentine I, II)
3 Troops, each: 2–3 × Valentine I, II
1 Squadron: Sqdn HQ (1 truck + LMG, 2 (4 man) crew secs)
3 Troops, each: 3 (4 man) SMG crew secs, 3 trucks + LMG

39th Royal Tank Regiment, ex of 74th Armoured Brigade (August 1942–January 1944)

RHQ (4 dummy tanks on trucks)
3 Squadrons, each: Sqdn HQ (4 × dummy tanks on trucks)
4 Troops, each: 3 × dummy tanks on trucks

Yorkshire Hussars Armoured Regiment (August 1942–December 1943)

RHQ (2 trucks + LMG, 4 (6 man) SMG secs
3 Squadrons, each: Sqdn HQ (2 trucks or cars, 3 (5 man) SMG secs)
4 Troops, each: 3 (5 man) rifle/SMG crew secs, 4 trucks + LMG

Cyprus Regiment (local recruits)

RHQ (4 rifle secs, 2 lorries, 1 car)
1st Infantry Battalion
Btn HQ (2 rifle secs)
4 Infantry Companies, each: Coy HQ (1 rifle sec)
3 platoons, each: 4 (6 man) rifle secs, 1 LMG, 1 Boys
Depot Infantry unit
1 Transport Company: 30 trucks
1 Pack Transport Mule Company: 90 mules 30 rifle armed crew

Notes
1. Radios were in all tanks and armoured cars, Carrier Pl HQ and other PHQs.
2. Infantry secs had Hawkins 75 anti-tank grenades.
3. The 39th RTR was in fact a dummy tank unit, part of the fictional 74th Armoured Brigade used successfully in North Africa just before El Alamein.
4. The 10th Indian Division arrived in August 1942 after being battered in the Gazala battles, and should be rated poor morale and poor training until March 1943.

2.29 GIBRALTAR GARRISON, 1939–1943

The Garrison's main combat elements were:
2nd King's Regiment, 2nd Somerset Light Infantry Btns (1939–Mar 1941)
1st Welsh Guards Inf Btn (September–November 1939 only)
4th Battalion Black Watch Inf Btn (July 1940–January 1941)
4th Devonshire Regiment Inf Btn (May 1940–April 1941)
1st Gibralter Infantry Brigade (March 1941–April 1943) (2nd King's Regiment, 4th Btn Black Watch, 1st Gibralter Independent Coy)
1st Gibralter Infantry Brigade (May–November 1943) (2nd King's Regiment, 2nd Royal Scots Regiment, 1st Gibralter Independent Coy)
1st Gibralter Infantry Brigade (November 1943–July 1944) (2nd Royal Scots, 1st Hertfordshire Regiment, 1st Gibralter Independent Coy)
1st Gibralter Infantry Brigade (August 1944–June 1945) (31st Suffolk Regiment, 30th Dorsetshire Regiment)
2nd Gibralter Infantry Brigade (April 1941–April 1943) (2nd Somerset Light Infantry, 4th Devonshire Regiment, +7th King's Own Rifle Regiment (June–September 1942))
2nd Gibralter Infantry Brigade (May 1943–December 1943) (2nd Somerset Light Infantry, 1st Hertfordshire Regiment, +2nd King's Regiment (November–December 1943))
9th Commando (January–February 1943)
3rd Commando (February 1943–July 1943)
2nd Commando (July 1943)
Troops were rated average morale and average training, with Commandos rated at excellent morale and good training.

SUPPORT UNITS

Garrison Support

Included:
Gibralter Tank Squadron (November 1942–1944): Sqdn HQ (3 × Valentine II then Sherman III)
4 Troops, each: 3 × Valentine II, then Sherman III)
3rd Heavy Coast Defence Artillery Regiment (1939–1941):
4th, 26th, 27th Batteries, sharing: 7 × 9.2" guns, 6 × 6" guns, 6 × twin 6pdr guns

3rd Heavy Coast Defence Artillery Regiment (1941–1945):
> 4th, 26th, 27th Batteries, sharing: 8 × 9.2" guns, 9 × 6" guns, 4 × 4" guns, 6 × twin 6pdr guns

19th Coast Artillery Regiment (1943–March 1944)
> 3 Batteries

18th Artillery Defence Regiment (December 1940–March 1944)
> 1 Field Battery: 1 Troop: 4 × 25pdr field guns, 6 trucks, 2 LMG
> > 1 Troop: 5 × 25pdr field guns, 6 trucks, 2 LMG
> 1 Medium Battery: 1 Troop: 2 × 9.2" coastal howitzers, static gunpit
> > 1 Troop: 4 × 6" 26cwt howitzers, 6 lorries, 2 LMG
> > 1 Troop: 3 × 6" 26cwt howitzers, 5 lorries, 2 LMG
> 1 Anti–tank Battery: 1 Troop: 5 × 75mm M1897 or Italian field guns, 6 trucks, 3 LMG
> > 2 Troops, each: 5 × 4.5"L15 howitzers, 6 trucks, 3 LMG

13th Heavy AA Regiment (March 1941–December 1942)
> 1 Battery: 2 Troops, each: 4 × 3.7" AA guns
> 2 Batteries (1942+), each: 16 × 3" twin AA rocket launchers, 4 2"single AA rocket launchers

82nd Heavy AA Regiment (July 1940–May 1943)
> 2 Batteries, each: 2 Troops, each: 4 × 3.7" AA guns
> 1 Battery: 1 Troop: 4 × 3.7" AA guns
> > 1 Troop: 4 × 3" 20cwt AA guns, 4 trucks

175th Heavy AA Regiment (April 1943–October 1944)
> 3 Batteries, each: 2 Troops, each: 4 × 3.7" AA guns

141st Light AA Regiment (August 1943–March 1944)
> 3 Batteries, each: 2 Troops, each: 4 × 40mmL60 Bofors, 1 Troop: 6 × searchlights

3rd Light AA Regiment (September 1941–August 1943)
> 3 Batteries, each: 2 Troops, each: 4 × 40mmL60 Bofors, 1 Troop: 6 × searchlights
> 1 Battery: 2 Troops, each: 8 × 20mm Oerlikon AA (1942+)

1st AA Z-Troop (1941+): 4 × 3" 20-round AA rocket launchers

1st Radar Battery (December 1941–1945): 6 × GL radar sets

1st, 32nd Fortress Engineer Companies (1939–45) manning searchlights

172nd, 178th, 179th, 170th, 180th Tunnelling Companies (June 1940–January 1944)

3rd Canadian Tunnelling Company (June 1941–January 1944)

Royal Navy AA assets (by December 1941): 8 × 4" naval AA guns, 20 × 20mm Oerlikon, 4 × 3" 20-round rocket launchers

Brigade Support

Infantry Brigade HQ (5 rifle secs, 4 lorries) with:
> 1 HQ Defence Platoon: 1 (7 man) rifle Pl HQ sec, 1 × 2" mortar, 1 Boys, 3 (10 man) rifle secs, 3 LMG

MAIN COMBAT ELEMENTS

Infantry Battalion

Btn HQ (5 rifle secs, 1 LMG)
4 Companies, each: Coy HQ (1 (13 man) rifle sec)
> 3 platoons, each: 1 (7 man) rifle Pl HQ sec, 1 Boys, 1 × 2" mortar,
> > 3 (10 man) rifle secs, 3 LMG
1 Support Company: Coy HQ (1 rifle sec)
> 1 platoon: 4 × twin AALMG, 4 Boys A/T Rifle in 2 rifle crew secs (1939–1942 only)
> 1 platoon: 2 rifle/engineer secs, 1 stores truck
> 1 platoon: 6 × 2pdr or 6pdr anti-tank guns (1943 only)
> 1 battery: 2 or 4 × or 6 × 3" mortars, 3–7 × Universal Carriers or trucks, 1 Boys
> 1 platoon: Pl HQ: 1 × Universal Carrier, 1 × Daimler S/C, 1 LMG (1940+)
> > 4 sections, each: 3 × Universal Carriers, 3 LMG, 1 Boys, 1 × 2" mortar, 1 rifle sec

1st Gibralter Independent Company

Coy HQ (2 rifle secs)
3 platoons, each: 1 (8 man) rifle Pl HQ sec, 1 × 2" mortar, 1 × Boys
> 3 (10 man) rifle secs, 3 Bren LMG

British Army Commando (1942–early 1943)

Btn HQ (6 rifle/SMG secs, 35 cycles, 1 car, 6 Jeeps, 8 × 15cwt trucks, 3 × 3-ton lorries)
1 Signals Platoon: 21 men
> 5 Commando Troops, each: Troop HQ (1 (6 man) SMG sec)
> > 2 Sections, each: 1 (2 man) rifle/SMG HQ secretary, 2 (14 man) rifle secs, 3 LMG, 2 Boys, 1 × 2" mortar

Notes
1. Radios were in all Coy HQ and all tanks. Artillery is rated Assigned FC until the end of 1942, when it becomes Flexible FC with 3 OP Teams per Battery.
2. Infantry had No.75 anti-tank grenades. In 1940 they may have No.68 rifle anti-tank grenades.
3. Rockets were 2" single shot types, and 3" twin barrel launchers and 20-round multiple launchers. All were on static mounts.
4. The Gibralter Tank Squadron was disbanded when its Shermans were handed to 15th Army HQ in Italy. The Shermans probably replaced the Valentines in mid 1943.

PART 3
AFRICAN THEATRES 1941-1945

3.1 SOUTH AFRICAN 1ST ARMOURED BRIGADE, SOUTH AFRICA, 1943-1945

The Brigade's main combat elements were:
> Duke of Edinburgh's Own Rifles Armoured Regiment
> Transvaal Scottish Armoured Regiment
> Regiment President Steyn Armoured Regiment
> Cape Town Highlanders Motor Battalion

Troops were rated average training and good morale.

SUPPORT UNITS

Brigade Support
1st Armoured Brigade HQ (6 × Stuart III, 2 radio vans, 3 × Scout Cars)

MAIN COMBAT ELEMENTS

Armoured Regiment
RHQ (4 × Stuart III, 1 recovery truck)
3 Squadrons, each: Sqdn HQ (4 × Stuart III)
> 4 Troops, each: 3 × Stuart III
1 Recce Troop: Troop HQ (2 × Daimler Scout Car)
> 3 Sections, each: 3 × Daimler Scout Car

Cape Town Highlanders Motor Battalion
Btn HQ (2 rifle secs, 2 trucks)
3 Companies, each: Coy HQ (1 rifle sec, 1 truck, 1 Boys)
> 1 platoon: 2 × 3" mortars, 2 × Vickers MMG, 4 trucks
> 3 platoons, each: 4 (6 man) rifle secs, 3 LMG, 1 Boys, 4 trucks
> 1 platoon: 2 × 2pdr A/T guns, 2 trucks
> 1 platoon: Pl HQ: 1 × Universal Carrier, 1 LMG
>> 3 Sections, each: 3 × Carrier, 3 LMG, 1 rifle sec, 1 Boys, 1 × 2" mortar

Notes
1. Radios were in all AFV and other PHQs.
2. Infantry had no anti-tank grenades.
3. The Brigade was the sole element of the 1st South African Armoured Division.
4. Brigade remained in South Africa.

3.2 SOUTH AFRICAN MOBILE FIELD FORCE, SOUTH AFRICA, JULY 1942–APRIL 1943

The Division's main combat elements were:
> 7th Armoured Brigade (9th Cape Corps Motor Battalion, First City Regiment, Pretoria Regiment Infantry Battalions earmarked for conversion to armoured regiments)
> 6th Armoured Brigade (8th Cape Corps Motor Battalion)

Troops were rated good morale and average training.

SUPPORT UNITS

Divisional Support
Included:
13th Armoured Car Commando: Coy HQ (4 × South African Armoured Recce Cars Mk.1)
> 6 Troops, each: 3 × South African Armoured Recce Cars Mk.1
26th Field Artillery Regiment:
> 3 Batteries, each: Battery HQ (4 rifle secs, 2 Boys, 4 AALMG, 6 trucks)
>> 2 Troops, each: 4 × 25pdr field guns, 5 trucks, radio truck
14th Field Park Company:
> Workshop Section, Stores Section
9th Anti-Tank Regiment:
> 3 Batteries, each: Battery HQ (1 rifle sec, 1 truck)
>> 3 Troops, each: 4 × 2pdr anti-tank guns, 4 trucks, 2 LMG
5th South African Air Force Light AA Regiment:
> 3 Batteries, each: Battery HQ (1 rifle sec, 1 truck)
>> 3 Troops, each: 4 × 40mmL60 Bofors, 4 trucks

Brigade Support
7th Armoured Brigade HQ (6 rifle secs, 4 lorries) with:
31st Air Force Armoured Car Commando: Coy HQ: 4 × South African Armoured Recce Cars Mk.1

6 Troops, each: 3 × South African Armoured Recce Cars Mk.1 (look like Marmon-Herrington Mk.1)
6th Field Artillery Regiment:
    3 Batteries, each: Battery HQ (4 rifle secs, 2 Boys, 4 AALMG, 6 trucks)
        2 Troops, each: 4 × 25pdr field guns, 5 trucks, radio truck
88th Field Engineer Company: Coy HQ (2 rifle secs, 2 trucks)
    3 platoons, each: 4 (12 man) rifle/engineer secs, 2 lorries, 2 LMG
6th Armoured Brigade HQ (6 rifle secs, 4 lorries) with:
30th Armoured Car Commando (as above)
21st Field Artillery Regiment (as above)
89th Field Engineer Company (as above)

MAIN COMBAT ELEMENTS

First City Regiment, Pretoria Regiment Infantry Battalions, each:

Btn HQ (5 rifle secs, 1 LMG, 2 lorries, 2 trucks, 1 car)
3 Companies, each: Coy HQ (1 rifle squad, 1 truck)
    3 platoons, each: 1 (6 man) rifle Pl HQ sec, 1 × 2" mortar
        3 (10 man) rifle secs, 3 LMG, 2 lorries
1 Support Company: Coy HQ (1 rifle sec, 1 truck)
    1 battery: 6 × 3" mortars, 6 trucks, radio truck
    1 platoon: 2 AALMG in 2 rifle crew secs, 2 trucks
    1 platoon: 2 rifle/engineer secs, 2 lorries
    1 platoon: 4 × 2pdr A/T guns, 4 trucks

Cape Corps Motor Battalion

Btn HQ (2 rifle secs, 2 trucks, 1 car)
3 Companies, each: Coy HQ (1 rifle sec, 2 trucks)
    1 battery: 2 × 3" mortars, 2 × Universal Carriers or light trucks
    2 platoons, each: 4 (8 man) rifle secs, 3 LMG, 1 × 2" mortar, 1 Boys, 4 trucks
    1 platoon: 4 MMG, 2 trucks or 4 × Universal Carriers
    1 platoon: Pl HQ: 1 × Universal Carrier,1 LMG, 1 car
        3 Sections, each: 3 × Carrier, 3 LMG, 1 rifle sec, 1 × 2" mortar, 1 Boys
1 Anti-Tank Company: Coy HQ (1 rifle sec)
    3 platoons, each: 2 × 2pdr or 6pdr A/T guns, 2 trucks

Notes
1.   Radios were in all Coy HQ, all armoured cars, and Carrier PHQs. Artillery is rated Assigned FC.
2.   Infantry had no anti-tank grenades.
3.   The Force never left South Africa, except elements of the 7th Brigade, which served in Madagascar.
4.   The 6th Brigade was planned to have two Infantry Battalions assigned to be then converted to armoured regiments, but this never happened.

3.3 SOUTH AFRICAN 16TH ARMOURED CAR BRIGADE, SOUTH AFRICA, SEPTEMBER 1942–1943

The Brigade's main combat elements were:
    21st North-East Rand Armoured Car Commando
    22nd Central Rand Armoured Car Commando
    23rd West Rand Armoured Car Commando
    South-East Rand Motor Battalion
Troops were rated good morale and average training, except engineers which were rated good training.

SUPPORT UNITS

Brigade Support

16th Armoured Car Brigade HQ (4 × Marmon-Herrington IV, 4 trucks + LMG, 2 cars) with up to:
    33rd Field Artillery Regiment:
        97th, 98th, 99th Batteries, each:
            Battery HQ (3 rifle secs, 2 Boys, 1 AALMG, 4 trucks)
            2 Troops, each: 4 × 25pdr or 18pdr field guns, 6 trucks, 1 AALMG
        33rd Anti-Tank Battery: Battery HQ (1 rifle sec, 1 truck)
            3 Troops, each: 4 × 2pdr, 4 trucks, 2 LMG
        18th Light AA Battery: Battery HQ (1 rifle sec, 1 truck)
            3 Troops, each: 2–4 × 40mmL60 Bofors or 6 × twin AALMG, 6 trucks
    56th Field Engineer Company: Coy HQ (2 rifle secs, 2 trucks)
        3 platoons, each: 4 (12 man) rifle/engineer secs, 4 trucks, 4 LMG

MAIN COMBAT ELEMENTS

Rand Armoured Car Commando

Coy HQ (4 × Marmon-Herrington Mk.III or Mk.IV)
6 Troops, each: 3 × Marmon-Herrington Mk.III or Mk.IV

Rand Motor Battalion
Btn HQ (2 rifle secs, 2 trucks, 2 LMG)
3 Companies, each: Coy HQ (1 rifle sec, 1 truck, 1 LMG)
1 platoon: 2 × 3" mortars, 2 × MMG, 4 trucks
3 platoons, each: 4 (8 man) rifle secs, 3 LMG, 1 × 2" mortar, 1 Boys, 4 trucks
1 platoon: 2 × 2pdr A/T guns, 2 trucks
1 platoon: Pl HQ: 1 × Universal Carrier, 1 LMG
3 Sections, each: 3 × Universal Carriers, 3 LMG, 1 rifle sec, 1 Boys

Notes
1. Radios were in all armoured cars and other PHQs.
2. Infantry had no anti-tank grenades. May have molotovs and dynamite satchel charges if in defence.
3. All troops were technicians, drivers and engineers from the mineral mines in the Rand in Transvaal, and were not allowed to serve outside South Africa.
4. Due to the high number of civil trained mining engineers the Brigade Engineers were rated as well trained, and able to produce improvised anti-armour weapons such as molotovs, box mines, demolition charges and satchel charges for the infantry if defending industrial areas.
5. The Brigade was also known as the Mine Engineer Brigade.

3.4   81ST WEST AFRICAN DIVISION, NIGERIA, MARCH–JULY1943
The Division's main combat elements were:
3rd West African Infantry Brigade (6th, 7th, 12th Battalions Nigeria Regiment)
5th West African Infantry Brigade (5th, 7th, 8th Battalions Gold Coast Regiment)
6th West African Infantry Brigade (5th Btn Sierra Leone Regiment, 4th Btn Nigeria Regiment, 1st Btn Gambia Regiment)
Divisional Recce Regiment (West African Divisional Recce Regiment)
Troops were rated good morale and average training

SUPPORT UNITS

Divisional Support
Included:
8th West African Field Park Company: engineer stores
1st West African Anti-tank/Anti-aircraft Regiment:
2 AA Batteries, each: Battery HQ (1 rifle sec, 1 truck)
3 Troops, each: 4 × 40mm Bofors, 4 trucks
2 Anti-Tank Batteries, each: Battery HQ (1 rifle sec, 1 truck)
3 Troops, each: 4 × 2pdr portees, 2 LMG
West African Divisional Recce Regiment HQ
(3 rifle secs, 3 LMG, 2 Boys, 3 × Light Recce Car, 3 trucks)

Brigade Support
3rd West African Infantry Brigade HQ (6 rifle secs, 4 lorries) with:
1 HQ Defence Platoon: 1 (7 man) rifle Pl HQ sec, 1 × 2" mortar, 1 Boys, 3 (10 man) rifle secs, 3 LMG
3rd West African Light Battery: 4 × 3.7" Mountain Guns, 350 unarmed porters, OP Team
7th West African Field Engineer Company: Coy HQ (2 rifle secs, 2 trucks)
3 platoons, each: 4 (12 man) rifle/engineer secs, 2 LMG
3rd Recce Squadron: Sqdn HQ (3 rifle secs, 1 LMG, 3 trucks, 1 Light Recce Car)
3 Troops, each: Pl HQ: 1 × Universal Carrier, 1 LMG, 1 Boys, 1 × 2", 1 × Light Recce Car
2 Sections, each: 2 × Light Recce Car
2 Sections, each: 3 × Carrier, 1 × Boys, 3 LMG, 1 × 2" mortar, 1 rifle sec
1 Troop: 4 rifle secs, 5 trucks, 1 Boys, 4 LMG
5th West African Infantry Brigade HQ (6 rifle secs, 4 lorries) with:
1 HQ Defence Platoon (as 3rd Bde above)
5th West African Light Battery (as above)
3rd West African Field Engineer Company (as above)
5th West African Recce Squadron (as above)
6th West African Infantry Brigade HQ (6 rifle secs, 4 lorries) with:
1 HQ Defence Platoon (as 3rd Bde above)
6th West African Light Battery (as above)
6th West African Field Engineer Company (as above)
6th West African Recce Squadron (as above)

MAIN COMBAT ELEMENTS

Infantry Battalion, West African, Gold Coast, Nigerian Regiments, each:
Btn HQ (4 rifle secs)
4 Companies, each: Coy HQ (1 rifle sec)
3 platoons, each: 1 (7 man) rifle Pl HQ sec, 1 × 2" mortar, 1 Boys,
3 (10 man) rifle secs, 3 LMG
1 Support Company: Coy HQ (1 rifle sec)
1 platoon: 4 or 6 × 3" mortars, 6 × Universal Carriers

1 platoon: 2 rifle/engineer secs, 1 lorry
1 platoon: 4 × twin AALMG, in 2 rifle crew secs

Notes
1. Radios were in all platoon HQs and above.
2. Infantry had no anti-tank grenades.
3. The Division was deployed in Nigeria until July 1943 when it was moved to India.
4. The Divisional Recce Regiment was split up as shown with one Squadron attached to each Infantry Brigade.

3.5   SOUTH AFRICAN CAVALRY DIVISION, SOUTH AFRICA, 1940–1941

The Division's main combat elements were:
    3 Cavalry Brigades (three Cavalry Regiments, also called Commando Battalions)
Troops were rated good morale and poor training if in home defence.

SUPPORT UNITS

Divisional Support

None known

Brigade Support

Mounted Rifle Brigade HQ (6 rifle secs, horses or trucks) with:
    1 Attached Mountain Battery: 4 × 3.7" Mountain guns, pack mules, Assigned FC

MAIN COMBAT ELEMENTS

Mounted Rifle Regiment Commandos

RHQ (6 rifle secs, horses, radio cart)
3 Squadrons, each: Sqdn HQ (2 rifle secs, horses)
        4 Troops, each: 1 (6 man) rifle Pl HQ sec, 3 (10 man) rifle secs, horses, 1 LMG
1 MG Squadron: Sqdn HQ (2 rifle secs, horses)
        4 Troops, each: 1 Vickers MMG, pack horses

Notes
1. Radios were in Btn HQ and above. Artillery is Assigned FC
2. Infantry had no A/T grenades.
3. Most of the Commandos were Afrikaans, and part of the Defence Rifle Associations. Many of these were opposed to the war against Germany.
4. No formal division was formed, other than the 5th "Motorised Division" in late 1941–mid 1942, but this list shows the equivalent cavalry force that would have been available in the case of invasion.
5. The 5th Motorised or Commando Division also had the 16th South African Armoured Car Brigade (see 3.3 above).

PART 4
SPECIAL FORCES ALL THEATRES
1940-1945

4.1 ROYAL MARINE BRIGADE, BRITAIN, DECEMBER 1939–JULY 1940

The Brigade's main combat elements were:
> 1st, 2nd, 3rd, 5th Royal Marine Battalions

Troops are rated good morale and average training.

> Teeth Arm Royal Marine Battalion: (each 300 men)
>> Btn HQ (1 rifle sec)
>>> 1 Firepower Platoon: 4 (7 man) rifle secs, 8 Bren LMG
>> 4 Rifle Companies, each: Coy HQ (1 (8 man) rifle sec, 1 Boys)
>>> 2 platoons, each: 4 (8 man) rifle secs, 1 × 2" mortar, 1 Boys, 2 Lewis MG

Notes
1. The 2nd Battalion landed as part of Force Sturges in Iceland in early May 1940.
2. In May 1940 the three battalions formed the 101st Brigade, later forming part of the Royal Marine Division (see below).
3. In June 1940 the 101st Brigade was earmarked for the reinforcement of Ireland if the Germans invaded there, or for the seizing of the Azores or Cape Verde Islands.

4.2 ROYAL MARINE DIVISION, ENGLAND, AUGUST 1940–JULY 1943

The Division's main combat elements were:
> 101st Royal Marine Brigade (1st, 5th RM Infantry Battalions, + 8th Btn Argylls Regiment Army Infantry Battalion (July 1940–April 1941))
> 102nd Royal Marine Brigade (2nd, 3rd RM Infantry Battalions)
> 103rd Royal Marine Brigade (7th RM Infantry Battalion, +8th RM Battalion (May 1941–August 1942), +9th RM Battalion (January 1941–1943), +10th RM Battalion (January 1942–1943))

Troops are rated good morale and good training.

SUPPORT UNITS

Divisional Support

Included:
31st Royal Marine Battery (1940–May 1942): Battery HQ (2 rifle secs, 4 trucks, 2 LMG)
> 1 Troop: 6 × 3.7" pack howitzers, 8 trucks, 2 LMG

15th Royal Marine Machine Gun Battalion: (mid 1941–1942 only)
> 3 Companies, each: Coy HQ (2 rifle secs)
>> 3 platoons, each: 4 × Vickers MMG

18th Mobile Battalion: (1941–1942 only)
> 6 Motorcycle Companies, each:
>> 2 platoons, each: 3x Universal Carriers, 3 LMG
>> 3 platoons, each: 3 motorcycle combinations, MMG, Boys

Royal Marine Field Artillery Regiment: (1941–August 1942)
> 31st Howitzer Battery: 6 × 3.7" pack howitzers, 8 trucks, 3 LMG
> 32nd Howitzer Battery: 4 × 3.7" howitzers, later 18pdr field guns, 6 trucks
> 1st, 2nd A/T Batteries, each: 1–4 Troops, each: 4 × 2pdr A/T guns on portees
> 1st Light AA Battery: 3 Troops, each: 2 × 40mmL60 Bofors
> 2nd Light AA Battery: 2 × 20mm Oerlikon, 2 × 40mmL60 Bofors AA, 4 trucks
> 1st, 2nd AA–A/T batteries, each: 3 Troops, each: 4 × 20mm Oerlikon or Hispano on trucks

1st RM Artillery Brigade:(September 1942–1943 only)
> Royal Marine Field Artillery Regiment: RHQ (4 rifle secs, 6 trucks, 2 LMG)
> 31st, 32nd Light Batteries, each: 4 × 3.7" pack howitzers, 6 trucks, 2 LMG, OP Team
> 1st, 2nd Field Batteries, each: 2 Troops, each: 4 × 25pdr guns, 6 trucks, 2 LMG, OP Team in AFV

Royal Marine Anti-Tank Regiment:
> 1st Battery: 4 Troops, each: 4 × 2pdr portees
> 2nd Battery: 1 Troop: 4 × 6pdr A/T guns, 4 trucks

Royal Marine Light AA Regiment:
> 1st, 2nd Light AA Batteries, each: Battery HQ (1 rifle sec, 1 truck)
>> 1 Troop: 4 × 40mmL60 Bofors, 4 trucks
> 1st, 2nd AA/A-T Batteries, each: Battery HQ (1 rifle sec, 1 truck)
>> 1 Troop: 6 × 20mm Polsten or Oerlikon on 6 trucks

1st Royal Marine Engineer Company (1941–1942): 240 men
Royal Marine Operational Engineer Battalion (1943)
> Btn HQ (20 rifle secs)

A, B, C, D Works Companies, each: 246 men
Electrical & Mechanical Section: 244 men
Landing Gear Assembly Party: 67 men
Fuel Gear Assembly Party: 60 men
1 Depot/Training/Replacement Battalion

Brigade Support

RM Infantry Brigade HQ (1940–1941) (4 rifle secs, 6 lorries, 2 cars)
RM Infantry Brigade HQ (1942–1943) (8 rifle secs, Humber Scout Cars, Universal Carriers, 8 lorries, 1 recovery truck)
with:
HQ Defence Platoon: 4 (8 man) rifle/SMG secs, 3 LMG, 1 × 2" mortar, 1 Boys
Signals Company
1 MG Company: Coy HQ: 1 rifle sec (1943 only)
    4 platoons, each: 4 MMG
    1 battery: 6 × 4.2" mortars, 7 × Carriers (in theory)
1 Recce Company: Coy HQ: 3 × Daimler Scout Cars (1943 only)
    3 platoons, each: 3 (11 man) rifle secs, 33 M/C Combinations, 9 LMG
    1 platoon: Pl HQ: 1 × Universal Carrier, 1 LMG
        3 Sections, each: 3 × Carrier, 3 LMG, 1 × 2" mortar, 1 Boys, 1 rifle sec

MAIN COMBAT ELEMENTS

Royal Marine Battalion 1940–1942 (each 300 men)

Btn HQ (1 rifle sec)
1 Firepower Platoon: 4 (7 man) rifle secs, 8 Bren LMG
4 Rifle Companies, each: Coy HQ (1 (8 man) rifle sec, 1 Boys)
    2 platoons, each: 4 (8 man) rifle secs, 1 × 2" mortar, 1 Boys, 2 Lewis MG

Royal Marine Infantry Battalion, September 1942–mid 1943 (up to 660 men)

Btn HQ (4 rifle secs)
1 Firepower Platoon: 4 (8 man) rifle/SMG secs, 8 Bren LMG or 2 × Vickers MMG, 2 × 3" mortars
4 Rifle Companies, each: Coy HQ (1 (8 man) rifle sec, 1 Boys)
    3 platoons, each: 4 (8–12 man) rifle secs, 1 × 2" mortar, 1 Boys, -63 LMG

Notes
1. Radios were in all Coy HQ and above. Artillery is Assigned FC until 1943, when it becomes Flexible FC, with OP Teams in Universal Carriers or Scout Cars.
2. Infantry had No.74 or No.75 anti-tank grenades.
3. In September 1940 the 101st and 102nd Brigades were deployed to Sierra Leone for the attempted invasion of Vichy Dakar in Senegal.
4. From October 1940 to 1941 the division planned for invasions of the Azores, Cape Verde Islands or Spanish Canary Islands if Spain joined the Axis, or to intervene in West Africa, or to invade Madagascar.
5. In 1942 the Division was earmarked for the invasion of North Africa but was not used as the army could not provide necessary transport, supply and additional artillery unit.
6. From mid 1943 the Division was disbanded to form the RM Commandos and landing craft crews for D-Day.

NOTES FOR WARGAMERS

The lists in this book do not include points values, and therefore can be utilised with any rules system.

If not using points values, the following method can be used to generate realistic battlegroups, particularly with regard to equipment and vehicles available. Indeed, this method could be combined with points values; the lists are designed to be flexible to the gamer's own needs.

- Agree with opponent or organiser on points limit, or on the number of 'teeth arm' or main combat element companies and support platoons to be fielded. A typical limit could be two companies and three support platoons.
- Select companies as desired from the main combat elements in the particular list, up to the limits imposed above.
- The battlegroup HQ is determined from the type of main combat element companies fielded: if one type is in the majority, then field that type's battalion HQ or equivalent; if equal numbers of 2 or 3 types are fielded then combine the battalion/equivalent HQs as the battlegroup HQ. For example, if 2 tank and 2 infantry companies are used, then the battlegroup HQ would consist of a combined tank battalion HQ and infantry battalion HQ; if a full battalion plus more than one company of another battalion is fielded, then use the full battalion's brigade or regimental HQ as the battlegroup HQ.
- Any main combat element recce or support companies can be split up so that individual platoons can be fielded as desired, being classed as support that does not need to be diced for.
- Brigade level support can be fielded as desired only if the appropriate brigade or regiment HQ is fielded, otherwise it must be diced for.
- Division, corps and army level support must be diced for. Any company at these levels can be split up and individual platoons fielded.
- Dicing for support: select the platoon or company type desired, then note the maximum number of that type of unit; multiply this by the number of main combat element companies being used; then multiply by the following number, to give the % chance of obtaining the desired unit:

Regimental/brigade level support	10
Divisional level support	5
Corps level support	1
Army level support	0.5

- Before rolling, it can be decided to split the resultant percentages, thus giving more than one chance of obtaining the unit type in question, e.g. 60% could be split into 2 rolls at 30% and so on.
- Any company HQ or battalion HQ can have two couriers attached, on foot, horse, motorcycle or jeep, as appropriate to that army list. Infantry battalions can add 2 snipers per infantry company, with morale and training one level above accompanying troops.
- Any platoon can be fielded one section or vehicle short to represent combat losses, and any company can be fielded one platoon short.

ARTILLERY FIRE CONTROL

Artillery batteries have three types of fire control noted in the lists, these being Obsolete, Assigned, and Flexible. Unless noted otherwise, the fire control of all batteries listed in this book is of the Flexible type unless stated otherwise. Descriptions are as follows:

OBSOLETE FC: The battery can only be used for pre-planned fire, on-table direct fire, or indirect fire controlled by runner or telephone. This is typical of armies without radios.

ASSIGNED FC: The battery is controlled by radio or telephone, but is assigned to a battlefield company HQ or the battlegroup HQ. It can only be controlled by that HQ, and there is no separate OP team. If the controlling HQ is lost in battle, then the battery is considered out of action for the rest of the battle. Alternatively the battery can be fielded up-front as a direct fire unit. This is typical of armies with poor training and limited radios; a commander from the artillery battalion has a vehicle at the battalion or regimental command post it is supporting.

FLEXIBLE FC: This applies to WWII German and post-July 1942 US and British armies only. The battery is allocated to the battlegroup HQ (BHQ) via an artillery rear-link (usually a radio van or armoured OP) vehicle which is fielded on-table. In addition, most batteries have one or two OP (observation post) teams, each of 3 men and a backpack radio, often in a vehicle or aircraft, who control the battery and can call down fire from other batteries in the same artillery battalion or regiment. If not in an aircraft, these OPs will also have a direct radio link to the BHQ.

In addition to the above, most corps or army batteries are used only for pre-planned or counter-battery fire, although they can be assigned or allocated to the BHQ as above.

TACTICAL DOCTRINE

To a large extent, modern mechanised combat is based around the battlegroup, in which a brigade mixes and matches its battalions to the task in hand, for example, by detaching an infantry company from its parent battalion and joining it with a tank battalion, or by attaching a tank company to an infantry battalion. British and Commonwealth units were notoriously bad at forming task-orientated battlegroups until after mid-1944, and even after this date their abilities were limited. Most forces would consist of a main combat element's battalion or regiment, with artillery assigned as required; other main combat element units would also be present, remaining under their parent command, even if assigned to support a particular unit. This was especially evident in North Africa, where armoured brigades repeatedly fought without their infantry support. It was only after 1944 that improvised battlegroups became common, more so in Italy and the Far East, where combined arms groups could be formed down to company level.

For the period covered by this book no mixed battalions were formed, and if two different battalions/regiments were tasked to attack the same target, they would often act virtually independently. Initial planning may have specified that they support one other, but this was little trained for, and so rarely happened effectively. The only exceptions to this were the tank brigades, which were designed to be split and assigned at the ratio of one troop per infantry company or one squadron per infantry battalion. However, again, cross-training was in limited in practise, and the tank brigades tended to be used as heavy armoured brigades for assault work.

After about July 1942 the British restructured their artillery support, such that it became the best in the war. Adopting the 'Flexible Fire Control' system described earlier in this appendix, British OP teams (or Forward Observation Officers) could order the fire of their own battery/troop, and given time could *order*, not *request*, the fire of all batteries up the chain of command. For example, once one troop was firing, the rest of the battery could then be ordered onto the same target, then the whole regiment (so-called 'Mike Target'), then all the divisional regiments ('Uncle Target'), and then all corps batteries ('Victor Target'), and army level batteries ('William Target'). Fire could be restrained and timed so that all shells landed together – Time On Target firing, but this was rarely done. British OP teams were highly trained and had good initiative in deciding the level of fire required for a certain target type – they would not request a corps heavy artillery regiment to destroy one A/T gun platoon holding up a tank advance, when one battery could do the job, but on the other hand, they could request everything up to offshore battleships when a Panzer corps presented itself, as happened in Normandy. However, British artillery prior to mid-1942, despite the fact that it had possessed separate OP teams as far back as 1940, did not have the training and radio support required to be rated 'Flexible Fire Control', so instead should be treated as 'Assigned Fire Control'.

SERIES BIBLIOGRAPHY

Atkin, Ronald *Pillar of Fire, Dunkirk 1940* (Sidgwick & Jackson, 1990)

Bellis, Malcolm *A Commonwealth Divisions 1939–1945* (Data File series No.11, 1999)

Bouchery, Jean *From D-Day to VE Day, The British Soldier Vol.2* (Histoire & Collections, 1999)

British Orders of Battle, Joslen, extracts provided by David Ryan

Command Post and Command Post Quarterly, various issues, GDW/Old Glory (1993–2000)

Conboy Ken and Paul Hannon *Osprey Elite 41, Elite Forces of India and Pakistan* (Osprey Publishing, 1992)

Dalzel-Job, Patrick *From Artic Snow to Dust of Normandy* (Alan Sutton Publishing, 1991)

Delaforce, Patrick *Churchill's Desert Rats: From Normandy to Berlin with the 7th Armoured Division* (Alan Sutton Publishing, 1994)

Delaforce, Patrick *Monty's Highlanders* (Chancellor Press, 2000)

Delaforce, Patrick *Monty's Ironsides* (Chancellor Press, 1995)

Delaforce, Patrick *Taming the Panzers, 3rd RTR at War* (Sutton Publishing Ltd, 2000)

Delaforce, Patrick *The Black Bull, From Normandy to the Baltic with the 11th Armoured Division* (Tom Donovan Publishing Ltd, 1997)

Delaforce, Patrick *The Polar Bears* (Chancellor Press, 1995)

Divisions of the British Army 1939–1945 2nd Edition (Malcolm Bellis, 2000)

Draper, Alfred *Dawns Like Thunder – the Retreat from Burma* (Leo Cooper, 1987)

Elphick, Peter *Singapore The Impregnable Fortress* (Hodder & Stoughton, 1995)

Expansion of the Armed Forces and Defence Organisations Plosad, Orient Longmans (notes supplied by David Ryan)

Farran, Roy *Winged Dagger, Adventures on Special Service* (Arms & Armour Press, 1986 reprint of 1948 original)

Featherstone, Donald *Tank Battles in Miniature 4* (Patrick Stephens Ltd, 1977)

Forty, George & John Duncan *The Fall of France* (Guild Publishing, 1990)

Gregory, Barry *British Airborne Troops* (Macdonald & Janes, 1974)

Harclerode, Peter *Go To It! The Illustrated History of the 6th Airborne Division* (Caxton Editions, 2000)

Hughes, David et al *The British Armies in World War Two – an Organisational History Vol.1* (Nafziger, 2000)

Hughes, David et al *The British Armies in World War Two – an Organisational History Vol.2* (Nafziger, 2000)

Hughes, David et al *The British Armies in World War Two – an Organisational History Vol.3* (Nafziger, 2001)

Hughes, David et al *The British Armies in World War Two – an Organisational History Vol.4* (Nafziger, 2002)

Jenner, Robin and David List *Osprey New Vanguard 32 – The Long Range Desert Group 1940–1945* (Osprey Publishing Ltd, 1999)

Kersaudy, Francois *Norway 1940* (Arrow Books Ltd, 1990)

Ladd, James *Commandos and Rangers of WW2* (Book Club Associates, 1978)

Ladd, James D *The Royal Marine 1919–1980* (Jane's Publishing Company Ltd, 1980)

Leasor, James *The Marine from Mandalay* (Leo Cooper Ltd, 1988)

Lord, Cliff *The Armed Forces of Aden 1839–1967* (David Birtles, Helion & Co, 2000)

MacDonald, Callum *The Lost Battle, Crete 1941* (MacMillan, 1993)

Mains, Tony *The Retreat from Burma* (W Foulsham & Co Ltd, 1973)

Neillands, Robin *The Desert Rats: 7th Armoured Division 1940–1945* (George Weidenfeld & Nicolson, 1991)

Norton, GG *Famous Regiments – The Red Devils* (Leo Cooper Ltd, 1971)

Notes on 10th Army in Persia, supplied by David Ryan, via e-mail

Notes on 1940 & 1943 Motor Battalion War Establishments, supplied by Gary Kennedy.

Notes on 2nd New Zealand Division, supplied by Rob Rowell

Notes on 9th Army in Palestine, supplied by David Ryan, via e-mail

Notes on British Air Landing Battalion, supplied by Gary Kennedy.

Notes on British Recce Regiments, supplied by Phil Shaw

Notes on Cyprus Garrisons, supplied by David Ryan, via e-mail

Notes on Indian Army OOB December 1941, supplied by David Ryan, via e-mail

Notes on Malaya Garrisons November 1941, January 1942, supplied by David Ryan

Notes on Middle East OOB February 1943, supplied by David Ryan, via e-mail

Notes on New Zealand garrisons, supplied by David Ryan.

Perrett, Bryan *Osprey Vanguard 13 – The Churchill Tank* (Osprey Publishing, 1980)

Perrett, Bryan *Osprey Vanguard 23 – British Tanks in North Africa 1940–1942* (Osprey Publishing Ltd, 1981)

Perrett, Bryan *Tank Tracks to Rangoon* (Robert Hale Ltd, 1978)

Pitt, Barrie *Special Boat Squadron, The Story of the SBS in the Mediterranean* (Century Publishing, 1983)

Plowman, Jeffrey *Armoured Fighting Vehicles of New Zealand 1939–1959* (JEP Publications, 1985)

Rolf Hedges (2000), *2nd Lothian addendum*. E-mail (17th October 2000)

Seaman, Harry *The Battle of Sangshak* (Leo Cooper Ltd, 1989)

Shille, Carl *The Fighting 52nd Recce* (Eskdale Publishing, 2000)

Stafford, David *Secret Agent, The True Story of the SOE* (BBC Worldwide Ltd, 2000)

Tank TV – The World of Fighting Vehicles, various issues, (Wellington, New Zealand, 1993–2000)

Tankette, The Miniature Armoured Fighting Vehicles Association Magazine, many various issues, Gary Williams (secretary), 45 Balmoral Drive, Holmes Chapel, Cheshire, CW4 7JQ

Verney, Major-General GL *The Desert Rats: The 7th Armoured Division in WW2* (Greenhill Books ,1990 reprint from 1954 original)

The Journal of the Society of Twentieth Century Wargamers, various issues, Mark Wheeler (Secretary), 25 Buttermere, White Court, Black Notley, Essex, CM7 8UY

Thomas, Nigel *Osprey MAA 238 Foreign Volunteers of the Allied Forces 1939–1945* (Osprey Publishing Ltd, 1991)

Van Der Bijl, Nick *Osprey Elite 57 – The Royal Marines 1939–1993* (Reed International Books, 1994)

Woodbine Parish, Michael *Aegean Adventures 1940–1943* (The Book Guild Ltd, 1993)

Zaloga, Steven J *Opsrey New Vanguard 53–M8 Greyhound Light Armoured Car 1941–1991* (Osprey Publishing, 2002)

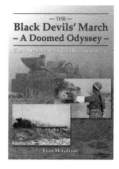

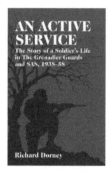